Inventions of Reading

By the same author:

Thomas Mann's "Goethe and Tolstoy": Notes and Sources
The Incredulous Reader: Literature and the Function of Disbelief

Co-editor:

The Current in Criticism: Essays on the Present and Future of
  Literary Theory (with Virgil Lokke)
The Comparative Perspective on Literature: Approaches to
  Theory and Practice (with Susan Noakes)

Inventions of Reading

Rhetoric and the Literary Imagination

CLAYTON KOELB

Cornell University Press

ITHACA AND LONDON

Copyright © 1988 by Cornell University

First published 1988 by Cornell University Press.

International Standard Book Number 0-8014-2182-9
Library of Congress Catalog Card Number 88–47732
Printed in the United States of America
Librarians: Library of Congress cataloging information
appears on the last page of the book.

The paper in this book is acid-free and meets the guidelines for
permanence and durability of the Committee on Production Guidelines
for Book Longevity of the Council on Library Resources.

In memory of Jane Koelb, my mother

Contents

Preface

When I first thought of the title *Inventions of Reading*, I imagined it to contain a possessive rather than an objective genitive. I conceived what follows as an exposition not of how someone invented reading but of how reading participates in the invention of other things, in this case literary texts. A particular mode of reading, which I will call *rhetorical construction*, occurs when a writer discovers in the discourse he or she reads a set of opposing meanings whose conflict can become the basis for a fiction. The invention of reading is the discovery process that can occur when a writer sensitive to the rhetorical complexities of even everyday language illustrates or elaborates those complexities poetically.

But some readers of this book, occasionally including its author, will want to understand the title in the other way. After all, the very principles of rhetorical construction outlined here suggest that both interpretations ought to be considered. In that case the chief candidate for the role of inventor of reading (*this* kind of reading, at least) is likely to be the person who thought up *Inventions of Reading*. Some may find the role in certain respects more villainous than heroic, with an aggressive form of interpretation imposing on innocent texts a reading that is "invented" in the sense of being made up out of the critic's head with no thought given to what the texts themselves intend. Others—once again including the author—may find rather congenial the idea that a critic should invent a mode of reading, but they might wonder why in the world I would retreat, in my very first paragraph, from embracing fully the rhetorical reading of my own title.

Although I would have to reject the first of these criticisms, with its assumptions about textual innocence, as a form of positivism already thoroughly dismantled by others, I surely need to reply to the second. Why am I not prepared to accept responsibility for being an inventor of reading? My answer has to be that I *am* prepared to do so, but with the important proviso that the responsibility must be shared. If I have discovered a mode of reading, I have been able to do so only because the authors of the texts I read had already discovered it. What I have discovered is their invention, and therefore in a certain sense the discovery is not mine at all. Since both cases are true—that I have invented this mode of reading and also that I merely rediscovered something already there—I defend both positions in the book.

If now I appear to advocate a kind of essentialism that understands rhetorical elements to be somehow "in" texts, and then I turn around and suggest that they are a matter of the reader's act of reading, it is because I really do mean both, since both are necessary for rhetorical construction to work. The rhetorical text and its reader cooperate in order to make rhetorical moments visible. I try to stress at various points in the argument, especially in chapter 1, that rhetoric is a relational concept referring to an interaction between a text possessing certain qualities and a reader possessing certain skills. Neither in itself is sufficient. I may at one moment lay particular stress on the text's qualities and at another emphasize the reader's skills, but that is a matter of my own rhetorical strategy.

I can happily accept the title "inventor of reading," knowing that it is by no means a lonely form of employment: it is one I share with many—ultimately including, I hope, some of those who make their way through *Inventions of Reading*.

My method is clearly not "historical" in the sense in which most critics use the term, but it is by no means antihistorical. Rhetorical criticism does not deny the existence of that "something outside language" that we call history; it suggests, rather, that history is necessarily mediated through consciousness, which is thoroughly linguistic. Historical facts play a crucial role in the analyses I present below, but those facts happen to be linguistic ones—the principal ones, after all, that I as a critic am in a position to deal with. I have a particular interest in the realities of language that make possible the invention of stories, realities that are themselves no less "historical" than class struggles or economic conditions. That Rabelais's French included expressions like

"Bran! En ta gorge!" or allowed an ambiguity between indicative and subjunctive in the phrase "le fondement vous escappe" is not less factual, not less historical, than other conditions that formed the possibility of his writing. Because of my interest in this aspect of history, I want to show how such linguistic "material facts" come into play in the production of literature. The inventions of reading are no less inventions of history.

Some matters of scholarly style deserve comment here. There is of course a large and important body of critical commentary on the authors treated in the book. Though this commentary is worth engaging in dialogue, there is simply not enough space to do that *and* keep a reasonable focus on my own topic. In any case, I really do not intend my readings of particular works as contributions to the scholarship on individual authors. I treat these authors only as part of a larger discussion of rhetorical construction which is usually, but not always, without precedent in the scholarship. This lack of precedent, I hasten to add, is merely a curious fact of literary history and no particular credit to me.

My choice of texts for analysis is also affected by personal style. Since rhetorical construction is a widely employed mode (like, say, irony), there is no special core group of texts to be cited as inherently paradigmatic. There is no set of principles internal to the concept that allows us to order inventions of reading about some absolute center. This means there are thousands of texts one might choose from, each having a legitimate claim on the attention of the rhetorical critic. The selection that emerges from these circumstances is necessarily arbitrary, then, but it is not unconsidered. I have chosen to illustrate what I find to be the most interesting varieties of rhetorical construction by reading a set of texts that match my particular capabilities and interests. There are more examples drawn from the mainstream German tradition than from any other, for example, because I know that tradition best, but I have tried hard to provide as a counterbalance discussions of works from other canons and even a few that are not strictly canonical. The selection is temporally and geographically as broad as I was qualified to make it and represents several national literatures, periods, and genres; but it is very much constrained by my own limitations.

Foremost among those limitations is a linguistic one: it is not possible to engage in this style of reading without a knowledge of the language in which the text was written. This constraint placed a severe but welcome restriction on my choices. In combination with the limitations in my knowledge of world literary history, it narrowed the field dramatically. Furthermore, it is clear that some texts reward more abundantly than others the reading practice I am trying to illustrate, and it only made sense to choose those most suitable to the method.

The contingent nature of the selection process is altogether in keeping with the theoretical thrust of the argument. Contingent relations, such as the fortuitous juxtaposition of two incompatible interpretations of a single text, can have enormously fruitful consequences. That circumstance is indeed one of the chief lessons of contemporary theory, and that is what this book seeks to illustrate in detail.

The contingent linguistic/historical situation in which I am embedded could not fail to have a powerful influence on the shape of my book. I will, in the first chapter, give an account of the most important influences that have contributed to my argument and acknowledge thereby that I do not in any sense stand apart from my own historical position. I owe a substantial debt to the deconstructive practice of Paul de Man, to J. L. Austin's version of speech–act theory, and to semiotics, not to mention classical rhetoric and the New Critical "close reading" in which I was trained. My project is also related, though less directly, to the work of Mikhail Bakhtin and, more recently, of Gregory Ulmer. What I find in all of these predecessors is a set of suggestions leading toward a practice of reading that understands texts as shaped in nontrivial ways by the conditions of their language. All writing presupposes acts of reading in that one can produce discourse only by taking apart the discourse of others and reusing the pieces. We must hear before we speak, read before we write.

I therefore situate myself in the wake of poststructuralism, in a period of realignment and of a continuing sense of crisis among professional critics. The level of unease is if anything on the rise, in part because of the recent discovery of the unhappy role the young Paul de Man apparently played in the political life of Belgium during the German occupation. It is still too soon to assess the significance of the pro-Nazi newspaper articles discovered by Ortwin de Graef and discussed in his forthcoming article "Paul de Man's Proleptic 'Nachlaß,'" but a preliminary examination suggests that de Man exploited the worst as well as the best possibilities of rhetoric—possibilities he later taught many of us to recognize. When the dust has settled, it will be necessary to come to grips with the ugly form of ethical engagement most visible in "Les juifs dans la littérature actuelle" (*Le Soir*, March 4, 1941) and others of its kind. It is clear, however, that no matter how deeply these pieces alter our view of Paul de Man's public career or taint the future reception of his work, they should not diminish the significance of his contributions to the theory of reading.

The sense of crisis in the critical community is also a response to the seemingly inexorable pressure pushing literary studies from the center to the margins of the academic enterprise. Some commentators see these two problems as related: the rise of poststructuralism has coincided with a dramatic decline in undergraduate interest in language and literature, and therefore the former must have caused the latter. This argument, no matter what its attractions, strikes me as both faulty in logic and innocent of historical consciousness. This is not the place, however, to develop a full-scale case against it. I mention it only to note my conviction that the opposite is true: with Ulmer and others, I believe that the elaboration of a concept of reading and writing derived from poststructuralism offers the best hope of restoring literary studies to a place of importance in the curriculum. One of the aims of this book, then, is to advance the notion that sophisticated rhetorical reading is not an arcane and sterile activity carried on only by professors addressing other professors; it is rather one of the principal methods used by creative people of the past and the present to conduct the business of inventing.

I am grateful to the Department of Germanic Languages at Princeton University for inviting me to spend a semester with them. Stanley Corngold, who initiated the invitation, deserves special thanks. The department asked of me only that I do a little teaching, and the time free from meetings, examinations, and other routine academic duties made it possible for me to write a substantial portion of the book. The occasion of a lecture at Princeton afforded me the opportunity to try out an early version of some of the material on Kleist in chapter 3. The comments I received after the talk were very helpful and led to significant revisions. I also had the opportunity to offer another portion of chapter 3, that on Hawthorne, as a lecture at the University of Kansas. I benefited equally from the comments I received there. Small portions of chapters 1 and 2 have appeared in print before as part of an essay ("Kafka's Rhetorical Moment") in *PMLA* 98, no. 1 (1983): 37–46.

I am pleased to acknowledge permission to reprint material from the following sources: Schocken Books, published by Pantheon Books, a division of Random House, Inc., for Franz Kafka, "Give It Up!," translated by Tania and James Stern and published in *Franz Kafka: The Complete Stories,* edited by Nahum N. Glatzer (copyright 1971 by Schocken Books); Fischer Verlag for Franz Kafka, "Gibs auf!," in *Franz Kafka: Sämtliche Erzählungen,* edited by Paul Raabe (1970); Carl Hanser Verlag for passages from Friedrich Schiller, *Sämtliche Werke* (1959) and Heinrich von Kleist, *Sämtliche Werke und Briefe* (1961); Oxford University Press, for passages from *The Divine Comedy of Dante Alighieri,* translated by J. D. Sinclair; Continuum Publishing for passages from Heinrich von Kleist, *The Broken Pitcher,* translated by Jon Swan, in *Heinrich von Kleist: Plays,* edited by Walter Hinderer, copyright © 1982 by The Continuum Publishing Company; Frederick Ungar Publishing Co. for passages from *Iphigenia in Tauris* by Johann Wolfgang von Goethe, translated by Charles E. Passage, English translation © 1963 by the Frederick Ungar Publishing Company, reprinted by permission of the publisher; Barron's Publishing Co. for passages from Friedrich Schiller, *Mary Stuart,* translated by Sophie Wilkins (1959); and Mr. George Trevelyan for passages from Heinrich von Kleist, *Penthesilea,* translated by Humphry Trevelyan and published by Continuum in *Heinrich von Kleist: Plays* (1982).

Samuel Jaffe not only offered support, advice, and consolation but also often served as a sounding board for inchoate ideas. Some of the subtler points made in the first chapter derive from our conversations while debriefing after long seminar sessions. Bernhard Kendler is a thoughtful and supportive editor, and it is my good fortune to be able to work with him. Kay Scheuer, Cynthia Gration, and the entire staff at Cornell University Press have earned my admiration and gratitude. Two anonymous readers for the Press deserve thanks for numerous suggestions toward improving the book. Most of all, I owe thanks to Susan Noakes, whose knowledge and judgment have been my greatest resource.

CLAYTON KOELB

Chicago, Illinois

Inventions of Reading

1 | *Ways of Beginning*

"Where do you get your ideas?"

It is one of the questions most frequently asked of authors of imaginative fiction, though apparently it is also one of the most difficult to answer. Even writers tired of hearing the question must understand, though, why readers are curious about the origins of the ideas underlying the stories they find so fascinating. It is hard to imagine, for example, that anyone could read Kafka's story "The Metamorphosis" without having the fantasy of asking the author where he got the idea of Gregor's transformation. The more unusual the concept, the more urgently we want to know something about its genesis.

It is certainly not my intention to revive the concept of "origin" as a privileged and determining moment for a literary text; hunting for origins of this kind is an enterprise of demonstrably limited value (once an origin is found, it immediately demands a search for its own origin, and so on), and it is in any case something very different from the project I have in mind. So much has been written in the past two decades criticizing the very notion of "origin," as that term has traditionally been used in philosophy and other humanistic disciplines, that today one hesitates even to use the word. The critique of origins has been carried out most forcefully by Jacques Derrida, whom Paul de Man aptly dubbed the "Archie Debunker" of contemporary thinkers.[1] Derrida's critique has had a substantial and in my view salutary effect

1. Paul de Man, *Allegories of Reading* (New Haven: Yale University Press, 1979), 9. He cites Nietzsche as another "de-bunker of the arche."

on the practice of recent literary criticism and especially literary theory. Though I may from time to time employ the word "origin" in my own writing, I mean it to be a synonym for what Edward Said calls a "beginning."² Said's notion is useful here because, as he defines it, a beginning is better understood as something made by a person, in this case an author, than as an ontologically privileged *arche*. While we would be hard pressed to find the ultimate and indisputable "origin" of any work of fiction, we can talk quite intelligibly about the beginning the author made in order to be able to write it.

Part of the task of making a beginning for a work of imaginative fiction is the difficult work of coming up with an idea, discovering or inventing some fictional situation that readers will find interesting. It is a classical rhetorical process to which classical rhetoricians gave the name *inventio*. This notion of "invention" was specialized, but in a way that is of considerable relevance here. Rhetorical invention was the activity that "found" thoughts; the orator extracted from the material he had (*res*) whatever "more or less hidden possibilities of thought" it might contain.³ Note carefully that invention was considered to be not finding or making the material (*res*) but developing interesting possibilities in it. By saying I am interested in investigating that part of making a beginning that has been called invention, I am explicitly denying any interest in hunting for sources, influences, or other matters pertaining to the establishment of a body of material. I do think, however, that there exist patterns among groups of authors in the ways they go about the necessary and difficult task of poetic invention, that such groups can be understood to share what we might tentatively call an "imaginative mode," and that their methods of invention can be investigated both theoretically and in concrete detail. This book aims to define and explore one such "imaginative mode."

I use the word "mode" here in part to stress that what is at issue is the specification of a "way of doing things," a process, and not of a literary taxonomy. My goal is not to define a genre. I realize that the distinction between "mode" and "genre" is neither certain nor stable and that the difference between a way of writing and a class of objects so written may in the end be only a matter of point of view. Indeed, I insist on it here partly to announce my point of view, but also because I

2. Edward Said, *Beginnings: Intention and Method* (New York: Basic Books, 1975).
3. Heinrich Lausberg, *Handbuch der literarischen Rhetorik* (Munich: Max Hueber, 1956), 146.

recognize that many kinds of works can be produced by the verbal imagination. A genre called "rhetorical constructions" would be far too huge and heterogeneous to be useful in any literary taxonomy. Even the small sampling of works treated in this book gives proof of this complexity. The diversity of these works helps to establish both the importance of inventive reading as an imaginative mode (because we find it so frequently) and its uselessness as a generic label (again because we find it so frequently). I mean to recognize, too, that rhetorical construction may play a crucial role in one aspect of a text but no role at all in the rest of it. Even Franz Kafka, whose example I will use to establish my topic, turns as often to observation of the world for his inventive impulse as he does to rhetoric. As Kathryn Hume has argued in another context, the desire to "describe events, people, situations, and objects with such verisimilitude that others can share your experience" seems to form one pole of every act of literary invention.[4]

To begin the process of defining just what inventive process I am interested in, we might profitably turn to a writer with a deep and abiding interest in the imagination—Samuel Taylor Coleridge. There is an entry in Coleridge's notebooks, albeit a rather cryptic one, perhaps no more than a reminder for future reference, that hints at a project with far-ranging implications: "Examine minutely the nature, cause, birth & growth of the *verbal* Imagination of which Barrow is almost the Ideal."[5] Exactly what Coleridge meant by the phrase "verbal imagination" will probably never be fully determined. The available evidence,[6] however, suggests he was alluding to the process by which structures of language (and not necessarily any structures of "thought" assumed to stand behind them—language, in other words, as the classical rhetorician's *res*) form the basis for a process of invention that gives rise to other structures of discourse, what we might call "thoughts" or "notions" or "stories," expressed in different, often more elaborate verbal form. In Isaac Barrow's sermons, cited by Coleridge as "almost the Ideal" examples of the verbal imagination, the (often lengthy) texts composed by Barrow find their beginnings in

4. Kathryn Hume, *Fantasy and Mimesis: Responses to Reality in Western Literature* (New York: Methuen, 1984), 20.

5. Kathleen Coburn, ed., *Notebooks of Samuel Taylor Coleridge* (New York: Routledge, 1957), vol. 1, note no. 1275.

6. For a more detailed discussion, see my essay "The Story in the Image: Rhetoric and Narrative Invention," *Modern Fiction Studies*, 33, no. 3 (1987): 509–22.

short selections from the Bible. Barrow assumes that the language of Scripture signifies intelligibly on every level and in every conceivable mode of reading. The infinite readability of the biblical text is never an embarrassment for Barrow but is always the occasion for greater feats of scholarly and rhetorical dexterity. The divine authorship of Scripture seems to mean for Barrow that all possible readings of a biblical passage always already exist as part of its intentional structure. That is to say that the text's construction (in the sense of "interpretation") is from the first a part of its construction (in the sense of "the way it is made").

What interests me about this notion is its potential applicability to the analysis of fiction. Whether Coleridge had any such possibility in mind I cannot say; it is at any rate immaterial. The purpose of my argument is to develop a concept that will be useful in talking about the construction of literary language, and Coleridge's diary entry is helpful in pointing the way. To that end I am grateful to have it, even though I can never be sure I have understood it rightly. The very sketchiness of Coleridge's text authorizes and promotes a certain imaginative descanting upon its provocative melody. It is the uncertainty of intention behind the entry, its relative lack of context, that makes it so fascinating and productive of further discourse.

The fascination provoked by the imprecision of Coleridge's notebook jotting will take us only so far, however. We will have to find something more specific than a bare reference to Isaac Barrow if the notion of a verbal imagination is to prove helpful in thinking about poetic invention. In the absence of further assistance from Coleridge himself, we may turn elsewhere for suggestions about sharpening the concept. A fortunate coincidence provides an opening in an unexpected direction: where Coleridge had described Barrow as the ideal exemplar of the verbal imagination, one of Kafka's most acute contemporary critics, Stanley Corngold, has ascribed to the author of "The Metamorphosis" a "linguistic imagination."[7] It is convenient to assume that the similarity of the two phrases reflects a substantial similarity at the conceptual level. If indeed Corngold's "linguistic imagination" is pointing toward basically the same inventive practice as Coleridge's "verbal imagination," we would have as a concrete point of departure not only the entirely nonfictional oeuvre of Barrow but also the stories and novels of Kafka.

7. "Kafka's *Die Verwandlung*: Metamorphosis of the Metaphor," *Mosaic* 3, no. 4 (1970): 106.

To understand the Christian scholar and clergyman Isaac Barrow as somehow doing the same kind of thing as the Jewish author of fantasy Franz Kafka might at first seem a mental contortion beyond the capabilities of the most agile theory. And indeed one would hardly want to minimize the differences between the characters, goals, and achievements of the two writers. Still, for all their evident differences, there is one feature in which they are strikingly similar, and it is precisely the way they go about the rhetorical task of invention. Both depend characteristically and essentially upon the process of "reading" (that is, construing) an infinitely readable text for the conceptual beginnings of their works. For Barrow, the texts to be read were always pieces of Scripture, and the methods for developing his ideas were refinements of a long tradition of sermon writing. Although Kafka occasionally also used passages from the Bible, the texts he chose were more frequently pieces of everyday language, commonplace expressions and tropes suddenly construed in unexpected ways by the developing fiction.

Let me illustrate Kafka's procedure with the example of one of his most famous short fictions, the miniature parable called "Give It Up!" The entire story consists of just these few sentences:

> It was very early in the morning, the streets clean and deserted, I was on my way to the station. As I compared the tower clock with my watch I realized that it was much later than I had thought and that I had to hurry; the shock of this discovery made me feel uncertain of the way, I wasn't very well acquainted with the town as yet; fortunately, there was a policeman at hand, I ran to him and breathlessly asked him the way. He smiled and said: "You asking me the way?" "Yes," I said, "since I can't find it myself." "Give it up! Give it up!" said he, and turned with a sudden jerk, like someone who wants to be alone with his laughter.[8]

8. I quote Kafka's fiction in English from *The Complete Stories*, ed. Nahum H. Glatzer (New York: Schocken, 1971), and in German from *Sämtliche Erzählungen*, ed. Paul Raabe (Frankfurt a.M.: Fischer, 1970). This passage is from *Stories*, 456, and *Erzählungen*, 358. "Es war sehr früh am Morgen, die Straßen rein und leer, ich ging zum Bahnhof. Als ich eine Turmuhr mit meiner Uhr verglich, sah ich, daß es schon viel später war, als ich geglaubt hatte, ich mußte mich sehr beeilen, der Schrecken über diese Entdeckung ließ mich im Weg unsicher werden, ich kannte mich in dieser Stadt nicht sehr gut aus, glücklicherweise war ein Schutzmann in der Nähe, ich lief zu ihm und fragte atemlos nach dem Weg. Er lächelte und sagte: 'Von mir willst du den Weg erfahren?' 'Ja,' sagte ich, 'da ich ihn selbst nicht finden kann.' 'Gibs auf, gibs auf,' sagte er und wandte sich mit einem großen Schwunge ab, so wie Leute, die mit ihrem Lachen allein sein wollen."

The effectiveness of this tale depends upon the readability of the phrase "breathlessly asked him the way" ("fragte atemlos nach dem Weg") and on the potential, here realized, for enormous differences among possible readings. The crucial narrative moment takes place when the policeman understands the narrator's request in a way that diverges radically from the way the reader is likely to have understood it. This difference in understanding is possible because the requirements governing reported illocutionary acts are quite different from those governing actual illocutions. The phenomenon is the same in both German and English as well as in many other languages. We can be far less specific in the report of an illocutionary act of requesting, promising, warning, or whatever than we would have to be in the performance itself; that is, we may say things like "He promised her something" or "He asked for directions," though obviously we may not say—to any real effect—"I hereby promise you something" or ask someone to give us directions without specifying where it is we want to go. We would not, unless we were seeking religious instruction, say to someone "Please, sir, kindly tell me the way." Such an utterance would seem foolish and indeed incomprehensible. We might very well say "Please tell me the way to the station" and report this later by saying "I asked him the way," because in a report a reference to an unspecified object is both possible and occasionally necessary.

Kafka's story cleverly exploits the gap between an illocution and the report of an illocution by moving from narration to dialogue at just that point where the policeman replies to the narrator's request. When the narrator reports that he went up to the policeman and "breathlessly asked him the way," we suppose this means that he said to the policeman something like "Please tell me the way to the station," but the policeman responds as if the man had said "Please tell me the way." Of course we do not suppose that the man would have actually posed such an inappropriate question, but the form of the *report* authorizes the reading. The policeman is in fact replying not to any actual illocutionary act of asking we can imagine the narrator performing, but to the form of the report. If the dialogue had begun earlier, with the request itself, the story would have lost its point completely: the policeman's reply would no longer be appropriate. "You asking me the way?" and so on is not a reasonable reply to "Sir, please tell me the way to the station." The policeman's response is justified only as a reading not of the man's actual request, but of his narration of it. There is a temporal gap between the narration and the policeman's quoted utterance, a gap that the narrative procedure carefully ignores. The narrative at one moment assumes (like all narratives) the priority of the events reported but then reports an event that presupposes the story, leading us back in an infinite regression of describing text and described action.

It turns out, then, that one of the characters in the story is also one of its readers, and he reads the narrative in a way that diverges widely from the way we read it—but not, we have to admit, in a way that is unjustified. We assume, because of the context, that the narrator's words "asked him the way" are a report of something like "Please tell me the way to the station." But the policeman could be right: the same words could be a report of the vague but philosophically provocative request, "Please tell me the way." Although we do not suppose the narrator would have been so distracted as to actually frame his request that way, it is a perfectly valid reading of the report. The phrase "breathlessly asked him the way" becomes the hinge on which a trivial, everyday matter turns into a portentous issue. In the policeman's reading, the narrator has not simply forgotten how to get to the station, he has lost his way in life, a loss that is not remediable by a hasty request to a patrolman on the street.

This characteristic example of Kafka's verbal (or linguistic) mode of invention can serve as a starting point for defining the "invention of reading." Kafka's text can function only because of the existence of another text, a piece of everyday language in this case, whose capacity for widely divergent interpretations opens up the space for narrative development. It is only because the phrase "asked him the way" can be understood as describing two very different sorts of utterances that the story "Give It Up!" can exist. The crucial action takes place in the gap between one meaning and the other, in the possibility that the rhetorical slide from our conventional reading of the phrase to the policeman's unexpected (though equally conventional) one reflects, at least in the world of the fiction, the possibility of an actual interchangeability. By forcing us to consider both interpretations of "asked him the way" at once, the parable urges us to consider the two as related on grounds other than the purely verbal. Perhaps having lost one's way to the station *is* somehow equivalent to having lost one's way in life, the story suggests. Certainly there are times when they feel the same.

The stinging effect of Kafka's story, we do not want to forget, comes in no small way from the fact that the two readings of the key phrase it offers are in a relevant sense incompatible. The narrative does not simply reconcile two somewhat different interpretations: it forces a confrontation between something commonplace and trivial on the one hand and something grandly significant on the other. The policeman's sarcastic reply, "You asking me the way?" ("Von mir willst du den Weg erfahren?"), implies that there is an enormous gulf between "me" and "the way"—that he is absolutely incapable of supplying the requested information. But in the other reading there would be no such gulf: a patrolman (*Schutzmann*) is just the person to ask about the way to the station. The narrator's asking of the policeman is therefore either exactly the right or exactly the wrong thing for him to have done. The impact of the parable depends on this confrontation, this sudden swerve, in which an action that at first seems utterly appropriate turns out to be disastrously wrong.

As presented in Kafka's parable, the phrase "asked him the way" represents an interpretive crux, a moment of undecidability that we have become familiar with under the name "aporia." The aporia in question here is not a feature of Kafka's text that we have discovered by our reading; it is rather a feature of the text Kafka read in order to write his story. And it is not something that Kafka's text reveals about the crucial phrase so much as it is something that text presupposes in order to do its work. My reading of Kafka's story is therefore not a deconstruction of that story, nor is it equivalent to the discovery that Kafka deconstructed the phrase "asked him the way." For this reason I prefer to consider Kafka's text, and as a consequence my reading of it,[9] a *construction* of the verbal imagination, because I see the story as structured by an act of construing. Such construction presupposes deconstruction in that it attends to fictions based on exploiting the narrative possibilities of language that is in a way *already* deconstructed. In Kafka's story, for example, it is clear that the action the narrative performs is not the deconstruction of the text it reads: the story does not

---

9. I do not mean to deny the difference between a text and a reading of that text (a distinction my argument requires) so much as to problematize it and thereby, perhaps paradoxically, assert the priority of the fictional construction to my critical reading. Cf. Paul de Man's comment on his deconstruction of a passage from Proust: "The reading is not 'our' reading, since it uses only the linguistic elements provided by the text itself; the distinction between author and reader is one of the false distinctions that reading makes evident. The deconstruction [in this case read *construction*] is not something we have added to the text but it constituted the text in the first place" (*Allegories of Reading*, 17).

simply point out the existence of the interpretive crux but goes further by exploiting the dramatic possibilities created by playing the two incompatible readings off against each other.

The distinction between deconstructive "pointing out" and constructive "exploiting" is meant to draw attention to the differing goals of two interrelated reading practices, one being a procedure for discovery and the other a way of making use of such discoveries. I might explain this distinction with an analogy to the oil industry.[10] It often requires highly trained experts with sophisticated technical skills to point out where the oil is; but it is a different matter involving different skills to exploit the oil once it is found. Exploitation depends upon discovery, to be sure, but does not follow automatically from it. It has been pointed out, for instance, that there is a huge amount of oil in certain shale formations, but the technology to exploit that oil profitably has not yet been developed. This is not to deny that in the proper circumstances discovery can function as a kind of exploitation: if one invests in oil stocks, it is clear that the discovery of oil itself, in advance of any development, can function as a kind of exploitation of the oil's economic power. I mention this as an acknowledgment that sophisticated deconstructors do indeed exploit their discoveries, even though they do not necessarily exploit the interpretive cruxes by way of rhetorical construction.[11]

The term "construction" therefore seems particularly appropriate to the activity I want to describe in that it foregrounds in a way its relation to deconstruction. Constructions of the verbal imagination make their narrative beginnings with texts that are already understood as undecidable in their meaning. The aporia produced by the availability of two (or more) incompatible readings is the rhetorical mo-

10. My example is, in a certain sense, a crude one. I am well aware of the metaphorical nature of this analogy and of the difference between finding oil and "finding" an aporia. But my point here has to do with the relation between finding and exploiting (or, if you will, "finding" and "exploiting") and not with that between finding and "finding." On the latter, see the discussion of seeing and "seeing" as it appears in Lewis Carroll's *Sylvie and Bruno* in my *The Incredulous Reader* (Ithaca: Cornell University Press, 1983), 87.

11. I persist, here and throughout the book, in distinguishing between reading and writing, between discovering and exploiting, between literal and figurative, and between writing criticism and writing stories. I do so not because I fail to see that such oppositions are deconstructible but because my discourse, like every other, requires a certain logocentric moment to come into being.

ment out of which the fiction is generated, not the moment of insight toward which it moves. Although these fictions, it is true, do make the deconstructive insight available to us, that is not their principal narrative tendency. The fictions I will be examining do not stop with the discovery of language's eternal and inevitable deconstructibility; they reveal rather an urge to put Humpty Dumpty back together again— perhaps tentatively, ironically, humorously, or (like Kafka) paradoxically—by inventing a fictional world whose structure allows all interpretations of the language being read to function at once.

Inventive construction based on the verbal imagination is not a form of deconstruction, though it certainly depends on the insights of deconstructive criticism as elements in its foundation. My reading of fictions based on this inventive practice is, however, like deconstruction as practiced by Paul de Man, essentially a form of rhetorical analysis. Not only is it concerned with the rhetorical issue of invention, but it tends to focus frequently on figurative language, because it is in tropes that writers so often find the possibilities for divergent readings that produce narrative space. Even when the language under construction is not strictly a trope, however, it is still likely to be an idiomatic expression, a commonplace, or some other turn of phrase wherein language is made to mean something other than what it says. In the case of "Give It Up!" the key phrase "asked him the way" is not a recognizable trope cataloged by classical rhetoric, but it is a conventional expression that regularly means something other than what it says. It is a kind of shorthand way of saying "asked him the way [to some specific place already mentioned]." The phrase becomes the impetus for a story when we realize that it can also be read as functioning according to a different interpretive convention, as if the word "way" were a shorthand for "way of living" or "method of discovering truth," as the policeman seems to read it. In the policeman's construction, we are in fact dealing with commonplace figuration, for the "way" (or "road" or "path") is an ancient and well-recognized trope for "teaching" or "rules of conduct."

In this book I will ordinarily use the term "rhetoric" to refer to language such as this—to language understood as readable under more than one interpretive convention—as well as to the activity of reading and writing such language. "Rhetoricity" will refer to a discourse's openness to radically divergent interpretations. As Paul de Man put it, rhetoric "allows for two incompatible, mutually self-destructive points of view," as for example in the so-called rhetorical question, where "a perfectly clear syntactical paradigm (the question) engenders a sentence that has at least two meanings, of which the one asserts and the other denies its own illocutionary mode."[12] Kafka uses as the impetus for his narrative the aporetic moment in which one cannot decide whether to read "asked him the way" as "asked him the way to the station" or "asked him the way to lead my life." Kafka apparently has an insight similar to de Man's about the rhetorical nature of this language, but he proceeds in a different way when he discovers such an aporia.

For de Man, the discovery of "two incompatible, mutually self-destructive points of view" in the same discourse is the goal of a critical practice (deconstruction) that seeks to reveal the intentionally rhetorical underpinnings of all literary language. For Kafka and other writers employing the same inventive mode, however, it seems to be a spur to the imagination, a challenge to create a fiction in which the incompatible readings have at least a chance of somehow fitting together on the narrative plane as well as the linguistic plane. This may not always be a happy outcome, as we readily see in the case of "Give It Up!" The possibility the story raises that having lost one's way to the station may not be so very different from having lost one's direction in life is hardly consoling. It does, however, retroactively legitimize the ambiguity of the phrase "asked him the way," whose two apparently imcompatible readings are shown to belong to the same narrative universe.

I do not wish to exclude from my usage more traditional meanings of the term "rhetoric," such as "discourse intended to persuade" or even "figurative language," and at times I will point out features of a text that are rhetorical in those senses. But as a general rule, I will intend "rhetoric" to have this special sense. It is in any case not a radical departure in the usage of the term: it is merely a more inclusive way of pointing out a feature of discourse especially visible in figurative language. It is intentionally broad; it is inclusive enough to have potential reference to all possible utterances—but only in very particular circumstances. The rhetoricity of any individual piece of discourse is not a quality that somehow resides in the nature of the discourse but derives from the circumstances of usage. The sentence "Hector is a lion" is readily considered a paradigmatically figurative expression, but it is easy to imagine circumstances in which the sentence would be neither

12. *Allegories of Reading*, 131, 10.

figurative nor rhetorical in either intention or effect. We are at the zoo, and we hear two custodians talking about the marvelous size, strength, and ferocity of Hector. "Hector?" we ask. "Can we see him?" "Yes, in the lion house," they say. "Hector is a lion." Nothing about this exchange would lead us to question the phrase further, given the circumstances stipulated. Only when the topic of discourse is known to be a person named Hector are we required to engage in a special interpretive act by shifting "lion" from its ordinary meaning (not applicable here, since we know that this Hector is a man) to a figurative one expressing bravery, strength, and aggressiveness.

Context clearly plays a central role in encouraging or discouraging the rhetorical reading of discourse. Only context allows us to differentiate a "genuine" from a "rhetorical" question, but context can also make the distinction difficult. To reuse de Man's famous example: when Edith Bunker asks Archie whether he wants his bowling shoes laced over or under, he replies, "What's the difference?" The context, for everyone except Edith, is saturated with Archie's impatience with his wife and calls for understanding this question as a rhetorical denial of any significant difference between lacing over and under. But Edith has survived living with Archie precisely by ignoring this impatience. Her context excludes it, and so she answers his question by explaining the difference between the two modes of lacing. The joke resides in Edith's "incorrect" interpretation of Archie's question as genuine. As de Man points out, however, there are contexts in which it would not be possible to adjudicate so neatly between the rhetorical and genuine uses of a question. He cites the closing line of Yeats's poem "Among School Children" as a particularly telling example. There is simply no way for the reader to know whether the question "How can we know the dancer from the dance?" is genuine or rhetorical. The context in effect encourages a rhetorical reading in which neither possibility may be excluded.

Since the rhetoricity of texts thus resides in the degree to which potentially conflicting acts of reading are encouraged, I conclude that rhetoric is at bottom a relational concept. Rhetoric really comes into being only in the interaction between a text and a reader, between an utterance and its interpreter. Because the reader involved in rhetorical construction is always a writer—"construction" being a concept that unites reading and writing—a new text necessarily results from this reading. The new text cannot be properly understood as existing in the splendid ontological isolation presumed by the New Criticism, because it cannot function in the absence of the rhetorical discourse it reads. A rhetorical construction is therefore always understandable as the *interpretant* of another text. C. S. Peirce defines the interpretant as "the idea to which [the sign] gives rise."[13] He stresses the productive nature of the relation between sign and interpretant when he says that a sign "addresses somebody, that is, creates in the mind of that person an equivalent sign, *or perhaps a more developed sign. That sign which it creates I call the interpretant.*"[14] A rhetorical construction can be profitably understood as the imaginative interpretant, a "more developed sign," created out of the interpretation of a text construed as a rhetorical sign. Peirce in fact proposes that the aspect of his nascent science of semiotics that would deal with the production of interpretants—that is, that would "ascertain the laws by which . . . one sign gives birth to another"—should be called "pure rhetoric."[15]

Although Peirce's use of the definite article in speaking of "the" idea a sign produces suggests some sort of unitary concept of the interpretant, it is clear enough from his discussion that a sign may have multiple interpretants, indeed an infinite number. Futhermore, since "the interpretant is nothing but another representation" and hence itself also potentially a sign, "it has its [own] interpretant again."[16] My book is therefore the set of interpretants generated by reading the set of texts I understand as interpretants of various other rhetorical texts. But my texts are plainly of a different character from those I read, in that my readings are rhetorical constructions not so much because I employ the invention of reading as because others, the authors of the fictions, have done so for me. My texts do not make fictions out of the possibility for multiple interpretation inherent in those texts. They are explicatory rather than narrative. I bring this up to stress the special nature of that

13. *Collected Papers* 1:339. Quoted by Umberto Eco, *A Theory of Semiotics* (Bloomington: Indiana University Press, 1979), 69.

14. C. S. Peirce, "Logic as Semiotic: The Theory of Signs" in *Semiotics: An Introductory Anthology*, ed. Robert E. Innis (Bloomington: Indiana University Press, 1985), 5. I have added the first set of italics.

15. "Logic as Semiotic," 6.

16. Quoted by Eco, *Theory of Semiotics*, 69.

set of interpretants I call "constructions" of inventive reading.[17] My mode of invention is not exactly the same as theirs.

I follow Peirce in the essential matter of finding rhetoric in an interaction, a productive relation, between two discourses. I am uneasy, however, with the identification of those two discourses with something called "thought." Thought certainly does enter the picture, but for me it does so in the interpretive process itself and not necessarily before. The texts read by practitioners of rhetorical construction are more often treated as pure material signifiers whose character as "thought" is open to question. Calvino's reading of the scientific report of the extinction of the dinosaurs is absolutely oblivious of the "thought" this discourse, construed as science, represents.[18] An even more dramatic example is Calvino's "The Distance of the Moon," which makes hash out of Sir George Darwin's "thought" cited in its headnote.[19] Rhetorical reading so often operates in this way, deliberately ignoring the intention of the text being read, even when that intention is quite clear, that it is better to divorce discourse from "thought." I suspect one of the attractions of rhetorical reading for imaginative writers is the opportunity to put the stamp of their own thought upon texts that may be understood as having no thought of their own. The new discourse generated by rhetorical reading is certainly the product of thought, but here again it might be best not to equate the text itself (the discourse conceived of as material signifier) with thought. The question of how one thought gives rise to another is certainly an interesting and important one, but it is not my question.

Even taking into account this substantial difference between Peirce's line of inquiry and mine, I think it will be clear that my project is more like a semiotic "pure rhetoric" than like what a number of historians of criticism have called "rhetorical criticism." This approach to literature is associated with, at the two historical extremes, Horace's *Ars poetica* and Wayne C. Booth's *The Rhetoric of Fiction*.[20] Their way of under-

17. Actually, the set of readings that constitute this book seems to be a more rigorous embodiment of Peirce's original definition of "pure rhetoric" than the set of imaginative works I read. The full text of the definition quoted in part above says of pure rhetoric that its "task is to ascertain the laws by which in every scientific intelligence one sign gives birth to another, and especially one thought brings forth another." This definition in its full form shows that Peirce's conception of rhetoric is not exactly like mine.

18. See chapter 4 below.

19. I discuss this example in detail in *The Incredulous Reader*, 160–64.

20. (Chicago: University of Chicago Press, 1961).

standing the poetic process is characterized by "a tendency to derive the rationale, the chief determinants of elements and forms, and the norms of such artifacts [i.e., literary works] from the legitimate requirements and springs of pleasure in the readers for whom it is written."[21] Horace conceives of the poet's task as winning the approval and admiration of an audience whose tastes and habits of thought are well understood. The form of a literary work is determined not by the nature of the subject matter but by the expectations of the audience: a play should have five acts, for example, because that is what the audience prefers and expects. The issue Booth addresses is more narrowly and perhaps more subtly framed, but it still concerns the fundamental problem of winning an audience's approval. Booth examines the means by which writers of fiction gain assent and sustained attention for texts that, unlike a telephone book or a set of accounts, hold no practical interest for the reader. M. H. Abrams calls this "pragmatic criticism" because it attends to the matter of what the author does to and for the audience to engage each reader's participation in the fiction. The author acts upon the reader by means of the text.

In the case of rhetorical construction, the energy flows more in the opposite direction. The reader in question here is none other than the author, who by performing an act of reading upon someone else's language is able to invent the language for his or her literary invention. The conceptual framework might properly be called pragmatic, but the locus of activity is elsewhere than it is for Horace or Booth. In Abrams's version of pragmatic criticism, the shape of a literary work is determined by the author's expectations about the work's potential audience; in rhetorical construction, the narrative content of the work is determined by the author's activity as an audience. Of course I do not mean to imply that writers like Boccaccio or Flannery O'Connor did not have expectations about their audiences or did not incorporate these expectations into their writing. I will in fact suggest quite strongly the contrary. I choose, however, to focus on the inventive practice of these writers rather than on the resources of their language as shaped by their literary goals. Rhetorical criticism would have, and indeed has had, much to say about works such as the *Decameron* and "The River"

---

21. M. H. Abrams, "Poetry, Theories of," in *The Encyclopedia of Poetry and Poetics*, ed. Alex Preminger et al. (Princeton: Princeton University Press, 1965), 642.

and the others treated in this book, but it moves in a different direction from mine.

A theoretical position that has recently emerged—so recently in fact that its principal exposition was published while I was writing the first parts of this book—may be the one closest in spirit to the enterprise of rhetorical construction. Although derived from Derrida, it is chiefly the creation of Gregory Ulmer, who names it in the title of his book *Applied Grammatology*.[22] Ulmer takes as his first task an attempt to give a coherent account of the kind of writing activity that could take place in the wake of Derrida's critique of logocentrism. He proposes applied grammatology as a praxis consonant with a postdeconstructive point of view, a "methodology . . . operating on every manner of inscription" and even "generating 'information.' The initial move is to examine the metaphors (verbal images) lining every discourse, in order to decompose or unfold and redirect the possibilities of meaning inherent in the material" (p. 314). We can start on the way to becoming grammatologists, Ulmer says, by agreeing "to let language do some thinking for us" (p. 315). Ultimately, grammatological composition (which Ulmer calls "Writing") can and must move beyond this beginning: "My argument is that applied grammatology will be characterized by a picto-ideo-phonographic Writing that puts speech back in its place while taking into account the entire scene of writing" (p. 157). Ulmer is therefore interested in the visual arts, in film, video, and various other forms of technological inscription, all of which belong to the scene of writing taken in its totality.

The argument that follows has a grammatological cast to it, though this is not so much my doing as that of the authors I read. I am not so much grammatological myself as the discoverer of grammatology in others, since I think one could view the practitioners of rhetorical construction examined here as grammatologists of a sort *avant la lettre*. These are writers who "unfold and redirect the possibilities of meaning inherent in the material" of received texts. By making their inventive beginnings with already-deconstructed language, they put themselves in just the position of Ulmer's grammatologist, who also uses language to make a beginning. But Ulmer's grammatologist belongs

---

22. *Applied Grammatology: Post(e)-Pedagogy from Jacques Derrida to Joseph Beuys* (Baltimore: Johns Hopkins University Press, 1985). Citations in the text below refer to this edition.

more to the present or future than to the past, participating in something Ulmer unabashedly defines as "the *inventio* of a new rhetoric" (p. xii). Both rhetorical construction and Writing may be described as inventive practices exploiting the possibilities of limitless readability in rhetorical discourse. Ulmer finds a paradigm in Derrida's manner of using a certain kind of figurative discourse, "the description of quotidian objects," as an inventive beginning generating an account of "the most complex or abstract levels of thought" (p. xii). This is a compositional strategy obviously very similar to rhetorical construction.

My reader may already suspect, even on the basis of this necessarily sketchy account of some of Ulmer's notions, that applied grammatology is a broader and indeed more radically innovative category than I would claim to have defined in these pages. Grammatological Writing is open in very interesting ways to all media through which one could disseminate information, while my concern remains very much centered upon speech. "The applied phase of grammatology," Ulmer says, "is meant to be . . . adequate to an era of interdisciplines, intermedia, electronic apparatus" (p. xiii); but my presentation of rhetorical construction has nothing to say about these matters, perhaps because I want primarily to demonstrate the relevance of rhetorical reading to the literature of past eras. Ulmer pitches his theory aggressively toward a future characterized by a variety of technologies for recording and manipulating information; I admit to being more inclined to show the existence of the constructive mode of invention over a long span of history. Where applied grammatology aims to be "the *inventio* of a new rhetoric," rhetorical construction proves to be an inventive practice of very long standing.

This only points up a fact I have no desire to obscure: the construction of inventive reading is not involved with the production of a *new* rhetoric but is very much part of the tradition. If there is an innovation in my approach, it is in projecting elements from the area of *elocutio* onto the field of *inventio*. Classical rhetoric did not think of elocutionary matters such as tropes as having any relevance for the issue of invention, since *inventio* was quite reasonably assumed to precede *elocutio* in the compositional process. I can only agree with this traditional view—which is, after all, both logical and serviceable—when the object of analysis is a single, isolated discourse. Taken as a discrete unit, the individual text can deploy its elocutionary forms only after the writer has gathered the necessary material (*res*) and worked out the discursive possibilities (*inventio*). In my view, however, no discourse ever actually exists in such isolation. All texts come into being in a world already occupied by other discourse, a world richly populated with other people's *elocutio*. The inventive potential of tropes is realized in the writer's act of reading this *elocutio* in the special way I have described.

The imaginative constructions in which I am interested, the products of the verbal or linguistic imagination, arise not primarily out of the making of rhetoric but rather out of rhetorical reading. Kafka did not make up the phrase "asked him the way" or create the interpretive aporia it can lead to. He takes this existing rhetoric and exploits its rhetoricity. The rhetorical imagination constructs its language by construing other language, by restructuring in a sense its deconstructed elements. This sort of rhetorical construction is evidently an intertextual enterprise. It arises out of a consciousness of language as a preexisting order carrying authority and enjoining a certain obedience. Kafka, to return to the example with which I made my beginning, was a writer filled with a kind of respect for everyday language ("gemeine Sprache")[23] that led him to think very seriously about the implications of even the most vulgar commonplaces of street language, expressions that were not typical of his own discourse. A good example is the insulting metaphor "Du bist ein Ungeziefer" (cf. English "You're a louse"). Though unquestionably a trope, the phrase is neither clever nor surprising; it is the commonest sort of verbal assault, equating the addressee with something low, dirty, and valueless, and Kafka could have heard it from countless sources, sometimes, at least in his imagination, directed at himself. But no matter where or how often he might have heard it, it seems entirely likely that he never said it. From what can be determined from reports by Kafka's family, friends, and acquaintances, it is quite possible that he never uttered such an insult to another human being.

While it will not be the business of this book to investigate in the manner of John Livingston Lowes[24] the sources of the language exploited by rhetorical construction, it is one of the defining characteris-

23. On this subject see Ruth V. Gross, "Rich Text/Poor Text: A Kafkan Confusion," *PMLA* 95, no. 2, (1980): 168-82.
24. I refer, of course, to his famous book *The Road to Xanadu: A Study in the Ways of the Imagination* (1927; rpt. Boston: Houghton Mifflin, 1955). I discuss Lowes's approach to the problem of literary invention in "The Story in the Image."

tics of this mode of writing that those sources, wherever they may be, lie outside the writer. A moment's reflection will reveal why this is a fundamental condition of the process. The effectiveness of an imaginative construction depends on the possibility of radically different interpretations of the same text. The fiction is interesting and convincing only so long as the reader accepts both readings as equally plausible, and this can most reliably happen when the text being read is already somehow a known quantity. To be able to assent to the fiction, the reader needs to test the readings offered against his or her own experience. While this sort of assent can be obtained for readings of the author's own language, assuming the author uses standard interpretive conventions, the fiction will be far more potent when the discourse being interpreted is in some sense already common property. Putting it another way, the reader is more likely to *care* about the interpretation of language that already somehow belongs to him or her, that is already part of the normal functioning of the world, than about a text newly minted for the occasion. The reader is also in a better position to judge, perhaps to be surprised by, the correctness of the divergent interpretations offered.

To return to the concrete: if "Du bist ein Ungeziefer" were not a perfectly ordinary expression with an accepted conventional figurative meaning, it would not be so surprising, distressing, or fascinating when Kafka has Gregor Samsa wake up one morning in a position to hear those words with "new" meaning. I put that "new" in quotation marks because the convention that would understand "Ungeziefer" literally as "verminous insect" is actually, for most everyday discourse, the more prevalent one. In the event one were in the position of having to address a bug in German, it would not be at all unreasonable to say "Du bist ein Ungeziefer." Kafka has arranged a situation in which one could properly address Gregor Samsa with these words in either the literal or the figurative meaning, or in both. Though no one actually thus addresses him in the story, the existence of the expression as part of a common stock of similar unremarkable phrases belonging to every speaker of German acts as a kind of anchor in the known universe for this story partaking so strongly of the supernatural. In the case of "asked him the way," we can see how much the parable depends on the ordinariness of the phrase to draw its reader in. All of us have from time to time "asked the way" and later said so, or wondered to ourselves if we hadn't perhaps lost the way, and because we have performed essentially the same act as the narrator we participate to some extent in his discomfiture.

Constructions like "Give It Up!" and "The Metamorphosis" live off the fact that the world was full of discourse before they were written. What might be a problem for Harold Bloom's poetic latecomers[25] is the very spark that ignites literary invention for Kafka and others like him. Instead of striving with Pope's poet to give the reader "What oft was thought, but ne'er so well express'd," these authors give us what has been expressed a thousand times before but perhaps never so thoroughly or imaginatively thought out, interpreted, and represented. In this regard, and others as well, rhetorical construction is very similar to what I have elsewhere called "logomimesis."[26]

Logomimetic fictions reproduce and elaborate structures found not in the nonlinguistic world but in the resources of language itself; they make the structures of fictional reality conform to patterns provided by tropes, topoi, and other preexisting texts. A story like "The Metamorphosis" is logomimetic in that it imitates the equation of person and bug proposed by phrases analogous to "You're a louse." The parable "Give It Up!" on the other hand does not so much imitate the phrase "asked him the way" as stage a confrontation between two plausible interpretations. "The Metamorphosis" stages such a confrontation also, but it does so by means of the logomimesis. Rhetorical construction is the general phenomenon of which logomimesis is a special (and particularly interesting) case. Some of the examples of rhetorical construction I will discuss in detail later in the book are highly logomimetic, while others are not.

Because they always occupy the disputed territory between two more-or-less hostile positions, it is useful to think of rhetorical constructions as enactments of a kind of dialogue. Now the word "dialogue" has become so fashionable, surpassing "intertextuality," "aporia," and maybe even "deconstruction" in the very recent past, that I hesitate to use it. But the issue is of such obvious relevance to my topic that I will have to take that risk. Anglo-American critics have seen an

25. The "ephebes" of Bloom's *The Anxiety of Influence* (London: Oxford University Press, 1973) struggle to make a place for their own writing in a universe already replete with discourse.

26. A definition and detailed discussion of this term can be found in *The Incredulous Reader*, 41–57.

abundance of dialogic readings, perhaps in surfeit, but to the good effect that we are now far more sensitive to the essential participation of a literary text and indeed of all language in interactions with other discourse. The substantial impact that Bakhtin has had on the institution of criticism is based on the needed correction he gives to a hermeneutic tradition that has tended to view all literary texts as locutions without interlocutors. My notion of rhetorical construction evidently moves in a similar direction, taking the interaction between text and text as one of its principal defining characteristics.

If we may take a passage from Voloshinov's *Marxism and the Philosophy of Language* as Bakhtin's or at least fundamentally Bakhtinian, we can see in brief how the notions I am developing here relate to the "dialogism" of Bakhtin and his circle: "A word is territory *shared* by both addresser and addressee, by the speaker *and* his interlocutor."[27] The texts read by works of rhetorical construction are clearly such shared words; but more importantly, the texts constructed out of these readings are a special kind of shared territory in that they belong equally to more than one interpretive possibility. The fictional text mediates between the two conflicting positions, giving space and support to each. Although we cannot without resorting to metaphor speak of "communication" as taking place between these two positions, there is a kind of dialogue in that two very different voices can be heard. Because of the constructed narrative, these are not simply two monologic discourses taking place at the same time; they interact by means of the fiction. I have already discussed, for example, how the situation presented in "Give It Up!" potentially alters the condition of conflict between the two readings of "asked him the way." The sudden appearance of the policeman's interpretation nurtures a suggestion that the two readings may not be mutually contradictory after all, that the inability to find the way to the station may be a symptom of the more serious problem of having lost one's way in life. But this remains at best only a suggestion. The essential difference between the two interpretations remains.

Katerina Clark and Michael Holquist have hit on a particularly apt formulation in characterizing Bakhtin's concept of dialogue as "com-

27. V. N. Voloshinov, *Marxism and the Philosophy of Language*, trans. Ladislav Matejka and I. R. Titunik (New York: Seminar Press, 1973), 86.

munication between simultaneous differences."[28] This concise phrase helps to show how near rhetorical construction comes to dialogism without really being the same thing. That I am dealing with structures of discourse whose fundamental building blocks are simultaneous differences should be clear enough from what has been said so far. It is in the area of communication that these rhetorical texts take on a character that is not quite dialogic. As I just pointed out, the interaction between the two readings presented is only figuratively communicative. The voices we overhear within the confines of a rhetorical construction may be thought of as engaged in a kind of dialogue, but it is not strictly speaking the Bakhtinian variety.

It is possible, however, to adopt a slightly different point of view that looks at the *other* dialogue in progress. When we come to consider the relation between constructed rhetoric and the texts it construes, one might well speak of a properly Bakhtinian dialogue between the imaginative writer and the community of speakers whose tropes, commonplaces, and interpretations thereof spark rhetorical invention. The writer is able to make his or her own meaning—something new, original, and unquestionably the product of a particular individual— by using language and interpretations of that language that are not at all original, that indeed function properly only because they are already the property of the community at large. The voice of the collective other is always vigorously present in rhetorical construction, speaking not only audibly but with authority. The rhetorical writer—Kafka, for instance—in effect says to the communal voice: "You are right, all of you, when you say (or understand) 'I asked him the way.' I can show you a situation in which virtually all your readings are appropriate." A construction like "Give It Up!" is both an expression of the writer's individual imagination and an acknowledgment of the community's control over both speaking and understanding.

The dialogue between the individual reader and the constitutive linguistic power of the community is at the essence of rhetoric. Rhetorical construction takes place in the space between a received discourse (what we might call "the texts themselves") and a particular interpreting consciousness. It functions best when both parties in the dialogue have certain qualities: the reader ought to be sensitive to the rhetorical potential of language, and the text should be situated in a context that

28. *Mikhail Bakhtin* (Cambridge: Harvard University Press, 1984), 9.

makes that potential visible. When these conditions are met there is no longer any question of conflict between the subjectivity of the reader and the objectivity of the text. If these terms have any meaning at all in such a situation, we would have to say that both partners in the dialogue are equally subjective and objective. The invention of reading tolerates no absolute opposition between reader and text, though it certainly allows the distinction. It does resist, however, the distinction between its practice of reading and any theory (such as this one) that seeks to account for it. How could there be any act of theorizing about rhetorical reading able to stand outside the dialogue, able therefore to avoid its own acts of reading? Since I am engaged in the construction of such a theory, my text inevitably consists of a set of readings. Here is the first: Construction is a matter of both structure (in the text) and construing (on the part of the reader). The proper way to start defining the concept of rhetorical construction is to read its language rhetorically. And that, of course, is how I have made my own beginning.

2 | *Rhetorical Moments*

The special act of reading that initiates the process of rhetorical construction merits a special designation: I call it a *rhetorical moment*.[1] I use the word "moment" both with the usual meaning of "instant" and in the relatively technical sense of "cause or motive of action," the latter in order to refer to the initiatory aspect of this kind of reading. The moment or instant of understanding is to be viewed not as the end point in a process of reception but rather as the beginning of an act of poetic activity. It is rhetorical because it considers the text before it to be legitimately comprehensible under two interpretive conventions at once. Because the character of the reader/writer is as important to the process as the character of the text being read, we may understand it as a kind of dialogic interaction in which the rhetoricity of an existing text is exploited to produce a new text, a rhetorical construction.

Since rhetorical constructions depend on the possibility of employing different interpretive conventions on the same text, the character and availability of such conventions are clearly determining features of rhetorical moments. By far the most frequent choice presented among interpretive modes involves possibilities of figuration, such as the decision whether to read "literally" (in what was once called the *modus rectus*) or "figuratively" (in the *modus obliquus*). Most rhetorical moments are therefore structured by what we might call a tropological uncertainty. We can profitably understand the rhetorical moment of

1. I used this term for the first time in "Kafka's Rhetorical Moment," *PMLA* 98, no. 1, (January 1983): 37–46.

24

"The Metamorphosis," for example, as determined by the possibility of reading a phrase like "You're a louse" literally and figuratively at the same time. We will find this sort of rhetorical moment again and again as we investigate the constructions of inventive reading. Other kinds of tropological uncertainties exist, some of them perhaps not very different from that based on the literal/figurative pair. We saw in "Give It Up!" a case where two forms of oblique reference were made to confront each other: "the way" was either a figure for the proper manner of conducting one's life or a conventional shorthand for "way to the station." One can understand this as two competing figurative readings or as literal against figurative, depending on one's point of view. We come up against the fact that the "literal" is, when examined closely, only a special case of figuration. This is an important linguistic reality, but it has only minor significance for this inquiry. "Literal" remains a convenient term to refer to a figure that has become conventionally transparent. What is important here is the possibility of two different readings, and it matters relatively little whether we think of them as literal and figurative or as two different forms of figuration. They are both products of tropological uncertainty.

Another genre of rhetorical moment arises out of the problem of deciding whether a given utterance is or is not an illocutionary act. Although not so frequent as moments of tropological uncertainty, beginnings made out of these performative uncertainties are frequent enough in literature to deserve particular attention here. While most languages have special modes of expression, including "performative verbs," to signal the performance of an illocutionary act, there are also many circumstances in which either the grammatical form or the contextual environment (or both) fails to provide sufficient information so we can decide one way or the other. An especially dramatic example of such a performative uncertainty forms the basis for one of the principal rhetorical moments in Kafka's novel *The Trial*.[2] The narrator reports in the opening sentence that the hero, Joseph K., "without having done anything wrong was arrested one morning."[3] It is not clear, however,

2. The discussion of *The Trial* that follows is an abbreviated form of an argument I made at length in "Kafka's Rhetorical Moment."

3. Franz Kafka, *The Trial*, trans. Willa Muir and Edwin Muir (New York: Modern Library, 1964), 6; *Der Prozeß*, in *Franz Kafka: Die Romane* (Frankfurt a.M.: Fischer, 1966), 260: "Ohne daß er etwas Böses getan hätte, wurde er eines Morgens verhaftet."

that K. ever is actually arrested, because the novel shows us no clear-cut illocutionary act of arresting K. The first K. hears of his "arrest" is from one of the warders who mysteriously appear in his room: "You may not go out," the warder tells K.: "you're under arrest" ("Sie dürfen nicht weggehen, Sie sind ja verhaftet") (*Trial* 5–6, *Prozeß* 260).

The warder's interjected "ja" has a peculiar effect on the performative status of his statement, because this particle is used only in cases where the speaker assumes that the listener already knows what he is talking about. To make an arrest, one would not normally say "Sie sind *ja* verhaftet"; one would say simply "Sie sind verhaftet," just as in English one would say "You're under arrest." In both German and English, usage requires that we perform the illocutionary act of arresting by using a locutionary structure that simply asserts a perlocutionary effect. (Other examples would be "You're fired" and "You're out." We never say "I hereby fire you" or "I hereby declare you to be out." Any umpire who came out with the latter would undoubtedly be killed, and deservedly so.) A locution like "You're fired" or "You're under arrest" is potentially rhetorical because there are no linguistic means by which one can determine whether the words are being used as performative. It is easy to imagine circumstances in which they would not be: "I just heard the bad news from John. You're under arrest. I'm sure it's all a mistake." As a (nonperformative) assertion, "You're under arrest" is true only if an illocutionary act of arresting has already taken place. But in K.'s case the reader knows of no such previous action and must therefore wonder if the warder is not (*a*) mistaken or (*b*) trying to perform his own act of arresting K. Does the warder have the authority to arrest people? And even if he did, would the expression "Sie sind ja verhaftet" do the job?

The case of Joseph K.'s arrest is a rhetorical moment mainly because of that "ja." If K. had already been arrested, it would make perfect sense to use it, to say in effect, "As you know, you're under arrest." Since we have no such knowledge, it might make more sense to assume that the warder's remark is indeed a performative. But that particle "ja" argues strongly against such a reading, since its assumption of the listener's agreement would radically undermine the intended act. Is K. ever arrested? The novel provides evidence in both the affirmative and the negative, so the reader can never be certain. The fiction of *The Trial* operates precisely in the space between the two possibilities.

Performative Uncertainty in Schiller's *Mary Stuart* and Sarraute's *The Use of Speech*

A striking example of the way even an apparently straightforward speech-act can become a rhetorical moment occurs in a crucial scene in Schiller's play *Mary Stuart*.[4] The issue is whether Elisabeth has ordered the execution of the woman she believes is her rival for the throne. The English queen clearly wants Mary out of her way, but it is equally evident that she does not want to bear the responsibility for her death. This ambivalence motivates much of her behavior throughout the play, as she tells Mortimer quite directly early in the action:

> I had supposed the law would act for me,
> And keep my own hand undefiled by blood.
> Her sentence is pronounced. What have I gained?
> It must be *executed*, Mortimer.
> And *I* must authorize the execution.
> I bear the blame, I'm hated for the act,
> I see no way to save appearances;
> That is the worst of it! (2.5)[5]

The whole point of this confession of her problem is to suggest to the apparently devoted Mortimer that he solve it for her by killing Mary "on his own initiative." She does not mention, of course, that to completely "save appearances" she would have to see to the immediate apprehension and execution of anyone responsible for the murder of the queen of Scots. Her strategy does not work, since Mortimer is in fact devoted not to Elisabeth but to Mary.

The rhetoric of the speech is revealing in its import, however. Elisabeth asserts her desire to let the law act ("die Gesetze handeln lassen")

---

4. I cite Schiller's play in German from F. Schiller, *Sämtliche Werke*, vol. 2 (Munich: Hanser Verlag, 1959), 549–686, and in English from *Mary Stuart*, trans. Sophie Wilkins (Woodbury, N.Y.: Barron's, 1959). For the convenience of readers of various editions, I refer to act and scene rather than to page numbers.

5. "Ich wollte die Gesetze handeln lassen, / Die eigne Hand vom Blute rein behalten. / Das Urteil ist gesprochen. Was gewinn ich? / Es muß *vollzogen* werden, Mortimer! / Und *ich* muß die Vollziehung anbefehlen. / Mich immer trifft der Haß der Tat. Ich muß / Sie eingestehen, und kann den Schein nicht retten. / Das ist das Schlimmste!"

while she herself remains separated from the action. A form of discourse, law, is supposed to perform actions apart from any human agency. The queen is disappointed, perhaps even surprised, to discover that, at least in an absolute monarchy, this does not happen: the law is an expression of human will, signified by the fact that the monarch must personally sign the order of execution. Elisabeth continues throughout the play, though, to search for some way to get the deed done and at the same time "wash her own name clean" ("ihren eignen Namen reinzuwaschen"), as Paulet puts it (2.7). The importance of a person's good name, especially the queen's, is stressed over and over in the course of the play (e.g. 1.8, 2.3, 2.8, and as discussed below, 4.11 and 5.15). One of the main elements in the play's action, in fact, concerns what will happen to the English queen's name and how she herself will use it.

Finally, after much wavering, Elisabeth signs the execution order Davison has brought her; but after signing it she gives it back to Davison, telling him to "take it away" ("Nehmt es zurück") and adding, "I give it / Into your hands" (4.11). It is peculiar that she should thus imply, first, that she is returning to Davison the same thing he gave to her, and second, that Mary's fate now rests in his hands. Davison cannot believe either of these implications and urgently seeks clarification: he asks, "You have decided?" The queen's reply clarifies nothing: "I was asked to sign this. / I did so. But a sheet of paper, signed, / Does not decide, or kill" ("Ein Blatt Papier entscheidet / Noch nicht, ein Name tötet nicht").

With the declaration that "a name does not kill," Elisabeth is denying the very principle that underlies all speech-acts. She is in effect denying that language (in this case a name) can do things (in this case bring about someone's death). It is the old "sticks and stones" argument, usually applied by a child who has in fact been deeply hurt by language as a way of salvaging some dignity. If names could indeed never hurt us, we would not feel the need to declare so loudly that they do not. In this case Davison can only counter with the assertion that in the proper circumstances (that is, *these*) names can surely kill: "Your signature [*Dein* Name], under this paragraph, / Decides and kills; it is a winged bolt / Of thunder when it strikes." Elisabeth is saying that she has not committed a deadly act; she has merely signed a piece of paper, and that under compulsion from the "fickle crowd" of her subjects.

Davison's position is that the queen's act of signing the execution order constitutes bringing about Mary's death as surely as swinging the axe.

Of course Davison could keep the execution order in his pocket, show it to no one, and stop the chain of events set in motion by the signature. Is that what the queen wants? If so, Davison is perfectly prepared to do it. He simply wants to be certain what his sovereign requires of him so that he, for whom "obedience / Is my sagacity," can obey. "In clear and simple words, say what you mean: / What shall be done with this decree of blood?" Elisabeth's reply appeals to an authority we would not, in this context, expect: "Its title states its meaning" ("Sein Name spricht es aus"). The name, the very thing to which she had only a few lines earlier denied the power to do things, is now invoked as an active force in the production of meaning. In a statement that sounds almost Heideggerian, she asserts that the name (of the document) "speaks forth" precisely "what shall be done" ("Was soll . . . geschehen"). Of course the possibility exists that the queen's invocation of the power of names is here meant as an ironic turnabout; that Elisabeth is in a sense simply throwing back in Davison's face the notion to which he had ascribed such power. But if it is irony, Davison does not take it so: he continues to ask for a direct clarification of the queen's intention. Does she want the order carried out immediately? Her reply is once again evasive: "I did not say so, and I dread to think it" ("Das *sag* ich nicht, und zittre, es zu denken"). For a person who has denied the power of words to do things, this is another unexpected turn. She is extremely careful to deny that she has *said* the order should be carried out at once, but she leaves open the possibility that she is (tremblingly) *thinking* just that.

Davison, who sees his office as nothing more or less than obedience to the wishes of his monarch, supposes that if the queen knows what she is thinking she ought simply to say it to him directly so he can put those thoughts into action. He repeats his appeals to her to "speak" ("sprich"), "say, make clear" ("sage, bestimme") what it is she expects him to do with the distasteful document, to which she replies that indeed she has already done so ("Ich *habs* gesagt"). She finally dismisses Davison, who still has no idea what he is required to do, with the injunction to "do your office."

That office is not the same in her eyes as in his. Davison supposes that it is the queen's role to initiate actions and his to carry them out.

But by denying power to her name on the document and by refusing to say what she might be thinking, Elisabeth is demonstrating that she wants not to be understood as the initiator of this action. In so doing she sets up another parallel/contrast between herself and the rival she wants dead. Schiller, in a nice stroke of irony, has Mary's confessor accuse her of exactly the same "crime" of which Elisabeth is guilty: "It may be that, with sly equivocation, / You did avoid the *word* that makes you guilty, / Although your *will* was party to the crime" (5.7). Although Mary offers a fairly convincing denial, made the more convincing by our knowledge that she had earlier reacted in shock at Mortimer's proposal to gain her release by killing Drury, Paulet, and even Elisabeth, if necessary, Elisabeth makes the distinction between "word" and "will" the foundation of her position. She wants the act carried out, but she cannot accept responsibility for being its beginning. Davison's "office" is now, much to his confusion, precisely what it has never been and to his mind could never be: to stand in the role of author of the execution order to which Elisabeth has put her name. But how can that be? How can one person take responsibility for the words of another? The tradition of reading to which Schiller and his audience belong has already answered the question. The author is no longer responsible for his or her words once the text has been delivered into the hands of a reader who interprets it. Elisabeth gives Davison a fully rhetorical text (consisting of both the document itself, duly signed, and her refusal to confirm that it represents her will) that he has no choice but to interpret. When the queen later discovers that Davison has in fact given the order to Burleigh, who in turn has carried it out, she professes to be incensed: "Did I not command / Most strictly that you guard it with great care?" (5.14). No, that is not what she commanded, and Davison says so. "Dare you assert / I lie? When did I order you to give / The writ to Burleigh?" "Not in plain words," he pleads, "but—." "So you presume to lay your own construction / Upon my words; lend them your bloody meaning?" ("Nichtswürdiger! Du wagst es, meine Worte / Zu *deuten*? Deinen eignen blutigen Sinn / Hineinzulegen?").

By engaging in deliberately rhetorical discourse, Elisabeth has coerced Davison into the act of interpretation (*Deutung*) for which she now condemns him. Every reader of the play understands that the queen is brutally misusing her poor secretary to relieve herself of the responsibility that indeed belongs to her. Readers also understand, without the need to call upon speech-act theory, that Elisabeth has arranged a situation in which she has both said and not said something, both performed and not performed the speech-act of condemning Mary to death. What may not be so clear to every reader is that Schiller returns in the final two scenes of the play to the very same issue that had been the crux of the discussion between Elisabeth and Davison earlier: the power and value of a name. In the same speech in which she accuses Davison of committing the crime of interpreting her, she also accuses him of misusing royal power: "—Shrewsbury, do you see how they misuse / My name?" ("Ihr sehet, wie mein Name / Gemißbraucht wird"). The playwright has made the queen tell the exact truth, though in a way she did not intend; for Elisabeth does not specify the agent responsible for misusing her name, she merely asserts that is has "been misused." The context makes clear enough that the agent she has in mind is Davison, and it is thus that Shrewsbury understands her. But, recalling the dialogue of 4.11, we realize that it is Elisabeth herself who has in the more profound sense misused her name in order to rid herself of Mary, rid herself of the responsibility for ridding herself of Mary, and provide herself with a convenient scapegoat to take on her own guilt. By refusing to acknowledge the power of her name to Davison, she has very much misused it. She has done what Shrewsbury supposes Davison must have done: "surrendered thy name" ("deinen Namen . . . preisgegeben"). In the event, it is the queen herself and not the secretary who has surrendered the royal name, not only to the "loathing of all the ages," but more directly by giving over her name (as signature on the execution order) to Davison while at the same time withholding from him any knowledge of her will. She did indeed surrender to him, quite deliberately, the power of her name.

But now she wants to reclaim for herself the power of her name, to deny in fact that she had ever meant to give it up. She asks Burleigh, who saw to the actual completion of the execution, if Davison turned the order over to him "in my name" ("in meinem Namen"). The question is important only on the assumption that the queen's name has a direct connection to the queen's will, an assumption Elisabeth confirms by saying, "And yet you carried out / This writ in haste, without asking my pleasure?" ("Und Ihr vollstreckt ihn, / Rasch, ohne meinen Willen erst zu wissen?"). We know, of course, that Burleigh would surely have had no better success than Davison at discovering the queen's will, but that is less important here than the implied admission that what is done in the queen's "name" must presuppose the queen's consent. She is still unable to admit, however, that her own inscription of her name did represent her will and did initiate Mary's execution.

Elisabeth's language in *Mary Stuart* contains a number of rhetorical moments, but it is worth remembering that the rhetoricity of the queen's discourse depends heavily on her ability to enforce her own interpretive decisions. Schiller relies on the fact that the audience will understand Elisabeth's intentions in spite of her deliberate obfuscation and will therefore find the way she reads her own discourse to be arbitrary and self-serving. The rhetorical moments the play turns on are for the most part of Elisabeth's own making, created out of expediency on the spur of the moment, as in the case of her insistence that an utterance everyone else takes to be performative (the signed execution order) is not. Because she is a sovereign ruler, her very word makes such an unreasonable claim reasonable in the eyes of her subjects. The play's spectators, however, who are not her subjects, cannot be forced into such agreement. Unlike the case of "Give It Up!" where the reader readily assents to both readings of "asked him the way," *Mary Stuart* gives us rhetorical moments that are perhaps more rhetorical for the characters in the fiction than they are for us.

Many literary works, though, make their rhetorical moments out of a performative uncertainty that the reader feels as acutely as the characters. Kafka wrote some of the most famous of them, but there are other writers who have also worked with particular success in this mode. Let me take a relatively recent example, Nathalie Sarraute's *The Use of Speech* (*L'usage de la parole*, 1980), an anthology containing a number of fictions that exploit the rhetorical space found in utterances capable of being understood as both performative and nonperformative at the same time. The "stories" presented in *The Use of Speech* are of special interest in a study of rhetorical construction because they are frankly presented as interpretations of everyday discourse. They are not so much narratives as a set of rhetorical readings of fictional situations or of historical situations imaginatively fictionalized. The focus is always on a single "use" (*usage*) of an expression that somehow exceeds or complicates the lexical norms of "usage" (also *usage*). The narrator is always careful to look for the contextual elements that are necessary to determine meaning and are especially necessary to the functioning of speech-acts and thus to pin down as precisely as possible the conditions that make a particular "use" differ from an abstractly defined "usage." In doing so, the narrator demonstrates a command of a certain kind of practical knowledge (*usage*, as in *l'usage du monde*) of the subtleties of speech that is also, in the course of the narrative, passed on to the reader.

It is important to note that what Sarraute attends to is the "use" not of language or its linguistic structure (*langue* in the technical sense), but of discourse, the particular speech of particular people (*parole* in the technical sense). Sarraute's title adverts to Saussure's distinction between *langue* and *parole* in an oblique way exactly because her title is not *L'usage de la langue*. The latter would be entirely appropriate for a book by a structural linguist interested in the processes by which the paradigms of *langue* are actualized in *parole*. From the viewpoint of a Saussurian linguist, the concept *parole* already contains the idea of usage, since Saussure defined parole as an "individual act" on the "executive side" of the linguistic process. One could say then that the phrase "l'usage de la parole" is almost tautological from the purely (Saussurian) linguistic point of view. It is far from tautological, however, when considered in terms of the theory of speech-acts. Leaving aside for the time being the legitimate sense in which all utterances are performatives, as Austin himself came to admit, there is still considerable utility in distinguishing between speech that does something (other than assert a proposition) in the very act of speaking and speech that does not—between "I promise I'll go" and "I think I'll go," for example. Use of the phrase "l'usage de la parole" suggests an interest in those special "individual acts" (Saussure's parole) that are doing something beyond simply saying, that are being *used* for some particular purpose, to affect the world in a certain way. A paradigmatic case is the story of Anton Chekhov's last words, "Ich sterbe" ("I'm dying"). Sarraute evidently thought the story deserved paradigmatic status, since she made it the first in her collection. There is a story in these words not simply or even primarily because a famous man uttered them, but chiefly because this man was a Russian and a physician. The narrator dismisses at the outset the idea that Chekhov's vocation as a writer or his great fame has anything to do with the inherent interest of this "Ich sterbe": "You may be sure that he wasn't thinking of leaving us any famous last words. No, not he, certainly not, that wasn't at all his style."[6] It is quite clear that Chekhov was addressing not his posterity, but the German physician who, along with Mrs. Chekhov, attended the dying man. But why would he do so? Why tell this German doctor what he certainly already knew? Sarraute suggests a compellingly logical explanation, that this "Ich sterbe" was not simply a description of the action Chekhov was performing but also the official pronouncement of death, the pronouncement that must be duly uttered by the attending physician: "Here is a word of good German make, a word this German doctor habitually uses to certify a death, to announce it to the family, a solid, strong verb: sterben . . . thank you, I'll take it, I too will know how to conjugate it correctly, I shall know how to use it properly and duly apply it to myself: Ich sterbe."[7] Chekhov's "Ich sterbe" is in this view an illocutionary act, something equivalent to "I hereby certify my death." The dying man makes use of the strength of the word, a strength that derives appropriately enough as much from its grammatical structure as from its character. The phrase "verbe fort" is a literal translation of the German grammatical terminology "starkes Verbum" that refers to verbs (like *sterben*) that mark differences in linguistic function by vowel ablaut. The word, like Chekhov at this moment, is "strong" from a purely linguistic point of view, but some of this figurative strength seeps over, as it were, into the physical world. By purely linguistic means, by uttering these words, Chekhov transforms a moment of absolute weakness into one of enormous strength. He does not passively die, he actively "certifies the event."[8]

He is also able to validate himself as a worker with words. Chekhov becomes not only his own attending physician but his own narrator. Like a character in a story, Chekhov may not die until his death is recounted by a storyteller. His death coincides exactly with the telling

6. I cite Sarraute's stories in English from *The Use of Speech*, trans. Barbara Wright (New York: George Braziller, 1983), and in French from *L'usage de la parole* (Paris: Gallimard, 1980). This passage is from *The Use of Speech*, 7; *L'usage de la parole*, 9. "Vous pouvez être certains qu'il n'a pas songé à nous laisser un mot célèbre de mourant. Non, pas lui, sûrement pas, ce n'était pas du tout son genre."

7. *The Use of Speech*, 9; *L'usage de la parole*, 11. "Voilà un mot de bonne fabrication allemande, un mot dont ce médecin allemand se sert couramment pour constater un décès, pour l'annoncer aux parents, un verbe solide et fort: sterben. . . merci, je le prends, je saurai moi aussi le conjuguer correctement, je saurai m'en servir comme il faut et sagement l'appliquer à moi-même: Ich sterbe."

8. *The Use of Speech*, 13; *L'usage de la parole*, 15. "J'établis le constat."

of his death in that he is alive before the words are pronounced and dead afterward. With his "Ich sterbe" Chekhov is able to write the final line of his own life story, thus taking control of an event that would otherwise seem beyond all control, indeed the very essence of loss of control. It is, as Sarraute understands it, the ultimate authorial act: "No one who has got where I am has been able to . . . but I, gathering together the last remnants of my strength, I fire this shot, I send this signal."[9] The ultimate narration brings order to a process ordinarily without such order in an elegant if distressing enactment of the word becoming flesh. The word "Ich sterbe" becomes on the instant a piece of flesh, a corpse.

The choice of the German strong verb *sterben* is dictated by Chekhov's desire both to perform in advance the function of the German doctor and to forestall the anticipated objections of his wife:

> To you [the doctor]. In your language. Not to her, also there by my side, not in *our* language. Not in our too soft words, words we have made supple, limp, by constant use, by tossing them about in the spray of our laughter as we fell back helplessly . . . oh, stop it, oh, I'm dying . . . light words which, our hearts beating with a superabundance of life, we introduced into our murmurs, gave vent to in our sighs . . . I'm dying.[10]

What Sarraute's Chekhov must prevent here at all costs is the melancholy reappearance of the figurative meaning of "je meurs" ("I'm dying"). Unlike the foreign word *sterben*, which is strong, the words of the native language (whose role is played in the narrative by French) are "soft, supple, limp" ("doux, assouplis, amollis") precisely because they are so often used in commonplace tropes. *Mourir* can mean "éprouver un sentiment avec une grande intensité," according to Larousse ("experience a feeling with great intensity"), a significance just the opposite of the one appropriate to these circumstances. Chekhov's employment of the German verb works to suppress the

9. *The Use of Speech*, 10; *L'usage de la parole*, 12. "Personne arrivé jusque-là où je suis n'a pu. . . mais moi, rassemblant ce qui me reste de forces, je tire ce coup de feu, j'envoie ce signal."

10. *The Use of Speech*, 11; *L'usage de la parole*, 13. "A vous. Dans votre langue. Pas à elle qui est là aussi, près de moi, pas dans notre langue à nous. Pas avec nos mots trop doux, des mots assouplis, amollis à force de nous avoir servi, d'avoir été roulés dans les gerbes jaillissantes de nos rires quand nous nous laissions tomber sans forces. . . oh arrête, oh je meurs. . . des mots légers que le coeur battant de trop de vie nous laissions glisser dans nos murmures, s'exhaler dans nos soupirs. . . je meurs."

elements of life that are so prominent in the everday use of *mourir*.

But Chekhov's act of suppression is the opportunity for the narrator to reveal what is suppressed. The narrator, ironically borrowing Chekhov's voice by means of the *style indirect libre*, discloses the figurative meaning and traces out in detail the contrast between Chekhov's present "Ich sterbe" and the lighthearted, lively "I'm dying" of the past. The story of Chekhov's death is to some extent, then, the revelation of what its hero attempted, in a sense very successfully, to banish from this moment of dying. By translating this "Ich sterbe" back into "je meurs," the story effects an uncanny return of figurative meaning that both validates and undoes the act it describes. "How clever of Chekhov," the narrator is telling us, "*not* to have said . . ." the very thing that I, the narrator, am saying here, now, and in great detail. But even that is not quite right, for the voice we hear actually revealing the banished figurative meaning is not the narrator's; we are made to "overhear" the traces of other voices, those of Chekhov and his wife, as if they were memories bubbling to the surface and embedding themselves in the narration. In the very moment when these voices are asserted to be past, no longer relevant, they return with particular clarity and vividness.

The story lives upon these rhetorical complexities. It is not too much to say that the narrative Sarraute presents in "Ich sterbe" exists only because she hears that phrase, in its context, as already thoroughly deconstructed. The pathos of Chekhov's last words is that they do indeed force consideration of the confrontation of life and death in the verb *mourir*. If Chekhov's strategy had been entirely successful, if he had actually succeeded in extirpating every trace of figurative life from the deadly literal import of his words, there would be no story. Sarraute and her readers are able to see that something has happened here only because language cannot completely cover its tracks. This language of the absolute distance of death is at once very far away and very near. The narration properly begins by emphasizing this paradoxically distant nearness of the words that form its subject: "They come from afar, they come back (as people say: 'It's coming back to me') from the beginning of this century, from a German spa. But in reality they come from much, much farther off."[11] The place "much, much

---

11. *The Use of Speech*, 7; *L'usage de la parole*, 9. "Ils viennent de loin, ils reviennent (comme on dit: 'cela me revient') du début de ce siècle, d'une ville d'eaux allemande. Mais en réalité ils viennent d'encore beaucoup plus loin."

farther off" is, of course, the realm of death itself, while the other place, the place from which the words come back, is in the realm of memory ("cela me revient," having the meaning "I'm beginning to remember it"). The story itself has at its disposal all the space between the remembered meanings of "je meurs" and the vastly distant, absolutely alien kingdom into which Chekhov projects himself by means of his "Ich sterbe."

There is also a substantial amount of narrative space opened up by the difference between the performative "Ich sterbe," the certification pronounced by Dr. Chekhov upon himself, and the equally plausible constative "Ich sterbe" that describes, perhaps with a tinge of desperate hope, the process taking place. The same circumstances that permit the narrator to posit the first interpretation also authorize the second, wherein one would understand the use of the German language as an attempt to get the attention of the physician so that he will be able to understand and possibly help:

> But perhaps, as he was raising the flagstones [of his own grave], as he was holding it above him with outstretched arms and was about to lower it on himself . . . just before he fell back under it . . . was there maybe something like a faint palpitation, a barely perceptible quivering, a minute trace of living hope . . . Ich sterbe . . . And what if the man observing him and who was the only one who could know, were to intervene, to grasp him firmly, to hold him back . . . No, though, there's no one, no voice . . . It's already the void, it's silence.[12]

If understood as constative, Chekhov's "Ich sterbe" would be part of a movement exactly opposite to the one proposed by the performative reading. Instead of verbally effecting his own death, Chekhov might be trying against all odds to avoid it. He might be saying to his German doctor (not to his wife, who has no medical skills), "I feel the forces of life ebbing away. Do something to help me! I'm dying!"

The story ends—and begins—in the impossibility of deciding between these two opposed meanings. Just as there are no formal

12. *The Use of Speech*, 13–14; *L'usage de la parole*, 15–16. "Mais peut-être. . . quand il soulevait la dalle, quand il la tenait au-dessus de lui à bout de bras et allait l'abaisser sur lui-même. . . juste avant que sous elle il ne retombe. . . peut-être y a-t-il eu comme une faible palpitation, un à peine perceptible frémissement, une trace infirme d'attente vivante. . . Ich sterbe. . . Et si celui qui l'observait, et qui seul pouvait savoir, allait s'interposer, l'empoigner fortement, le retenir. . . Mais non, plus personne, aucune voix. . . C'est déjà le vide, le silence."

grounds that will assure us whether "Ich sterbe" (or "You are under arrest") is a descriptive statement or an illocutionary act, so are there no clear markers to determine whether these words belong on the side of life or of death. Paradoxically, the illocutionary "Ich sterbe," though it embraces death, verbally conjures death into being, is in its quality as a volitional act a sign of life, while the constative "Ich sterbe," though it shrinks from death, cooperates with death in its passivity. This "use of speech," then, discloses a scandal: this utterance cannot be securely confined to either the realm of life or the realm of death. It resonates with unsettling echoes of M. Valdemar's last words in Poe's "The Facts in the Case of M. Valdemar": "Dead! Dead!" The hypnotic trance under which M. Valdemar has existed "in articulo mortis" shatters with these words, and Valdemar collapes into a "nearly liquid mass of loathsome—of detestable putridity." The corpse articulates the fact of his own death: Ich sterbe.

Sarraute's tale of Chekhov's last words is not a horror story, of course, and there is not the least hint of anything loathsome or detestable about the writer's death. Quite the contrary: the story leaves an impression of great dignity and even the possibility of great achievement. Where Poe had stressed the intrusion of death into life, Sarraute has emphasized the opposite. Still, the one has contaminated the other in such a way as to open the question of the presence of death in what is here the paradigm of living processes, storytelling. We are not allowed to forget that the whole dialogue of this narrative, its whole action, consists in words signifying death. The story of the death of the storyteller is the story of storytelling, the story of something that exists only on the margin between the living and the dead. It is an old idea whose monuments are well known. Works like Mann's *Doktor Faustus* and "Death in Venice" are among the more familiar examples. What is specially relevant here is the commonplace figurative association between death and the literal, life and the figurative—or if you will, between death and the signifier and life and the signified. Sarraute's story is about that kind of storytelling that exists in the space (or moment) between figurative life and literal death. It is, in short, about fiction that results from rhetorical construction. Not only is it a story about a moment of transition—Chekhov's transition from speaking person to silent corpse—but it also derives its narrative energy from the conflict between a "living" and a "dead" reading of "Ich sterbe."

There is a certain sense, by no means trivial, in which the words "Ich sterbe," with the full set of associations Sarraute has given them, are an adequate paraphrase of every rhetorical fiction. The thrust of rhetorical construction is always to find a generative, "living" moment in a textual aporia that can be—and frequently is—valorized negatively as the emergence of annihilating contradiction. Sarraute presents a Chekhov who is able, by means of rhetoric, to make something out of nothing, to make the act of saying "I am not" into a way of proclaiming "I am." This rhetorical feat does not prevent Chekhov's death or transform it into anything like life, but it does take from "nothing's ability to noth," as Kenneth Burke has put it, the impulse for making something that is. The diegetic structure of "Ich sterbe" echoes this procedure by making out of the irremediable conflict between the literal and figurative, in one strand of the story, or in another the performative and constative readings of Chekhov's words, the space in which she inscribes her text. The negative moment becomes positive, though not by eliminating or somehow reconciling the negativity. The metaphor that most adequately expresses the generative, positive potential in a negativity that remains negative is the one to which I have constant recourse in these pages: space, that nothingness without which there could not be something.

It is perfectly logical, therefore, in the perspective of this inquiry, that Sarraute's stories in *The Use of Speech* frequently take as the generative texts pieces of language that are regularly understood as, in effect, nothing. The story "Mon petit" ends with an ostensibly rhetorical question that apparently reasserts the insignificance, the actual nothingness, of the phrase "mon petit" from which the story derives: "How could we live if we were to take umbrage at the slightest little thing, if we didn't very reasonably just let pass such words, which after all are quite insignificant and innocuous, if we were to make such a fuss about so little—about less than nothing?"[13] If the question is indeed what is traditionally described as "rhetorical," we read it as in effect asserting that it would be impossible to live "if we were to take umbrage at the slightest thing," and so on, if indeed "we were to make such a fuss" over little phrases. Since people do in fact live, the reasonable conclusion to be drawn is that the narrator is merely pointing out that we accommodate ourselves to life by deliberately not "making a fuss" over insignificant things.

13. *The Use of Speech*, 106; *L'usage de la parole*, 112. "Comment vivrait-on si on prenait la mouche pour un oui ou un non, si on ne laissait pas très raisonnablement passer de ces mots comme toute insignifiants et anodins, si on faisait pour si peu, pour moins que rien de pareilles histoires?"

There is very good reason, however, to think that we might read this as a genuine question looking for an answer. For one thing, Sarraute uses the phrase "faire de pareilles histoires" (literally, "make such stories") to express "make such a fuss," and in this context such a figure has a special resonance. The figure for "making a fuss" is making stories; but that is exactly what has been done by this narrator, for the etiology of "Mon petit" is quite correctly described as "faire pour si peu une histoire." Since the text in front of the reader is evidence that people can and do make a fuss and make stories out of little phrases, it is difficult for us to take the sentence as a rhetorical question denying the possibility of doing so. For another thing, the tale just told presents strong evidence that these little phrases like "mon petit" are far from innocent and innocuous and are well worth making a fuss over.

The narrator gives us a situation in which the phrase "mon petit" (translated as "my dear") is used in a conversation "between two people whose relationship is that of perfect equality."[14] But to whom does one say "mon petit" in appropriate usage? To someone who is literally small, of course, a child; or to someone who is metaphorically small, someone inferior on the social, economic, or moral scale. But this "mon petit" is explicitly not one of those that comes "from someone in a superior position, from someone older . . . in short, from someone who is presumed to possess the obvious, recognized superiority that these words may express."[15] The "mon petit" in Sarraute's story is thus readily interpretable as an act of aggression, an attempt by one person to assert over another a superiority that is not otherwise evident. "This is when the drama, or perhaps you would rather call it a game, to which you are invited, begins."[16]

The dramatic potential lies in the dilemma facing the person upon whom this "mon petit" has been visited. What is he going to do? It is inconceivable that a person addressed as "mon petit" by a supposed equal will not at least suspect that he is being insulted, but what can he do with this suspicion? Is it really worth making an issue over, making

14. *The Use of Speech*, 98; *L'usage de la parole*, 104. "Entre deux personnes qui sont dans des rapports de parfaite égalité."

15. *The Use of Speech*, 98; *L'usage de la parole*, 104. "Venu de quelqu'un de plus haut placé, de plus âgé. . . bref de quelqu'un qui posséderait une supériorité évidente, reconnue, que ce mot exprimerait."

16. *The Use of Speech*, 99; *L'usage de la parole*, 105. "C'est alors que le drame ou, si vous aimez mieux, le jeu auquel vous êtes conviés commence."

"une histoire"? It is entirely possible that this "mon petit" was inadvertent, that "the words merely escaped him, they're padding, connecting words he sometimes happens to use without the slightest intention of aggrandizing himself."[17] So, very probably, the listener simply pretends not to have noticed.

The protagonist of "Mon petit" suspects, but does not know for certain, that the "mon petit" he has heard functions as a kind of covert performative, something like "I hereby call you 'inferior creature.'" We properly identify "name calling" as an act, and though Austin did not list it as one of the performative verbs—for good reasons—this act is prima facie illocutionary, since it takes place in the act of speaking. One performs the illocutionary act of name calling not by using a performative verb but by calling the name. If his interlocutor has indeed "called" him "mon petit," the protagonist has every reason to object, to defend himself by saying, "Ne me dites pas mon petit" ("Don't call me 'my dear'"). There is the possibility, however, by no means distant, that no act of name calling was intended. The "nonperformative" use of "mon petit" would be analogous to the use of "man" or "sweetheart" or "baby" in the speech of certain Americans. This colloquial use of "man" is primarily phatic, and it is frequently heard in speech addressed to females without the slightest hint of irony. If this "mon petit" were such a phatic device, a way of maintaining communicative contact rather than "saying" something, it would be inappropriate to take umbrage. That would be, in every sense, a case of "prendre la mouche" (literally, "to take the fly"), and in this instance of going after the fly with a cannon.

The tension upon which the story "Mon petit" lives resides entirely in the confrontation between these performative and nonperformative readings of the two words. Either they are an insulting act of aggression or they are "less than nothing," phatic filler with nothing particular to signify. There would be no story—or at least no story in which Sarraute would be interested—if both possibilities were not present. If one person simply insulted another by calling him a name it could conceivably be called a story, but not a very interesting one. The rhetorical and emotional potential for elaboration would be extremely

---

17. *The Use of Speech*, 105–6; *L'usage de la parole*, 111–12. "Ce mot lui a échappé, c'est une cheville, un mot de liaison dont il lui arrive parfois de se servir sans aucune intention de se grandir."

small. If, on the other hand, it were clearly a case of phatic padding, there would be little or no cause for narration. Sarraute's protagonist is a genuine protagonist because he is faced with a difficult choice with which we can sympathize. He must either react to this "mon petit" or ignore it, and he stands to be hurt if he makes the wrong choice. Although the stakes are by no means life and death, they are high enough in terms of human anxiety to legitimize the narrator's allusion to the "drama" about to unfold before us.

The story also counts as "dramatic" in its thorough reliance on a dialogic situation. Although the play has only one line, and that one line is recited not by the star but by a supporting actor, the utterance in its context is still quite clearly not monologue but dialogue. Sarraute focuses upon the dialogic aspects, in Bakhtin's sense, by emphasizing the interpersonal way meaning comes into being. What this "mon petit" means, and what it does, depends upon both the intentions of the speaker and the attitude of the listener. The narrative device by which this is achieved is the simple expedient of allowing the reader access to the thoughts of one party and the words of the other. We do not know what, if anything, the protagonist says, and we remain entirely ignorant of what his interlocutor thinks. But between the words of the one and the thoughts of the other there is a complex and shifting dialogue that fully engages us in the fictional situation.

"Mon petit" is also dialogic in another way, the more fundamental way in which all fiction based on rhetorical construction is dialogic. It depends on the possibility of an interaction between two conflicting voices, neither of which ever subjugates or effaces the other. If we understand dialogue in Bakhtin's sense of communication between simultaneous differences, rhetorical fictions such as "Ich sterbe" and "Mon petit" are paradigmatic cases of dialogism, since the narrative arises out of reading some text as a structure of simultaneous differences. The coming together of these differences in rhetorical language—tropes, puns, and so on—may seem coincidental, but the process of rhetorical construction finds in the space between the differences a kind of pretended or assumed interaction that at times seems very close to communication. "Ich sterbe," for example, is the result of a process of invention that seeks to construct the one situation in which all the conflicting meanings of "I'm dying" are applicable. "Mon petit" sets up a case in which both potential readings of the phrase, as either phatic filler or devastating insult, are fully realized.

The fictional situation becomes the mode of interaction between these sets of simultaneous differences.

The fictions that result from the application of rhetorical construction are, however, still fictions, and that means they partake of that disquieting aspect of rhetoricity described by Paul de Man. Fictions simultaneously assert and deny their own illocutionary mode, they at once affirm and deny the very things they can be understood to "say." For this reason one has to be careful about thinking of rhetorical interaction as "communication." Sarraute appears to be acutely conscious of this property of rhetorical discourse, and in the last story in her collection, "Je ne comprends pas" ("I Don't Understand"), she explicitly draws our attention to it. The story, in brief, dwells in the space between "je ne comprends pas" as an assertion of incomprehension and the same phrase interpreted as a profound act of understanding. Suppose that the discourse one is confronted with is egregious, incoherent nonsense: to say in response to such stuff "je ne comprends pas" would be not an expression of personal inadequacy but a justified accusation. If I do not understand it is not because I am incapable of understanding but because you are incapable of being understood. To say "I do not understand" is to demonstrate that I have understood perfectly.

How would the speaker of nonsense react to such a "je ne comprends pas?" If the speaker were seeking understanding, his reaction could of course only be pleasure:

> At these words, "I don't understand," the crook, the pervert, the torturer, the oppressor, with gratitude and joy streaming from his eyes, turns round to the person who has proffered them, he places his hands on his shoulders, he presses them, he takes his hand, he shakes it . . . "Ah, bravo, thank you . . . if you only knew . . . I was already losing hope, it's so rare, it practically never happens . . . however hard I try to accumulate absurdities, incoherence . . . pick out desultory words and string them together at random . . . however much I shamelessly borrow from our most barefaced charlatans, go to the extreme limits, there's nothing to be done, no one turns a hair, everyone accepts, acquiesces . . . But you! . . . Ah, what a bit of luck."[18]

18. *The Use of Speech*, 149–50; *L'usage de la parole*, 155–56. "A ces mots, 'Je ne comprends pas,' voici que l'escroc, le pervers, le tortionnaire, l'oppresseur se tourne vers celui qui les a proférés, la reconnaissance, la joie ruissellent de ses yeux, il lui pose

In such a situation the space between understanding and not understanding would truly have been turned into a space of communication. Here, noncomprehension is precisely equivalent to comprehension, and the two potentially contradictory readings of "je ne comprends pas" have been perfectly resolved.

But the fiction seems just a little too pat. Since when do "perverts, torturers, and oppressors" greet their unmasking with joy and gratitude? Only in fiction do they do so, and only in the most outrageously fictional fictions at that. Sarraute ends her story with a confession: "Really, though, it might be thought that this beautiful, this too beautiful story has in the end turned out to be no more than a fairy tale."[19] This last story of *The Use of Speech* is the only one in which the structure of differences inherent in the phrases chosen for fictional contextualization resolves itself into perfect communication, and it announces itself as a fairy tale and nothing more. If these dialogic exercises show the possibilities for interaction in rhetorical space, they do not let us forget that such space arises, after all, out of a structure of differences.

Tropological Uncertainty in Rabelais's *Cinq livres*

Fictions like "Ich sterbe" and "Mon petit" show the degree of sophistication and complexity attainable by constructions whose rhetorical moments are based upon performative uncertainty. Engaging as they are, however, they do not adequately illustrate the prevalent mode of rhetorical construction, which tends to find its inventive impulses in moments of tropological uncertainty. Literary works based on this latter principle can easily be found in all periods and genres, and

---

les mains sur les épaules, il les serre, il lui prend la main, il la secoue. . . 'Ah bravo, Ah merci. . . si vous saviez. . . je perdais déjà l'espoir, c'est si rare, ça ne se produit presque jamais. . . j'ai beau m'efforcer, accumuler les absurdités, l'incohérence. . . prendre au hasard et assembler des mots sans suite. . . j'ai beau emprunter sans vergogne aux plus éhontés de nos charlatans, aller jusqu'aux extrêmes limites, il n'y a rien à faire, personne ne bronche, tout le monde accepte, acquiesce. . . Mais vous!. . . Ah, c'est une chance. . .'"

19. *The Use of Speech*, 151; *L'usage de la parole*, 157. "Mais vraiment c'est à croire que toute cette belle, trop belle histoire n'était finalement rien d'autre qu'un conte de fées."

probably in all literatures.[20] I will take as an example to treat in detail the work of another French author, for the sake of continuity, but for the sake of variety, one from a different historical period. After the serious little stories of performative uncertainty in modern life, let us turn to an outrageously comic long story of tropological uncertainty from the Renaissance, the *Cinq livres* of François Rabelais.

Rabelais begins his story of Gargantua—the second book he wrote, though the first in order of narration—with a somewhat perplexing prologue in which the author, announced as "M. Alcofribas," seems to recommend two contradictory modes of reading his book. On the one hand, he proposes that the reader must go beyond the "literal meaning" ("sens litéral") as Odysseus went past the Sirens and "interpret in a more sublime sense" ("à plus haut sens interpréter") the material of his book. The reader is encouraged to behave like the philosophical dog of Plato's *Republic*, to gnaw upon the bone of the text until it can be broken open to reveal the marrow, which, "more delicious than great quantities of other meat," will nourish the reader intellectually so that "very high sacraments and dread mysteries" will be revealed. On the other hand, the voice of the author maintains with equal vigor his innocence of any allegorical intentions: "I never spent—or wasted— any more—or other—time in the composing of this lordly book, than that fixed for the taking of my bodily refreshment, that is to say for eating and drinking." M. Alcofribas confesses in fact that "I gave no more thought to the matter [of allegorical meaning] than you, who were probably drinking at the time, as I was."[21] In the second edition, Rabelais added a prefatory poem "To the Reader" ("Aux lecteurs") advising that this book "teaches you no great perfection, / But lessons in the mirthful art" ("Vrai est qu'ici peu de perfection / Vous apprendrez, sinon en cas de rire") and adding that his heart was incapable

20. Although my competence is limited to a few languages and literatures of Western Europe, colleagues and students with knowledge beyond mine have found works based on tropological uncertainty in several non-Western literatures.

21. I cite Rabelais in English from *The Histories of Gargantua and Pantagruel*, trans. J. M. Cohen (Harmondsworth: Penguin, 1955), and in French from *Les cinq livres de Rabelais*, 2 vols., ed. Roger Delbiausse (Paris: Editions Magnard, 1965). I have profited greatly from Delbiausse's very helpful annotations. These passages are from *Gargantua and Pantagruel*, 39; *Les cinq livres* 1:61. "Les dictant, n'y pensasse en plus que vous, qui par aventure buviez comme moi? Car, à la composition de ce livre seigneurial, je ne perdis ni employai onques plus ni autre temps que celui qui était établi à prendre ma réfection corporelle, savoir est buvant et mangeant."

of choosing any other subject ("Autre argument ne peut mon coeur élire").[22]

It is simple enough, and true enough, to explain this contradiction as the result of trying to address two audiences at once, the thoughtful and the official.[23] We can easily suppose that Rabelais wanted the majority of his audience to find allegorical marrow in this jolly bone of a book, especially in passages such as those dedicated to the founding of the abbey of Thélème, where a strain of social reformatory zeal is evident. At the same time, it was clearly in Rabelais's interest (as he had good reason to know) to convince the authorities that his writings had no social, political, or religious implications at all and meant no more than what they literally said. The Sorbonne theologians had condemned the first book of Pantagruel's adventures as obscene, and Rabelais would surely have wanted to assure these powerful enemies that they had nothing to fear from his harmless jests. If one audience could be expected to read alethetically (looking for the truth hidden by an incredible surface), another, he could hope, would be willing to read it lethetically, letting their disbelief in these outrageous narratives remain firmly in control and understanding the marvelous events recounted here not as the outer covering of some inner truth but as purely verbal fun with no relation whatever to the real world. While the philosophically and theologically minded Rabelais might have desired alethetic readers, the political realist wanted those with the power to do him harm to remain steadfastly lethetic.

While it makes good sense to accept this explanation for the contradictory position M. Alcofribas takes in the prologue to *Gargantua*, we need not assume that it is the only explanation. Aside from the political considerations, there were good literary reasons for the author of these amazing adventures to present himself as at once the advocate of both the strictly literal and the aggressively figurative reading of his book. The adventures of Gargantua and Pantagruel owe their existence in part to their author's ability to interpret other texts in just this way, to produce rhetorical moments by reading both literally and figuratively at the same time. Over and over again we find in these tales the operation of rhetorical construction.

---

22. *Gargantua and Pantagruel*, 36; *Les cinq livres* 1:59.
23. Cf. Cohen's introduction to his translation of *Gargantua and Pantagruel*, 23.

Rabelais's rhetorical practice and its complicity with the problem of political prudence are both visible in the narrative of Gargantua's birth (*Gargantua*, chaps. 4–6). Although the reader's attention is ostensibly focused on the set of events described, the narrator seems at least as much concerned with the issue of his reader's belief as with the tale he is telling. In fact, the narration of events is preceded by an address to the reader demanding credulity: "This was the manner in which Gargamelle was brought to bed—and if you don't believe it, may your fundament fall out!"[24] The injunction to believe is buttressed by the threat of a curse, a rhetorical strategy common enough to provoke little comment were it not for the odd confrontation between what is being demanded and what is being threatened. The spiritual and lofty matter of believing is juxtaposed to the physical, disreputable matter of the loss of one's anus. Such scandalous conjunctions are the bread and butter of comic narratives, of course, in that the pretensions of the lofty intellect are undermined by the reminder that we are, after all, animals with anuses; but more than that seems to be at issue here. If Rabelais had simply wanted to undercut the high-minded language of belief, he had at his disposal far more earthy terms than *fondement* with which to shock the reader. The phrase "le fondement vous escappe" ("may your fundament fall out") is actually rather high style for such a low subject. The word *fondement* is an aristocratic term, welcome in the best society, where it is more likely to appear in philosophic discourse (cf. English "foundation") or in a discussion of architecture than in reference to the anus. The verb *escapper* (modern French *échapper*) is also rather more noble than synonyms like *tomber,* and it too has a spiritual as well as a physical meaning.

There is actually no grammatical reason why we should not read the phrase "si ne le croyez, le fondement vous escappe" as if the main verb were not subjunctive but indicative: "If you don't believe it, the foundation [or base] escapes you"; or more bluntly, "If you don't believe this, you're missing the point." This interpretation carries a message rather different from the first, for instead of demanding our belief on pain of physical disruption it posits our belief as a consequence of logic. On the literal plane, disbelief threatens to bring about bodily harm, but

---

24. *Gargantua and Pantagruel*, 47; *Les cinq livres* 1:67. "L'occasion et manière comment Gargamelle enfanta fut telle, et, si ne le croyez, le fondement vous escappe!"

it is a threat we certainly cannot take seriously, since nothing in our experience suggests any connection between the loss of one's credulity and the loss of one's anus. On the figurative plane, however, the argument is more compelling, since the intellectual issue of our belief is intimately connected to the intellectual issue of grasping the basis of something, an argument, say, or a course of reasoning, or a structure of allegory. If we read literally, lack of belief in the literal narrative is threatened (incredibly) by bodily harm; if we read figuratively, lack of belief in the allegorical narrative is exposed as intellectually inconsistent. This sentence, then, solicits the belief of literal and presumably lethetic readers only jokingly, but that of allegorizing, alethetic readers quite seriously.

Even if we insist on attending to the literal level, as Alcofribas seemed to recommend in his prologue, the ground we find is shifting and uncertain. The injunction to believe is supported by a threat that is an outrageous non sequitur and therefore not to be believed. Since the announced purpose of the literal level is amusement, however, the reader can accept such shifts not only with equanimity but with positive joy. Non sequiturs are silly, and silliness is exactly what we are looking for. Furthermore, a non sequitur is by definition outside the logical structure of the discourse; its purport can be safely ignored because it identifies itself from the outset as *hors d'oeuvre*.

Rabelais caps all this, finally, with a bigger joke. He takes the very piece of language that we had to read either as figurative, serious, and logical or as literal, silly, and beside the point and makes it, in its literal sense, an essential part of the narrative: "Her [that is, Gargamelle's] fundament fell out one afternoon, on the third of February, after she had overeaten herself on *godebillos*."[25] What we are to believe, on pain of losing our fundaments, is that Gargamelle lost her fundament. The narrator proceeds to supply a lengthy explanation of the circumstances surrounding this event, and suddenly what had been a non sequitur is a narrative sequitur and the center of our attention. Something the literal reader could dismiss as nothing more than purely verbal sideplay has been transformed by an act of logomimesis, shifted at a stroke from the margin to the center of the story. It is a wonderful rhetorical moment.

The space for this tale of Gargamelle's anus—which takes up, with all its attendant elaborations, over two chapters—appears as if by mag-

---

25. *Gargantua and Pantagruel*, 47; *Les cinq livres* 1:67. "Le fondement lui escappait une après-dînée, le IIIe jour de février, par trop avoir mangé de gaudebillaux."

ic out of the confrontation between the logical figurative and illogical literal readings of "le fondement vous escappe." The literal reader is surprised but not disappointed, since the story is now based upon the literal reading of the text we had been puzzling over. But the figurative reader is not disappointed either, since the literal "fondement," Gargamelle's anus, has been disclosed to be a figurative "fondement" as well, since it is now the base or foundation for the narrative. If this "fondement" does not escape us, we will give to Rabelais's tall tale all the belief—to paraphrase Samuel Johnson—due to tall tales. That belief resides precisely in acknowledging the propriety of making a "fondement" (anus) into a "fondement" (foundation). This acknowledgment by no means constrains us to suppose that there is any connection between this text and the structure of the real world, however; even the reader sensitive to figurative meaning is authorized to read this adventure with the salt handy.

Belief and disbelief engage in a peculiar intercourse throughout the narrative of Gargantua's birth, partly because the story is both outlandish and familiar, partly because the narrator emerges periodically to discuss explicitly the credibility of his story. After explaining that Gargantua was unable to emerge from his mother's womb in the normal fashion (because of this misfortune with her fundament and its consequent tightening of her sphincter muscles) and therefore was obliged to be born through her ear, he wonders if his reader's credulity has not been strained past tolerance:

> I doubt whether you will truly believe in this strange nativity. I don't care if you don't. But an honest man, a man of good sense, always believes what he is told and what he finds written down. /Does not Solomon say in Proverbs 14, "Innocens credit omni verbo, etc," and Saint Paul, I Cor. 13, "Charitas omnia credit"? Why wouldn't you believe it? Because, you say, it lacks probability [*apparence*]. I say to you that you should believe it in perfect faith for this very reason. For the masters of the Sorbonne say that faith is the evidence of things not seen [*de nulle apparence*]./ Is this a violation of our law of faith? Is it against reason or against Holy Scripture? For my part I find nothing written in the Holy Bible that contradicts it.[26]

26. *Gargantua and Pantagruel*, 52 (material between slashes appears only in the earliest editions, and the translation of that earlier material is mine); *Les cinq livres* 1:71–72. "Je me doute que ne croyez assurément cette étrange nativité. Si ne le croyez, si ne m'en soucie, mais un homme de bien, un homme de bon sens, croit toujours ce qu'on lui dit et qu'il trouve par écrit. / Ne dit pas Salomon Proverbiorum 14: 'Innocens credit omni

Rabelais makes a move here that is both amusing and very daring: he creates for his discussion of belief a rhetorical space that lies between "croyance" understood as an epistemological matter (belief that a statement is true) and "croyance" as a religious category essentially equivalent to faith (*foi*). He opens up this space initially by referring to Gargantua's birth as "this strange nativity" ("cette étrange nativité"), thereby reminding his reader of the marvelous nativity fundamental to the faith of all Christians. Although it might not be appropriate to cite Scripture in defense of such "pantagruelism," as its author dubbed it, it is surely appropriate in reference to *the* nativity. Of that nativity a Christian could certainly say, "si ne le croyez, le fondement vous escappe." But the teller of Gargantua's story is no longer willing to do so. He says merely, "If you don't believe it I don't care" ("si ne le croyez, je ne m'en soucie"). Our belief is or is not a matter of urgent concern—depending, of course, on what the object of that belief is construed to be.

Belief in something that does not merit belief is called credulity, while belief in something that does merit it (even in the absence of sensory evidence) is called faith. The discussion of belief that surrounds Gargantua's birth occupies the territory somewhere between credulity and faith and therefore entails a substantial risk of the appearance of impiety. It was probably to reduce this risk somewhat that Rabelais cut out both the quotations from the Bible and the reference to the gentlemen of the Sorbonne. In doing so, however, he had to sacrifice one of his better jokes and one of the key rhetorical moments supporting the structure of his pseudo-argument. The joke is based upon the French translation of the Vulgate version of Paul's Epistle to the Hebrews, 11.1 "fides est argumentum rerum non apparentium," which is rendered as "foi est argument des choses de nulle apparence."[27] Because *apparence* can mean both "semblance" (of truth) and "manifestation," the French sentence can be read as defining faith as the proof either of

---

verbo, etc.,' et Saint Paul, prime Corinthio 13: 'Charitas omnia credit?' Pourquoi ne le croiriez-vous? Pour ce (dites vous) qu'il n'y a nulle apparence. Je vous dis que pour cette seule cause vous le devez croire en foi parfaite. Car les Sorbonnistes disent que foi est argument des choses de nulle apparence. / Est-ce contre notre loi, notre foi, contre raison, contre la Sainte Ecriture? De ma part, je ne trouve rien écrit ès Bibles saintes qui soit contre cela."

27. Cf. Delbiausse's note, *Les cinq livres* 1:72.

that which is not manifest or of that which is unlikely. Paul (and the "Sorbonnistes") obviously meant the first; Rabelais impertinently supposes the second and thereby argues that the very improbability of his narrative is, on the testimony of Saint Paul and the Sorbonne theologians, the strongest evidence in favor of its believability.

That this is an impudent joke should not prevent us from recognizing its kinship to a tradition beginning with Plato's arguing that the craziest, most improbable discourse is likely to be the most "philosophical" and thus closest to the truth. One of Socrates' principal points in the *Phaedrus* is that madness is a proper symptom of a philosophical turn of mind. The discourse of philosophical (or poetic, or erotic) *mania* will always seem incredible from the point of view of common opinion (*doxa*), because common opinion never penetrates past the appearance of things. Plato would have found Rabelais's argument both familiar and congenial. What Plato would have objected to, of course, is the rhetorical basis of that argument, the play on the meanings of *apparence*. Though Plato's Socrates is by no means above using all the tricks of the Sophist rhetoricians, it is evident that Plato wished ardently that such devices could be eliminated from philosophical discourse. Rabelais has embraced them, and so thoroughly that much of the time it is difficult to imagine how to "interpret in a more sublime sense" this verbal tomfoolery.

But the narrator has, in addition to rhetoric and philosophy, both theology and scholarship to back up his claim that his story of the remarkable birth of Gargantua is worthy of credit. The theological argument is the familiar one that with God all things are possible: "If it had been His will women would have produced their children in that way, by the ear, for ever afterwards."[28] If one were to object that, though God may indeed will whatever he chooses, there is no reason to believe he ever willed this particular thing, Rabelais is ready with scholarly examples drawn mainly from classical learning. He points out that "Bacchus [was] begotten by Jupiter's thigh," Minerva from Jupiter's brain, and so on, and that Pliny devotes an entire chapter of his *Natural History* to "strange and unnatural births" at least as outlandish as this one. Conspicuously absent from this list of remarkable births is the story of a child born to a mother who never had carnal

---

28. *Gargantua and Pantagruel*, 53; *Les cinq livres* 1:72. "S'il voulait, les femmes auraient dorénavant ainsi leurs enfants par l'oreille."

knowledge of a man, but neither Rabelais nor his reader could fail to supply (at least unconsciously) the missing example.

Rabelais has written his own version of the story of the marvelous birth of the divine king, and if it seems impossible . . . Well, Rabelais tells us, we have believed a dozen other impossible things before breakfast. By telling us this he has not so much gained belief for his own story—which he surely never wanted in the first place—as forced the reformulation of the question of belief itself. If we try to distinguish between things worthy and unworthy of belief purely on the grounds of "apparence," there is no choosing between the nativities of Gargantua and Jesus. Only the naive reader would see this move as either promoting Gargantua or parodying Christianity. It suggests rather that there might be other grounds for making the choice, other issues more fundamental than *vraisemblance*. And if we don't believe that, "le fondement nous escappe."

This suggests, further, that the "more sublime sense" that Master Alcofribas wished his readers to find coexists perfectly well with the "literal" sense he says was the sum total of his intention. The discussion of belief carried out in and around the story of Gargantua's birth has foregrounded rhetorical reading of that very word ("belief" as credulity versus "belief" as faith) and, in the very act of giving evidence in favor of crediting his story, has demonstrated that it is not worth our faith. The idea of "faith" in these circumstances is ludicrous, not because of the story's miraculous features but because there is nothing in it that rewards the trouble of believing it. The promised reward of Christian faith, to cite the contrasting example of greatest relevance to Rabelais's project, is everlasting life. The more closely we attend to the literal events recounted in Rabelais's five books of marvelous adventures, the more likely we are to understand the difference between faith and credit, and that understanding is surely an aspect of the "more sublime sense" that these books aim at. It is as if we were to discover that, having chewed through the bone to get at the marrow, the very process of chewing had brought us many of the benefits we hoped to gain by eating the marrow. Even if there were no other allegorical intentions in these pages—and we have good reason to think that such intentions exist—the literal level itself, drawing attention to the problematic status of its own discourse, fulfills an allegorical function.

To return to my central topic, however, it is easy to see that the space between alternative readings of words like *fondement* and *appar-*

ence is the territory upon which Rabelais has established his linguistic kingdom. The tension between literal and figurative (and between other alternatives) generates the energy that makes such unpromising material as the fall of Gargamelle's anus into a story that is amusing and intellectually stimulating. Rabelais was certainly perfectly well aware of the rhetorical basis of his narrative wonderland, to such a degree indeed that he even turns the process of rhetorical construction loose upon the trope I just used here ("linguistic kingdoms") to characterize rhetorical construction itself. One of the most famous chapters of *Pantagruel* is that in which the narrator walks along Pantagruel's extended tongue into the giant's mouth, where he finds "more than twenty-five inhabited kingdoms, not counting the deserts and a broad arm of the sea."[29] The storybook worlds whose origin are in Rabelais's mouth and that emerged by means of his tongue are now discovered in Pantagruel's mouth and are entered by means of his tongue. The phrase "royaumes de la langue" (or "de la gorge"), which is in the modus obliquus an apt description of Rabelais's books, is understood here in the modus rectus as a set of actual places inside of one of Rabelais's characters. The narrator tells us that he has written "a great book entitled *History of the Gorgians*" (i.e., *History of the Throat Dwellers*), a title that could have been used equally well for the collected five books about Gargantua and Pantagruel. Rabelais makes rhetorical fun out of the fact that what has passed through his mouth has now been inserted into the throat of Pantagruel. After the narrator emerges from his stay of six months in his master's mouth, Pantagruel asks him what he has been doing:

When he noticed me, he asked: "Where have you come from, Alcofribas?" "From your throat, my lord," I replied. "And since when were you there?" said he. "Since the time when you went against the Almyrods," said I. "That's more than six months ago," said he. "And what did you live on? What did you drink?" "My lord," I replied, "the same fare as you. I took toll of the tastiest morsels that went down your throat." "Indeed," said he, "and where did you shit?" "In your throat, my lord," said I. "Ha, ha. You're a fine fellow," said he. "We have, by God's help, conquered the whole country of the Dipsodes. I confer on

29. *Gargantua and Pantagruel*, 275; *Les cinq livres* 1:232. "Plus de vingt-cinq royaumes habités, sans les déserts et un gros bras de mer."

you the wardenship of Salmagundia." "Many thanks, my lord," said I. "You reward me beyond my deserts."[30]

This passage depends on a logomimesis practiced upon a commonplace exchange of insults one could have heard on almost any French street in Rabelais's time: "Bran!" "En ta gorge!" (approximately: "You shit!" "In your throat, pal!") These are tropes, of course, having nothing to do with actual excrement. One person accuses another of being no more valuable than dung, and the other pays him back by saying he is so low that his throat is the proper repository of this dung. Rabelais, however, has constructed a situation in which it is both reasonable and necessary for Alcofribas to use Pantagruel's throat as a privy. The literal sense of these insults is suddenly foregrounded. But that is not the whole story, because the figurative sense is not effaced by this literalization. Even though he says, politely, "En votre gorge" instead of "En ta gorge," Alcofribas has still brought into his discourse the context of insult that these words inevitably carry with them. What will the huge, fearsome Pantagruel do if he takes the narrator's words in the conventional way?

There is a little drama here, a moment of tension in which Pantagruel must decide how he is going to react to this "usage de la parole." The tension is dissipated when the giant laughs and behaves not as if Alcofribas has insulted him, but on the contrary as if he has done some great service. It is a wonderful comic stroke. It is outrageously unexpected, another typically Rabelaisian nonsequitur, but it is more. It sets up another rhetorical shift, the capper that ends the series of jokes: Alcofribas receives his reward with the conventional reply, "You reward me beyond my deserts" ("vous me faites du bien plus que n'ai déservi envers vous") that now stands forth no longer as a

---

30. *Gargantua and Pantagruel*, 275; *Les cinq livres* 1:232. "Quand il m'aperçut, il me demanda: 'Dont viens-tu, Alcofrybas?' Je lui réponds: 'De votre gorge, monsieur. — Et depuis quand y es-tu? dit-il. — Depuis (dis-je) que vous alliez contre les Almyrodes. — Il y a (dit-il) plus de six mois. Et de quoi vivais-tu? Que buvais-tu?' Je réponds: 'Seigneur, de même vous, et des plus friands morceaux qui passaient par votre gorge j'en prenais le barrage. — Voire, mais (dit-il), où chiais-tu? — En votre gorge, monsieur, dis-je. — Ha! ha! tu es gentil compagnon (dit-il). Nous avons, avec l'aide de Dieu, conquêté tout le pays des Dipsodes; je te donne la châtellenie de Salmigondin. — Grand merci (dis-je), monsieur; vous me faites du bien plus que n'ai déservi envers vous.'"

conventional formula but as a substantially understated pristine truth. Alcofribas receives the wardenship of a province in return for the "service" of shitting in his master's throat, and by all conventional standards he has deserved something more like punishment than reward. But it is language rather than conventional standards that takes the lead here. The episode between Alcofribas and Pantagruel seems to have emerged out of a desire to validate commonplace tropes, to find that situation in which the phrase "vous me faites du bien plus que n'ai déservi envers vous" can be transformed from gentle hyperbole into radical understatement.

Language takes the lead on almost every page of the five books: there is a plenitude of rhetorical moments here perhaps unmatched by any work in the Western canon. One of the characters most aggressive in forcing confrontation of the literal with the figurative is Panurge, though in this trait he only follows the lead of his creator. Panurge sees the structure of language as a paradigm that the structure of his world should follow, and he is prepared to take on from time to time the responsibility of making sure that the paradigm is properly heeded. Given charge of the prisoner King Anarch, Panurge dresses him in a "beautiful belt of blue [*pers*] and green [*vert*] because Anarch, in making himself the enemy of Pantagruel, had acted in a "perverse" ("pervers") manner.[31] Similarly, he explains that his fondness for using burning glasses to drive people mad in church is linguistically justified, "for he said that there was nothing but a spoonerism separating a woman mad at mass [folle à la messe] and one yielding in the buttock [molle à la fesse]."[32] He is even ready with a learned philological excuse for stealing from the collection plate in church. The money, he says, is his by right:

> For really the pardoners give it to me when they offer me the relics to kiss and pronounce the words: "*Centuplum accipies* [you will recieve a hundredfold]," which is as much as to say that for one penny I am to take a hundred. For *accipies* is said after the manner of the Hebrews, who use the future tense instead of the imperative, as you have it in the Law, where it

31. *Les cinq livres* 1:229.
32. *Les cinq livres* 1:198 (translation mine). "Car il disait qu'il n'y avait qu'une antistrophe entre femme folle à la messe et femme molle à la fesse."

reads *Diliges Dominum* ["you will love the Lord"], for *dilige* ["love"]. So when the bearer of pardons said to me: "*Centuplum accipies*" he meant *centuplum accipe* ["take a hundredfold"].³³

While this argument is certainly a clever piece of rhetorical interpretation, it obscures as much as it displays the rhetorical complexity of this episode. Panurge's scholarly explanation that the pardoner's "centuplum accipies" is not so much a prophecy as a commandment has a certain credibility, based as it is upon the well-recognized Hebraicism, incorporated into the Latin Bible, substituting the future for the imperative. What Panurge glosses over (quite literally) is the transition he has made from spiritual to secular in his reading of the phrase. The pardoner's "centuplum accipies" is a trope for the promised acquisition of spiritual riches by the faithful; it is not and could not be a reference to monetary wealth. Nothing in the Christian religion could lead one to expect money in any quantity as the reward of virtue. Panurge's reading of the pardoner's phrase transfers it not only from the future indicative to the imperative but also from the spiritual, figurative realm it ordinarily occupies (but which is of little value to Panurge) into the secular, literal realm where Panurge can make use of it. Panurge requires the structure of this world, not the next, to comply with the structure of language as he construes it.

Panurge is a great manipulator of figures, and some of his most notable adventures come about in the effort to validate those figures as literal as well as metaphorical truth. When the English scholar Thaumaste challenges Pantagruel to a learned disputation, Panurge offers to stand in his master's stead. He boasts that he has argued with devils and bested them, so "you need have no doubts about this vainglorious Englishman. I'll make him shit vinegar to-morrow, before the whole world."³⁴ This is a variation on a common, earthy trope for extreme emotional discomfort, *pisser vinaigre*, and promises merely that Panurge will discomfit his opponent in the debate. It comes as no

---

33. *Gargantua and Pantagruel*, 227; *Les cinq livres* 1:200. "Car les pardonnaires me le donnent quand ils me disent, en présentant les reliques à baiser: *Centuplum accipies*, que pour un denier j'en prenne cent. Car *accipies* est dit selon la manière des Hébreux, qui usent du futur en lieu de l'impératif, comme vous avez en la Loi: *Diliges Dominum,* et *dilige*. Ainsi quand le pardonnigère me dit: *Centuplum accipies*, il veut dire: *Centuplum accipe*."

34. *Gargantua and Pantagruel*, 233; *Les cinq livres* 1:204. "Pour ce, soyez assuré de ce glorieux Anglais que je vous le ferai demain chier vinaigre devant tout le monde."

surprise, however—not in this book—that one result of the contest is that Thaumaste "got up in great alarm, but as he did so let a great baker's fart—for the bran followed it—pissed very strong vinegar, and stank like all the devils. Upon which the spectators began to hold their noses, since he was shitting himself with anguish."[35] This is a typically Rabelaisian logomimetic moment in which the actions of the story punctually carry out the program implicit in vulgar tropes.

This rhetorical game can be played with the highest as well as the lowest forms of figurative discourse, as Panurge's revisionary reading of "centuplum accipies" demonstrates. Rabelais is both willing and able to create an impudent tall tale out of a literalizing, logomimetic reading of Scripture, as he does in chapter 38 of *Gargantua*, "How Gargantua Ate Six Pilgrims in a Salad." Alcofribas tells how six pilgrims from the neighborhood of Nantes take shelter by chance in Gargantua's garden, among the giant lettuces that grow there, and are plucked up by accident when the giant picks a few of these great vegetables for a salad he suddenly craves. The pilgrims are too frightened to speak and end up in the salad bowl along with the lettuces and a dressing of salt, vinegar, and oil. Gargantua stuffs everything, pilgrims and all, into his mouth, but the pilgrims manage to take shelter behind his teeth and avoid being either crushed by his molars or washed into his stomach by the huge quantity of wine he drinks. Gargantua eventually dislodges the pilgrims with a toothpick, and (while the giant goes to relieve himself) they flee, only to have their road cut before them by the stream of Gargantua's urine. They are obliged to cross a great canal, and narrowly escape further disaster when all but one fall into a net trap that had been set out for wolves. The only lucky one, Fournillier, cuts the others free, and all finally reach a safe shelter where they can reflect upon their good fortune and upon the remarkable fact that "this adventure had been predicted by David in the Psalms." A pilgrim called Lasdaller ("tired of going") provides the outrageous *applicatio* of Psalm 124 (Vulgate 123):

Cum exsurgerent homines in nos, forte vivos deglutissent nos [When men rose up against us, then had they swallowed us up alive], when we were eaten

---

35. *Gargantua and Pantagruel*, 236; *Les cinq livres* 1:206. "Thaumaste, de grand ahan, se leva, mais, en se levant, fit un gros pet de boulangier, car le bran vint après, et pissa vinaigre bien fort, et puait comme tous les diables. Les assistants commencèrent s'étouper les nez, car il se conchiait d'angustie."

in a salad with a grain of salt; *cum irasceretur furor eorum in nos, forsitan aqua absorbuisset nos* [when their anger blazed forth against us, then had the waters swept us away], when he drank down the great gulp; *torrentem pertransivit anima nostra* [the torrent had gone over us], when we crossed the great canal; *forsitan pertransisset anima nostra aquam intolerabilem* [then had gone over us the seething waters], with his urine, with which he cut our road. *Benedictus Dominus, qui non dedit nos in captionem dentibus eorum* [Blessed be the Lord, who did not yield us a prey to their teeth]. *Anima nostra, sicut passer, erepta est de laqueo venantium* [We are like a bird escaped from the fowler's snare], when we fell into the trap; *laqueus contritus est* [the snare is broken] by Fournillier, *et nos liberati sumus* [and we have escaped].[36]

While one cannot argue with Rabelaisian scholars who tell us that in this passage "Rabelais is making fun of the customary way in which churchmen apply Scripture to all the events of life,"[37] we also cannot help but notice how well this particular *applicatio* works. The events of the pilgrims' adventure do indeed show a remarkable agreement with the literal meaning of the Vulgate psalm, even down to the marvelously unspiritual reading of "aquam intolerabilem" as urine. Of course it is outrageously silly, but much of the outrageousness comes from the absurd appropriateness of the psalm to the adventure. The capper on the series of jokes comes when we realize that we have been set up; the psalm works as a gloss on the episode because the episode was in fact composed out of a deliberately naive, literal reading of the psalm. Rabelais thus makes sure that we take these pilgrims (both Alcofribas's story of the pilgrims and the pilgrims' scriptural gloss on the story) the way Gargantua did: *cum grano salis.*

The tale of the six pilgrims is one of the more elaborately worked out logomimetic narratives in the five books; often Rabelais merely tweaks the story in a new direction by a sudden, comic swerve from

---

36. *Gargantua and Pantagruel*, 122; *Les cinq livres* 1:123. "*Cum exsurgerent homines in nos, forte vivos deglutissent nos,* quand nous fûmes mangés en salade au grain de sel; *cum irasceretur furor eorum in nos, forsitan aqua absorbuisset nos,* quand il but le grand trait; *torrentem pertransivit anima nostra,* quand nous passâmes la grande boire; *forsitan pertransisset anima nostra aquam intolerabilem,* de son urine, dont il nous tailla le chemin. *Benedictus Dominus, qui non dedit nos in captionem dentibus eorum. Anima nostra, sicut passer, erepta est de laqueo venantium,* quand nous tombâmes en la trappe; *laqueus contritus est* par Fournillier, *et nos liberati sumus.*

37. Thus Delbiausse in his note on the passage: *Les cinq livres* 1:123 (translation mine).

figurative to literal. In one of the skirmishes of the Picrocholean war, Gargantua's troops find themselves facing a force of the enemy outnumbering them ten to one. The warrior-monk Friar John advises the giant to lead his men ahead, since numbers (he says) are less important than courage, then he takes matters into his own hands by crying, "Charge, devils, charge!" ("Choquons, diables! choquons!") to Gargantua's men. "Hearing this, the enemy thought that these were real devils, and so began to fly headlong."[38] The enemy's literal interpretation might at first seem more credulous than is possible for anyone, and of course it is; at the same time, however, here we are reading a book about a person so huge that he can rest by leaning on the towers of Notre Dame, and it is this very person who leads the army of "devils." The reader, no less than the soldiers of the Picrocholean army, can never confidently assign hyperbolic language to the comfortable realm of the purely figurative. When, for instance, a lady Panurge wishes to bed finds his extremely direct and unromantic proposition offensive, she thrusts him back "more than three hundred miles" ("plus de cent lieues") and gives him a tongue-lashing. Since neither the lady nor Panurge is a giant, and since they continue to converse after this mighty shove, it would be reasonable to suppose that these three hundred miles are only hyperbolic figuration. But on second thought, given the enormous scale upon which events take place in these stories and the total disregard for the laws of physics regularly displayed here, there is equally good reason to take the narrator at his word. If the reader, safely removed from any real-life contact with this fictional world, is obliged to consider reading literally outrageous hyperboles such as these "hundred leagues," the army of Picrochole, having no other world to live in than the world of the fiction, cannot be expected to do otherwise. A reader with any inclination to feel superior to the credulous soldiers would be an "hypocrite lecteur" indeed, since both reader and soldiers are clearly "semblables" and "frères."

It is not too much to say that almost every character in the five books becomes caught up in the problem of reading, of having to face a seemingly undecidable choice between incompatible interpretations of

---

38. *Gargantua and Pantagruel*, 132; *Les cinq livres* 1:130. "Ce qu'entendants, les ennemis pensaient certainement que fussent vrais diables, dont commencèrent fuir à bride avallée."

the same text. Even when the characters make their choices, however, the reader is left suspended. A very large portion of the *Tiers livre* is taken up with exposition and explication of texts that can be read two ways. The chief matter in this book is Panurge's consideration of marriage and the lengthy series of advisers he consults on the issue. The advice Panurge receives is invariably capable of being read in different and conflicting ways and thus of advising either for or against his marriage. In this way the whole story of the third book is the discovery of rhetorical space. A try at the Vergilian lottery (opening the text of Vergil at random and reading the passage found as divine counsel) yields predictable results. On the first try they open to the line "Nec Deus hunc mensa, Dea nec dignata cubili est," in which Pantagruel finds a prediction that "your wife will be a whore, and consequently you will be a cuckold,"[39] while Panurge proclaims that "this augury denotes that my wife will be modest, chaste, and faithful."[40] On trying a second time they come upon "Membra quatit, gelidusque coit formidine sanguis," and Pantagruel promptly declares that it means "she'll beat you, back and belly."[41] Panurge, just as quickly, declares the opposite: "the prognostication applies to me, and says that I shall maul her like a tiger if she annoys me."[42] The third verse drawn is "Foemineo praedae et spoliorum ardebat amore." Both Pantagruel and Panurge agree that this prophesies a wife who will steal, but Pantagruel reads it *in malo* and Panurge *in bono*. The giant supposes that the wife will out and out rob her husband, while the companion thinks that she will love him so much that she will steal little things of his in order to get his attention.

Panurge subsequently consults a dream, a sibyl, a dumb man, an old poet, an astrologer, a physician, a philosopher, and a fool, and the results are always the same: under one construction the advice is against marriage, under another (invariably Panurge's own) it is in favor. As the third book nears its conclusion with still no decision in sight, the giant and his followers resolve to take a journey to consult

---

39. *Gargantua and Pantagruel*, 317; *Les cinq livres* 2:34. "Il dénote que votre femme sera ribaude, vous cocu par conséquent."

40. *Gargantua and Pantagruel*, 318; *Les cinq livres* 2:35. "Ce sort dénote que ma femme sera prude, pudique et loyale."

41. *Gargantua and Pantagruel*, 319; *Les cinq livres* 2:36. "Elle vous battra dos et ventre."

42. Ibid. "C'est de moi qu'il pronostique, et dit que je la battrai en tigre, si elle me fâche."

the Oracle of the Bottle regarding Panurge's marriage. In this way space is opened up for not one but two more books, for it is not until the thirty-fourth chapter of the fifth book that the company finally reaches the Oracle and not until the end of the book that the story of the pilgrimage to the Oracle is concluded. It is not too much to say, then, that almost the entirety of the last three books of the *Cinq livres* occupies the space between "Marry!" and "Do not marry!" This issue, in turn, arises out of the transformation of the literal into the figurative, when Panurge's purchase of an earring with a flea set in it becomes suddenly the "puce en l'oreille" of the common trope, a "flea in his ear" about getting married. As one rhetorical moment creates the possibility of further discourse, it creates as well the conditions for the generation of further rhetorical moments. The process is potentially endless. Rhetorical endings are always potential rhetorical beginnings.

There is in this sense nothing surprising about the otherwise very surprising conclusion of *Gargantua*, the book that had opened with a prologue apparently advising both literal and figurative reading of its contents. It ought to be surprising in that it seems to undercut radically the allegorical pretensions of the material on the founding of Thélème, some of the most "serious" material in all the five books. Alcofribas reports that a great bronze plate was found when men were digging the foundations of the Thelemite abbey and that on this plate was inscribed a lengthy "prophetic riddle," which he quotes in its entirety. The poem looks very much like an earnest and moral attempt at a kind of *consolatio* for those engaged in difficult labors and victimized by political strife. Upon hearing it all the way through, Gargantua sighs heavily and says, "This is not the first time that men called to the Gospel faith are persecuted," and asked directly what he thinks is the poem's meaning he replies, "Why, the continuance and steadfastness of Divine Truth" (163). Friar John, however, has another interpretation: "You can read all the allegorical and serious meanings into it that you like, and dream on about it, you and all the world, as much as ever you will. For my part, I don't think there is any other sense concealed in it than the description of a game of tennis wrapped up in strange language."[43]

---

43. *Gargantua and Pantagruel*, 163; *Les cinq livres* 1:151. "'Ce n'est de maintenant que les gens réduits à la créance évangélique sont persécutés . . . .' 'le décours et maintien de vérité divine.' 'Donnez-y allégories et intelligences tant graves que voudrez, et y ravassez, vous et tout le monde, ainsi que voudrez. De ma part, je n'y pense autre sens enclos qu'une description du jeu de paume sous obscures paroles.'"

He goes on to explicate various features of the poem in terms of tennis, providing at the least a plausible alternative to Gargantua's reading.

What makes this zany reading particularly amusing is that it reverses the relationship that we might have supposed to obtain between literal and allegorical readings. In the rest of *Gargantua*—and indeed generally throughout the five books—the literal level is down to earth, often vulgar, concerned with the ordinary events of the material world, while the figurative level (if we find one) is spiritual, elevated, and noble. That is after all what the author's prologue led us to expect, for it speaks of a literal sense containing "matières assez joyeuses" and of another "plus haut sens" that we must find by cracking the textual bone. In the case of the prophetic riddle, however, the literal sense is abstract, intellectual, and straightforwardly moral, while Friar John's allegorical reading is "assez joyeuse," materialistic, and even trivializing, bringing the high-flying language of the poem very much down to earth. With the help of Friar John the reader thus returns from the spiritual world of Thélème back to where he started, a physical reality that may emerge just as well from figurative as from literal reading.

Gargantua explicitly manifests the allegory of its own reading in such a way as to wave in the reader's face, as it were, the scandal of all deconstructible language. It flaunts aporetic moments of reading in exactly the same way that it flaunts excrement, genitalia, and other indelicate matters that it is improper to discuss in polite society. Rabelais's language is like the burlesque comic's banana peel: it constantly brings us back down to material reality, even (and especially) in those moments when it seems to be moving into the realm of the "plus haut sens." Friar John's reading of the prophetic riddle nearly cancels the difference between literal and figurative upon which the rhetoric of the narrative lives; but this is not really a surprise when we think back on the prologue. The principal joke of the prologue was in fact the cavalier gesture of canceling out the claim of an allegorical intention that had just been carefully set up. Alcofribas patiently built up his delicate rhetorical structure, and Alcofribas himself casually knocked it down with yet more rhetoric. If there is a single story in the *Cinq livres*, it is this very process. Rhetoric is the use of language that both affirms and denies a difference, and rhetorical construction is the narrative practice that finds its home in the space opened up by rhetoric. Rabelais's stories of Gargantua and Pantagruel exist comfortably, if outrageously, in that space.

3 | *Facts and Figures*

Rhetorical construction can clearly be a wonderful comic device. A good example is the case discussed in the previous chapter where a lady offended by Panurge's amorous advances pushes him back more than "three hundred miles." If we heard this same expression used in a conversation on a street corner, we would unquestionably understand it as a trope and think no more about it. The context provided by the outlandish adventures of the fairy-tale giants Gargantua and Pantagruel, however, sets the stage for tropological uncertainty about every hyperbole employed anywhere in the narration. The undecidability surrounding such hyperbole quickly infects all the figurative language used by anyone, whether character or narrator, to the point that we come to accept the interchangeability of literal and figurative as part of the structure of Rabelais's fictional world.

Rhetorical moments arising out of tropological uncertainties occur often in Rabelais's five books, and their frequency is due at least in part to the comic and frankly fantastic nature of the narrative. In this fictive world nothing is forbidden. The loosening or abandoning of constraints creates countless situations in which language we would ordinarily read figuratively suddenly calls for literal reading. We laugh, and our laughter serves as a powerful justification for the free interplay of rhetorical readings. We might be led to wonder, though, how tropological uncertainties can come into being in fictions that are not comic fantasies. How would an author of "serious" literary works—tragic dramas, let us say, or stories that end in catastrophe—contrive a situation that opens up the question of whether to read literally or figuratively? Are there predictable methods by which circumstances of tropological uncertainty can be produced?

The discussion of performative uncertainties in the previous chapter suggests a few possibilities. One alternative is akin to what Nathalie Sarraute does in *The Use of Speech*. In the story "Mon petit" she sets up a performative uncertainty by letting her own narrative voice discover a performative reading where we probably would not have found one. The narrator imagines a very special situation in which the use of "mon petit" could be interpreted both as the phatic filler we might ordinarily construe it to be and as an illocutionary act of name calling. In the same way, a practitioner of tropologically based rhetorical construction might take something we suppose to be a simple, literal fact and treat it unexpectedly as a trope, forcing us to reevaluate the relation between facts and figures.

A second alternative is actually a particularly interesting special case of the first. This transformation of facts into figures occurs when one historical fact, the author's personal name, becomes the leading trope in a fictional discourse. The reader ordinarily considers such a fact to lie outside the structure of the text, to belong to what Gérard Genette calls the "paratext," and to have no relevance to the reading process. But a name is a text, too, just like a trope. Many names indeed are tropes (or were at the time of their origin), though their figurative import is regularly ignored. The raw and unpromising fact of a personal name is therefore subject to rhetorical reading and is capable of generating an imaginative moment giving rise to a story.

A third alternative would be an analogue of Schiller's Elisabeth: a forceful character, intent for some fictionally relevant reason upon reading in an unconventional way, might simply insist so often upon hearing the literal where we hear the figurative (or vice versa) that the structure of the story becomes dominated by the clash between our conventional mode of reading and the character's unconventional one. As Elisabeth actually makes a performative uncertainty where ordinarily there would have been none, so another character in another work might create tropological uncertainties out of a need to interpret tropes in a special way. Such a character is Kleist's Penthesilea, who struggles mightily—and with surprising success—to turn figures into facts.

Figures into Facts: Kleist's *Penthesilea*

Penthesilea opens with an extended metaphor in which Odysseus compares the battling armies of the Greeks and Amazons to a pair of fighting wolves:

> You see upon this field
> The armies of the Greeks and Amazons
> Locked in dread conflict like two rav'ning wolves
> And, by the gods, neither can tell the cause!
> If Mars in anger, or our lord Apollo,
> Do not restrain them, or the Thunderer
> With levin-bolts do not divide the hosts,
> They die, in hate inseparable,
> The fangs of either deep in other's throat.[1]

This image, first applied to the two armies in general, is later narrowed to the leaders of the warring groups, Achilles and Penthesilea. The Amazon queen, in her pursuit of Achilles, is presented as more wolfish than the wolf:

> Not more untiringly the rav'ning she-wolf
> Pursues through snow-lapped forests still her prey
> That she has marked her with gaunt, hungry eye,
> Than throughout all our battle she Achilles.[2]

Achilles too, in this same scene, appears transformed metaphorically into a hunting canine. Odysseus describes him in a famous image as

1. I cite Kleist's play in English from Humphry Trevelyan's translation in *Heinrich von Kleist, Plays*, ed. Walter Hinderer (New York: Continuum, 1982); and in German from Kleist, *Sämtliche Werke und Briefe*, 2 vols., ed. Helmut Sembdner (Munich: Hanser Verlag, 1961). This passage is from *Plays*, 167; *Sämtliche Werke* 1:323. "Du siehst auf diesen Feldern, / Der Griechen und der Amazonen Heer, / Wie zwei erboste Wölfe sich umkämpfen: / Beim Jupiter! sie wissen nicht warum. / Wenn Mars entrüstet, oder Delius, / Den Stecken nicht ergreift, der Wolkenrüttler / Mit Donnerkeilen nicht dazwischen wettert: / Tot sinken die Verbißnen heut noch nieder, / Des einen Zahn im Schlund des anderen" (vv. 3–11).

2. *Plays*, 171; *Sämtliche Werke* 1:327. "So folgt, so hungerheiß, die Wölfin nicht, / Durch Wälder, die der Schnee bedeckt, der Beute, / Die sich ihr Auge grimmig auserkor, / Als sie, durch unsre Schlachtreihn, dem Achill" (vv. 163–66).

behaving like a "hound" ("Dogge") who falls upon a stag and, despite the hunter's efforts to call her off, holds on, "her teeth firm closed in the shaggy throat" ("verbissen in des Prachttiers Nacken") (vv. 213 ff.). The word *verbissen* occurs in both this and the opening image, and though biting is not explicitly mentioned in the description of Penthesilea, it is certainly implied by the adjective *hungerheiß*. The very beginning of the play, then, overwhelms us with pictures of animals, carried away by blood lust, killing each other with their teeth.

This and similar imagery later in the play cannot escape the reader's notice and has been extensively commented upon by critics. Achilles and Penthesilea are made to be linguistically identical to ravening, biting (or bitten) animals, not only by Odysseus but by other Greeks (cf. vv. 346, 403, 480), by various Amazons, and even by Achilles and Penthesilea themselves. The trope appears so often that within the context of the world of the play it becomes a commonplace. While this is something we might expect in a drama so prominently concerned with overpowering passion in its most destructive form, especially a drama so self-consciously "classical" in its rhetoric as this (Homeric/Vergilian extended metaphors are common), few readers are quite prepared for what Kleist finally does with his master trope. He has it acted out, literally (though one-sidedly), by Penthesilea upon Achilles: she, along with her hunting dogs (*Doggen*), bites him to death.

This is rhetoric with a vengeance, as if the trope set up at the beginning of the play comes back to haunt the poor Greeks who initiated it. The rhetoric goes further, though, in that it becomes conscious of its own construction and finally enunciates its central principle through the mouth of Penthesilea:

> How many a girl, her soft arms fast entwined
> About her man's neck, says she loves him so
> Beyond words she could eat him up for love.
> And then, poor fool, when she would prove her words,
> Sated she is of him—sated almost to loathing.
> Now, my beloved, that was not my way.
> Why, look, when my soft arms were round thy neck,
> I did it word for word; it was no pretending.
> I was not quite so mad as they would have it.[3]

3. *Plays*, 266; *Sämtliche Werke* 1:426. "Wie manche, die am Hals des Freundes hängt, / Sagt wohl das Wort: sie lieb ihn, o so sehr, / Daß sie vor Liebe gleich ihn essen

Penthesilea uses a trope different from the wolf/dog metaphor that began the play, but she is talking about the same process that earlier imagery initiated: the transformation of figurative language into narrative/dramatic action. The queen explains her grisly act as simply suiting the action to the word, in this case a "word" conventionally associated with romantic love. Her explanation proposes a radical reinterpretation of the trope of hyperbole. We ordinarily assume that this figure arises out of the ability of language to present a situation as somehow *beyond* what it could reasonably or possibly be. The hyperbolic gap between the language of the trope and reality is thus understood to arise out of something excessive or superfluous in language. Penthesilea, on the other hand, proposes that the hyperbolic gap is the result not of linguistic excess but of reality's insufficiency: not reality but language is the norm. The girl described in the Amazon's speech is unable to live up to the standard proposed by the trope; but Penthesilea herself *is* able to do it, is able to make up the distance between ordinary reality and the trope's proposed ideal of absolute desire.

She has also made up the gap between the figurative language of the play's first scene and the reality from which it originally diverged. In both cases language provides Penthesilea with a norm apparently authorized and approved by the community. These tropes are not the artifacts of some particular "poetic" consciousness but the common property of everyone who uses the language. This is even the case with the biting/bitten animal imagery inaugurated by Odysseus in the opening scene, since that image is used so often and by so many characters in the course of the play that it finally cannot be identified as the special, original invention of any particular person. Inside Penthesilea's world, the language that identifies Achilles and herself as prey and predator is so pervasive that it has the same endoxal status as "eating him up for love." In fashioning her behavior according to such figures, she is in a sense closing the gap between what society says (the "ideal" proposed by the trope) and what it does. From such a point of view, she has behaved like a model citizen—even and especially in the act

---

könnte; / Und hinterher, das Wort beprüft, die Närrin! / Gesättigt sein zum Ekel ist sie schon. / Nun, du Geliebter, so verfuhr ich nicht. / Sieh: als *ich* an deinem Halse hing, / Hab ichs wahrhaftig Wort für Wort getan; / Ich war nicht so verrückt, als es wohl schien" (vv. 2991–99).

that places her, from another point of view, outside both the Amazon and the human communities.

But she has done something else, something perhaps more disquieting to many of Kleist's readers than the gruesome maenadic blood lust of the conclusion: she has usurped the traditional male prerogative of striving for, and achieving, an unthinkably distant ideal, represented here by the implicit norms embodied in socially sanctioned tropes. She has taken the conventional notion of women as misusers of language—those who talk too much themselves and misunderstand the speech of others[4]—and transformed it into a program for female heroism. Figurative language is her program for surpassing what ordinary people are capable of. Her efforts may misfire, but they are *her* efforts, and indeed they are extraordinary, considerably more interesting than anything Achilles does in the play. This is a reversal of conventional expectation, as indeed the play makes explicit. It was, after all, not Penthesilea but Achilles who was supposed to be the hunting dog "verbissen in des Prachttiers Nacken" according to Odysseus's hyperbole. It is precisely because Penthesilea and not Achilles carries out the program implicit in this understanding of hyperbole that the play belongs to her and not to him. In the terms on which she seeks to be judged, the Amazon queen has achieved something as admirable and amazing as it is horrifying and inhuman.

Penthesilea is no less horrified by her act than is the audience. She realizes that in overcoming the gap between ordinary reality and the absolute proposed by hyperbolic language she has crossed other boundaries as well. Her great achievement, based on language, is also, because it is based on language, infected by the possibility of error (*Versehn*):

> So—it was a mistake. Kissing—biting—
> Where is the difference? When we truly love
> It's easy to do one when we mean the other.[5]

---

4. On this topic see Susan Noakes, "On the Superficiality of Women," in *The Comparative Perspective on Literature*, ed. Clayton Koelb and Susan Noakes (Ithaca: Cornell University Press, 1988), 339–55.

5. *Plays*, 265; *Sämtliche Werke* 1:425. "So war es ein Versehn. Küsse, Bisse, / Das reimt sich, und wer recht von Herzen liebt, / Kann schon das eine für das andre greifen" (vv. 2981–83).

What Humphry Trevelyan's English translation inevitably misses is that Penthesilea's explanation is based on these phonological similarity between the German words *Küsse* ("kiss") and *Bisse* ("bite"). The paronomasia simply escapes the translation altogether, but it is at the very heart of the matter, because once again this rhetoric proposes that something from the linguistic realm (the similarity of "Küsse" and "Bisse") can be directly carried over (*metapherein*, but in the opposite direction) into the sphere of the ordinary world, making an equation between the *acts* of kissing and biting. This is the same logomimetic principle that authorizes the acting out of metaphorical language: the reality of the story is presented as imitating what in "ordinary" circumstances is understood as belonging to the structure of language alone. It is only the structure of German phonology that proposes the similarity of kissing and biting, but Penthesilea, here as elsewhere, is prepared to understand that structure as an analogue of the structure of the (ideal) world. Her biting of Achilles is thus justified rhetorically in two ways, both by the metaphor of the ravening canine and by the "mistake" made possible by paronomasia.

It is important to understand that it is part of Penthesilea's character to take language seriously, to read figurative expressions as a kind of program for action. It is this readiness to take figure for fact that allows Prothoe and Achilles to deceive Penthesilea earlier in the play into believing that she has defeated Achilles in battle, when in fact the opposite is the case. While it is also true, as Ruth Angress has pointed out, that "steeped in her own desires and just recovering from her breakdown, Penthesilea is an easy dupe,"[6] the later course of the action authorizes us to find in the success of this deception a sign of something deeply rooted in the Amazon queen's character. When Prothoe suggests that Achilles, who is standing nearby weaponless, is himself the prisoner, Achilles obliges with a gallant metaphor. In answer to the queen's question, "My prisoner he?" the Greek hero replies, "In every way that's fair, thy prisoner I! / My only will to flutter out my life / In the soft durance of thy heavenly eyes."[7] That this is only a figure is

---

6. Ruth K. Angress, "Kleist's Nation of Amazons," in *Beyond the Eternal Feminine: Critical Essays on Women and German Literature*, ed. Susan L. Cocalis and Kay Goodman (Stuttgart: Akademischer Verlag Hans-Dieter Heinz, 1982), 129.

7. *Plays*, 219; *Sämtliche Werke* 1:377–78. "Er wär gefangen mir? . . . / In jedem schönren Sinn, erhabne Königin! / Gewillt mein ganzes Leben fürderhin, / In deiner Blicke Fesseln zu verflattern."

clearly signified in two ways, first by the formulation "in every way that's fair" ("in jedem schönren Sinn") with which Achilles opens his declaration, and then by the explicitly figurative phrase "in the soft durance of thy heavenly eyes" ("in deiner Blicke Fesseln"). Penthesilea is able to take this discourse as literally true, Achilles as her actual prisoner, in part because her native mode of understanding tends in that direction. She cannot fail to have understood the metaphorical intent of Achilles' words, that they are a declaration of love. Her later words in this scene show that she has so understood them. But for her the tenor of the metaphor does not obliterate the vehicle. That vehicle, the language of imprisonment, disarmament, and defeat, continues to signify in its own terms as well. If Achilles is her figurative prisoner of love, then he must be her actual prisoner of battle as well.

The high priestess is one character in the play who learns, though too late, that figurative language directed at Penthesilea can have results far different from those intended. The priestess's ironic request for forgiveness from the queen for Penthesilea's release from Achilles, her rhetorical wish for the return of the prisoners the Amazons lost in the rescue, becomes a script for Penthesilea to act out. What the priestess wants is not for Penthesilea to rush out to battle to regain the prisoners but rather for her to acknowledge that her behavior with regard to Achilles has been shameful and contrary to Amazon custom. When she claims that Penthesilea's rescue has in fact been a "mistake" ("Versehn"), she is applying heavy sarcasm, not asking Penthesilea to correct the mistake. And certainly when she pronounces the queen "free, in the name of the people," from all her traditional obligations as an Amazon, she does not suppose that Penthesilea will go ahead and engage in an act that places her outside all human society.

The priestess soon realizes that her ironic speech is having undesired consequences. When Achilles' herald brings the proposal for combat between the two lovers, Penthesilea quickly accepts, saying, "You shall have all the prisoners again!" Since that is not at all what the priestess really wants, she tries to ameliorate the effect of her earlier words: "If my hard words have stung thee, Penthesilea. . ."[8] The queen interrupts her with a reassurance that is anything but reassuring: "Not vainly, be assured, were those words spoken."[9] It does not mat-

---

8. "Wenn dich mein Wort gereizt, Penthesilea . . ." (v. 2401).
9. "Du sollst nicht umsonst gesprochen haben" (v. 2403). *Plays*, (244–45; *Sämtliche Werke* 1:404.

ter that from the priestess's own point of view her ironic words have been proved quite useless; Penthesilea is prepared to take the text presented to her and carry out what she understands as its literal significance.

One of the metaphors the high priestess had used in her sarcastic denunciation involved the bonds in which Achilles had held Penthesilea. The priestess set the queen free, she said, to do whatever she wished, including the following: "Kannst ihn mit flatterndem Gewand ereilen, / Der dich in Fesseln schlug, und ihm den Riß, / Da, wo wir sie zersprengten, überreichen" (vv. 2331-33).[10] I quote in German because Trevelyan's translation cannot reproduce the rhetorical complexity of the original. The end of the quoted passage, "ihm den Riß . . . überreichen," is difficult both grammatically and semantically. The priestess apparently means that Penthesilea may return to Achilles the gap hewn in her bonds by the Amazons in freeing her so that he can close it up and thus bind her again. But her words also have an erotic implication (probably intended), that Penthesilea is free to give her cleft to Achilles in sexual intercourse. What the priestess certainly could not have meant is that the queen should give her lover a "Riß," a set of fractures, tears, and wounds, and make them "überreich," multiply them in great profusion. Penthesilea validates the priestess's words, demonstrates that she "did not speak in vain" ("unsonst"), by using her newly declared freedom from all moral bonds to act out the unintended, overly literal meaning of the phrase "ihm den Riß überreichen." The queen tells us as much at the end of the play when she confesses, "I tore him apart" ("Ich zerriß ihn") (v. 2975).

By the play's end, Penthesilea is so adept at transforming rhetoric into reality that she is able to stab herself to death with a metaphor. What is perhaps more important for the play's poetic success, the audience is by now well prepared to accept—albeit with astonishment—such a remarkable feat:

> For now I will step down into my breast
> As into a mine and there will dig a lump
> Of cold ore, an emotion that will kill.
> This ore I temper in the fires of woe

10. *Plays*, 242; *Sämtliche Werke* 1:401. "With fluttering kirtle thou canst now pursue / Him who has made thee captive and canst give him / Those chains, by us hewn through, to weld again."

> To hardest steel; then steep it through and through
> In the hot, biting venom of remorse;
> Carry it then to Hope's eternal anvil
> And sharpen it and point it to a dagger;
> Now to this dagger do I give my breast:
> So! So! So! So! Once more! Now, it is good.[11]

It is precisely the Amazon queen, and only she, who can accomplish this feat, because she has demonstrated in no uncertain terms the ability to make the structure of her world conform to the structure of language. Among other remarkable features of this speech's rhetoric is its dialeptic division of the self into a multitude of linguistic entities:[12] the acting agent (ich); the arena of action (in meinen Busen); the source of various materials, implements, and forces (Gefühl, Glut, Gift, etc.); and finally the object of the action (reich ich meine Brust). This is to say that, in the act of cutting herself figuratively with the metaphorical dagger, she is cutting herself to pieces rhetorically. Language once again provides both the means and the justification for one of the play's most important actions, in an echo of the earlier, climactic slaughter of Achilles. As she then tore him to pieces (literally) in conformity with structures of language, so now she tears herself apart figuratively and linguistically. In Penthesilea's world, in which the norms are provided by language and reality struggles to conform, it is entirely understandable that the dismemberment of the grammatical self should be sufficient violence to destroy the physical body.

This self-dismemberment, which takes place both through and at the behest of language, not only repeats the gesture of her tearing Achilles apart, but also doubles the founding act of the Amazon state. It is a tearing apart of the breast by an act of almost superhuman self-control that makes Tanais the first and unquestioned monarch of the newly proposed female community. This feat is itself remarkable, but as Penthesilea relates it the event has the additional surprising feature of

---

11. *Plays*, 267; *Sämtliche Werke* 1:427. "Denn jetzt steig ich in meinen Busen nieder, / Gleich einem Schacht, und grabe, kalt wie Erz, / Mir ein vernichtendes Gefühl hervor. / Dies Erz, dies läutr' ich in der Glut des Jammers / Hart mir zu Stahl; tränk es mit Gift sodann, / Heißätzendem, der Reue, durch und durch; / Trag es der Hoffnung ewgem Amboß zu, / Und schärf und spitz es mir zu einem Dolch; / Und diesem Dolch jetzt reich ich meine Brust: / So! So! So! So! und wieder!—Nun ists gut" (vv. 3025–34).

12. The term "dialeptic" refers to the figurative division of entities ordinarily taken to be indivisible. See *The Incredulous Reader*, chap. 6.

being the reply to an utterance whose origin is never identified. As Tanais ascends the altar steps to take as symbol of her authority the golden bow of the Scythian kings,

> An awful voice was heard uttering these words:
> "'Twill but invite menfolk to mockery,
> A nation such as this, and 'twill succumb
> To the first onset of its warlike neighbors;
> For never can weak women, hampered still
> By the full-swelling bosom, learn to use
> The taut bow's deadly swiftness, as can men!"[13]

Tanais's response to this (perhaps divine) voice gives her new nation both a rite of passage and a name:

> She tore away her right breast, baptizing
> Thus all these women who would wield the bow
> —Herself, ere she had finished, swooned away—
> The Amazons, that is: the breastless ones![14]

It is a matter of some importance that Penthesilea does not identify the source of the voice that motivates Tanais's deed. While we may interpret this circumstance, as Trevelyan does in his translation, as indicating that the source is a divinity, other readings are possible. One of the women assembled to witness the coronation might have raised such an objection, perhaps even the high priestess herself. It might even have its source in Tanais's own mind. All we know about it is that it is "a voice" (not even an "awful" voice, as Trevelyan would have it) and that Tanais finds its words deserving of a response, not in word but in deed. I suggest that much of Penthesilea's action is similarly a response to an authoritative voice whose origin may not be precisely determinable. Her explanation of her biting of Achilles follows such a

---

13. *Plays*, 230; *Sämtliche Werke* 1:389. "Ließ eine Stimme also sich vernehmen: / 'Den Spott der Männer werd er reizen nur, / Ein Staat, wie der, und gleich dem ersten Anfall / Des kriegerischen Nachbarvolks erliegen: / Weil doch die Kraft des Bogens nimmermehr, / Von schwachen Fraun, beengt durch volle Brüste, / Leicht, wie von Männern, sich regieren würde'" (vv. 1976–82).

14. Ibid. "Riß sie die rechte Brust sich ab, und taufte / Die Frauen, die den Bogen spannen würden, / Und fiel zusammen, eh sie noch vollendet: / Die Amazonen oder Brustenlosen!" (vv. 1986–89).

pattern in that the language it seeks to obey is simply a common phrase in universal circulation: "I love you so much I could eat you up." It is the sort of thing that "manche" ("many a girl") has said and will say. It is a kind of endoxal sentiment that belongs to the speech community as a whole. The concern expressed by the sourceless voice at Tanais's coronation also has this endoxal quality, for the community as a whole seems to share it. After the voice is heard, "base fear began to sweep the people" ("die feige Regung um sich griff") (v. 1985). And of course Tanais would not have acted as she did unless she participated in this apparently communal opinion.

I stress this point because I see Penthesilea as a character deeply committed to following the precepts and ideals of her community. While she may ultimately fail and become an outcast, freed by her own declaration from the "Gesetz der Fraun," that is, from the Amazon code, she strives always to keep faith with something not unlike that "vernommene Stimme" to which Tanais hearkened. By following an ideal derived from structures of language rather than laws, she is in a certain sense following what might be seen as a "higher authority." Penthesilea does indeed break faith with the Amazon code, not only by her terrible cannibalistic desecration of Achilles' body but—probably more centrally—by her very decision to pursue a particular man, a man of her choosing, rather than accepting as her mate one falling to her by the chance of war. This decision is not, however, an act of willful self-indulgence but rather is an effort to be a dutiful daughter, to conform to the script written by her dying mother. The authority of maternal speech is, from Penthesilea's point of view, the source of all the state's authority to begin with. In following the former even when it conflicts with the latter, she is doing nothing different from what idealists from Plato onward have recommended: she is true to herself, to an internalized moral structure without formal legal standing.

Penthesilea's choice dramatizes a situation that we can easily imagine Kleist saw as his own. The martial ideals of the Amazon state, with their requirement of unwavering obedience to a code of duty, were hardly a matter of poetic fancy for Kleist, whose family tradition put him squarely in the position of a Prussian Penthesilea. Kleist ultimately had to choose adherence to an authority other than the martial code in which he was brought up, and that authority turned out to be poetic language. It was, as Kleist understood it, an unreliable authority, but having given up military duty and scientific truth as even worse alternatives, it was the one he felt most comfortable with. This language, the dwelling place of that "Gefühl" Kleist saw as the best chance for the direct apprehension of metaphysical truth, was not the creation of the individual Heinrich von Kleist but the common possession of his community. There is little question that he saw in at least some of his poetic efforts a form of keeping faith with that community, even if the community itself did not recognize it. The dedicatory poem prefaced to *Prinz Friedrich von Homburg*[15] emphasizes the social situation of the poet (Barde), whose poetic activity, described on the one hand simply as "Klänge ("noises")" and on the other as "Gefühle" ("feelings"), finds its place in the midst of a crowd of people ("Volksgedränge"). The poet is also described as "fromm," a term that in this context probably refers not so much to his religious piety (which is not an issue) as to his standing as a dutiful member of the community, as in the old phrase "ein frommer und getreuer Knecht." The poem expresses the poet's desire for the community's approval, which he will consider he has gained so long as "one in the circle of the crowd" ("eine . . . in der Kreis der Menge")—that is, the Princess Amalie of Hessen-Homburg—offers him the crown of success ("Und krönt ihn die, so krönen sie ihn alle").

Penthesilea's grammatical and metaphorical self-dismemberment at the play's end acts out her complex relation to her community. Like the sounds made by Kleist's "frommer Barde," Penthesilea's actions both reconcile her to and separate her from her fellows ("Jetzt trösten, jetzt verletzen seine Klänge"). While acknowledging that she is no longer like Tanais and thus no longer the Amazon queen, with respect to her duty to the law, her suicide links her on a figurative level with Tanais's most socially significant act. To the degree that her act of self-destruction is also, verbally and metaphorically, a tearing out of her breast, it is an attempt to insist upon her integration into the society from which she is apparently estranged. If metaphor has the power to put asunder, it also has the ability to join together.

Another metaphor is at work here as well, for when Penthesilea descends within herself to search out the means to destroy herself, she is entering a realm now occupied by her beloved enemy, Achilles. She has eaten him, incorporated him literally within herself. Her act of descent into herself is also a *descensus averno*, a journey into the under-

---

15. *Sämtliche Werke* 1:629.

world occupied by the fiercest of Greek warriors. The rhetoric of her final gesture, of giving her breast to the dagger (not the other way around), is the language of the bride going to her beloved. The dagger/emotion *is* Achilles, whom she will now allow to penetrate her as victor, after consuming him as victim. She keeps faith with the code of the Amazons, which sets forth a procedure whereby a woman can possess a man sexually, by taking him in (her conquering arms), *before* he penetrates her. The language that Penthesilea uses earlier in the play, as she explains to Achilles the customs of her tribe, anticipates the language of the conclusion: "And clip him to me with harsh arms of brass / Whom rather I would press to this soft breast."[16] Thus, in her suicide, Penthesilea receives Achilles within herself for the second time, but now returned to his status as aggressive, powerful, penetrating male. Having had her victory, she allows him his.

Penthesilea's mouth is the active principle that masters and orders all the elements of this disquieting play. Kleist's plot brings together the aspects of eros, aggression, nourishment, and language that belong to various metonymies of the mouth. At first it is the tooth of aggression that holds the center of attention, the tooth mentioned by Odysseus at the outset of the action (v. 11). This tooth returns at the end, both in the form of Penthesilea's biting and of the dagger, the figurative tooth (and penis) of Achilles. In the midst of all the violent aggression, however, eros, language, and even nourishment take an important place.

The themes of sexuality and language, like the theme of aggression, lie close enough to the surface of the play's discourse to be relatively evident to even the casual reader. But eating (I mean here sustaining, comfort- and life-giving nourishment) at first glance seems to be present only ironically, as a descant on the pervasive note of aggression that often overwhelms everything else. Actually, there are indications that Penthesilea's eating of Achilles may be as much an acting out of a desire to incorporate her mother (or at any rate the mother's breast) as of Bacchic excess. In the first place, it is remarkable that at her first sight of Achilles, Penthesilea's first thought is of her mother: "Oh, such a man as this, dear Prothoe, / My mother, Otrere, never can have

---

16. *Plays*, 228; *Sämtliche Werke* 1:387. "Und ihn mit ehrnen Armen mir ergreifen, /Den diese weiche Brust empfangen soll" (vv. 1898–99).

seen!"[17] Her immediate and all but uncontrollable desire for him is thus, in some unspecified way, connected to an aspect of her relationship to her mother. Later, after Penthesilea has been convinced that she has defeated Achilles in battle and the festival of their mating is in preparation, she explains to him and to Prothoe that Otrere had on her deathbed urged her daughter to follow the call of Mars and do battle with the Greeks at Troy. Otrere even prophesies, in her very last words, that "you will crown the son of Peleus" with the bridal crown. Penthesilea explains that she came to Troy less to please Mars than to please "the shade of Otrere," adding one of the most direct and unambiguous statements in the entire play—"I loved her" (v. 2172). She even goes so far as to confess that, even before she had ever seen Achilles, her dreams were filled with the image of the hero "whom my mother chose for me."[18]

Penthesilea's love for Achilles develops as a direct replacement of, and consequence of, her love for her mother. This connection between Achilles and Otrere is such a strong one that Penthesilea's turn from a desire to possess Achilles sexually to the need to destroy him utterly would not likely break it. In fact, this turn is itself motivated by a desire to be true to a maternal wish,[19] since her initial interest in Achilles was awakened by her mother's words. Penthesilea is motivated by an absolute need to defeat in battle the man she mates with, in keeping with what she describes as a maternal injunction: "The ban was laid by word of our first mothers, / And we are dumb before it, son of Thetis."[20] The Amazon queen, like all the Amazons, must fall silent before "the word of the first mothers" and obey this fundamental principle of their society. Penthesilea's relation to Achilles is thus a product of obedience to the maternal word in two ways.

For Penthesilea—even, or rather especially, the frenzied Penthesilea of the play's climax—Achilles must be a powerful metonymy of the mother. In the monstrous action of the final battle between them,

17. *Plays*, 169; *Sämtliche Werke* 1:325. "Solch einem Mann, o Prothoe, ist / Otrere, meine Mutter, nie begegnet!" (88–89).

18. *Plays*, 236; *Sämtliche Werke* 1:395. "Den mir die Mutter ausersehn" (v. 2184).

19. Penthesilea's desire must be seen as deeply ambivalent, since her suicide precisely undoes her mother's wish in giving her birth.

20. *Plays*, 229; *Sämtliche Werke* 1:387. "Der ersten Mütter Wort entschied es also, / Und dem verstummen wir, Neridensohn" (vv. 1909–10).

when Penthesilea performs the uncensored bidding of her unconscious, as it were, all the elements of her complex desire are brought to
the surface and acted out. Along with the aggressive, erotic, and linguistic aspects appears this strange but carefully prepared and motivated transformation of Achilles' body into the body of the mother:
she "Strikes deep her teeth into his snowy breast."[21] What is perhaps
most telling is that, while the dogs chew upon the right side of his
breast, she is described, at the close of Meroe's *récit*, as occupied with
his left. But we know, from Penthesilea's own detailed explanation,
that it is only the left breast that an Amazon warrior retains, and thus
only on the left side that an Amazon child could suckle. Penthesilea
undergoes a kind of regression in her frenzy, taking comfort from the
(metonymic) mother's breast in the act of keeping faith with all of the
maternal "words," both those that require her to love (kiss, receive
within herself) this man and those that require her to defeat him "on
the bloody field of war."[22]

One might wonder why Kleist went thus out of his way to associate
Achilles with Otrere and Penthesilea's frenzied attack on his body with
her filial attachment to the nourishing maternal breast. It would be
something of a trivialization to see the action of the play simply as the
attempt of a grieving child to repossess the comforting body of a
departed parent. At the same time, one cannot ignore the unmistakable
pattern of replacement (Achilles for Otrere) that the text offers, even if
one hesitates to understand this pattern in terms appropriate to a psy-
choanalytic investigation. The pattern could, and does, have an importance quite apart from the evidence it might offer about the state of
Penthesilea's psyche. That importance derives from Otrere's position
in the Amazon community.

It is important to remember that Otrere is not simply Penthesilea's
mother but also the previous ruler of the Amazon state. She is thus the
functional equivalent of Tanais and her successors, those authorities to
whom Penthesilea refers collectively as "the first mothers." Otrere is
not just Penthesilea's mother, she is the mother of the state and the
representative of the community's laws and standards. Obedience to
Otrere is for Penthesilea a double obligation: it is both her filial and her

21. *Plays*, 254; *Sämtliche Werke* 1:413. "Den Zahn schlägt sie in seine weiße Brust" (v. 2670).
22. *Plays*, 228; *Sämtliche Werke* 1:387. "Im blutgen Feld der Schlacht" (v. 1898).

political duty. By connecting Achilles so strongly to Otrere, Kleist has sharpened Penthesilea's moral dilemma. On the one hand, the figurative Achilles is made particularly attractive to the young queen precisely by his close association with the authority she has been brought up to respect. In mating with him, she can doubly fulfill the Amazon law. On the other hand, the actual Achilles remains always an alien, a male, and because she must seek him out, one forbidden to her by that same Amazon law. Ultimately there is little alternative for Penthesilea but to find a gesture by which she can both possess and reject Achilles at the same time. In her climactic Bacchic frenzy she finds the necessary gesture.

This mother/lover at whose breast Penthesilea feeds is a creation, from Penthesilea's point of view, of maternal speech. He has his beginning for her in Otrere's dying utterance, in which she "names the name" of the son of Peleus. This act of naming him brings him into being as the object of Penthesilea's desire, and the "words of the first mothers" set forth the conditions under which that desire may be fulfilled. Since maternal words are something before which an Amazon must fall silent (*verstummen*), Penthesilea speaks her obedience silently, with a mouth that bites/kisses the breast of the one she most desires. She has made her facts, in this ecstatic moment, conform as closely as possible to the authority of figures.

The power of rhetoric to generate and control complex events, so thoroughly explored in *Penthesilea*, evidently much occupied Kleist at this time in his life. In the more playful mood of *The Broken Jug*, he again set up a situation in which the distance between figurative language and its literal acting out is made vanishingly small. The opening scene presents the village judge Adam complaining about a fall he took, apparently for no reason, and observing philosophically that "each man bears, / Within himself, his own stumbling block."[23] Evidently inspired by this moral pronouncement, Adam's clerk Licht turns the judge's fall into another figure:

> You take your name from an unsteady sire who,
> When things were just beginning fell,

---

23. The translation is by Jon Swan. *Plays*, 3; *Sämtliche Werke* 1:177. "Jeder trägt / Den leidgen Stein zum Anstoß in sich selbst" (vv. 5–6).

> And still is famous for his fall.
> Surely you wouldn't . . .
> [. . .] Follow suit?[24]

Adam denies this metaphorical accusation of sexual impropriety, insisting that he fell right here:

> LICHT. Unbildlich hingeschlagen?
> ADAM. Ja, unbildlich.
> Es mag ein schlechtes Bild gewesen sein.[25]

While Adam here insists on the distinction between language that is not figurative (*unbildlich*) and that which is, his practice, in the same breath, is to create another figure (*Bild*) about "cutting a wretched figure" ("ein schlectes Bild sein"). What neither Licht nor the audience can know at this point, though, is the truth about Judge Adam's attempt to seduce a village girl. The figure of "Adam's (sexual and moral) fall" proleptically announces the truth of the situation, a truth Adam himself is struggling to hide by stressing the "wretched figure" he must have made in his literal fall.

This punning on "Bild" at the play's beginning is all the more complex for the fact that Kleist prefaced his manuscript with an explanation of the story's origin in a picture (*Bild*) he saw in Switzerland.[26] This picture, which he describes in some detail, was an etching copied from an "original" painted, Kleist reports, by a Dutch master. But Kleist supposes that this Dutch original was based on "a historical fact" ("ein historisches Faktum"), though he could never indeed find out anything more about it. The play as a whole, then, is presented as "bildlich" in the sense of deriving from a picture, a picture of a picture in fact; but also as "unbildlich" in that all of these "Bilder" are supposed to have their origin in historical reality, albeit a historical reality that is no longer discoverable.

When Adam asserts in the same breath that his fall is both "unbildlich" and "ein schlechtes Bild," he is repeating the gesture made by

---

24. Ibid. "Ihr stammt von einem lockern Ältervater, / Der so beim Anbeginn der Dinge fiel, / Und wegen seines Falls berühmt geworden; / Ihr seid doch nicht—? [. . .] Gleichfalls—?" (vv. 9–12).

25. Ibid. (vv. 14–15). "You literally fell, you mean. — I did. And must have cut a wretched figure doing so."

26. See *Sämtliche Werke* 1:176.

the play itself in relation to its alleged origin. The questioning of the opposition between literal and figurative, between what belongs to the realm of image and what belongs to "historical fact," is the premise on which the play is based. A substantial portion of the humor in the piece derives from figurative language that is, ironically, true. The audience begins to suspect very early on that it was Adam himself who committed the crime he now must judge, attempting to seduce Eve and breaking the jug in his flight when Eve's fiancé arrived to save her. When Adam makes comments such as, "If it wasn't Lebrecht [who committed the crime], call me a rogue" ("Ich bin ein Schelm, wenns nicht der Lebrecht war") or, "Still, if *you* can solve this, call me a knave" ("Doch wenn Ihrs herausbekommt, bin ich ein Schuft"), he is telling the literal truth. As John Gearey correctly points out, Adam "does not use these expressions out of slyness. They are a part of his natural manner of speaking";[27] that is to say, he uses these figures *as figures*. It is only the larger context that shows them to be "unbildlich." It would be incorrect to say that such lines as these are *apparently* figurative but actually are literally true: they are better understood as genuinely figurative under one interpretive convention and genuinely true in another.

In *The Broken Jug* Kleist set up a situation in which the literal and the figurative easily interchange. It is, after all, a comedy. In *Penthesilea*, on the other hand, there is no such easy intercourse between the two: there is a gulf between them that can be crossed only with great effort and at great cost. Penthesilea's heroic stature derives not so much from her high social rank or her singleness of purpose as from her ability to create a small corner of the world in which that gulf is momentarily obliterated. It should be paradise, as it was for Adam and Eve before the Fall, when man's language and God's were the same. But it turns out to look far more demonic than divine, because this language we use is fallen speech, one subject to "Versehn" ("mistake"). The ideal posited by hyperbolic language that Penthesilea manages to attain is one already corrupted by the possibility of error.

But if Penthesilea's linguistic achievement is ultimately highly questionable, the same cannot be said of *Penthesilea*. The play attains an extraordinary degree of integration, as *The Broken Jug* had done as well, by working through the poetics implied by its own rhetoric.

27. *Heinrich von Kleist: A Study in Tragedy and Anxiety* (Philadelphia: University of Pennsylvania Press, 1968), 84.

Kleist appears to be putting into practice, in a remarkably sophisticated way, the advice he offered in the little essay "Über die allmähliche Verfertigung der Gedanken beim Reden" ("On the Gradual Development of Thoughts While Speaking"), written just before he completed *The Broken Jug* and began work on *Penthesilea*.[28] Here the notion of making a beginning with language is presented, lightly but directly. Kleist limits himself in the essay to *spoken* language, proposing that, while it is often maintained that one should think before one speaks, it is often advisable to speak first, letting the ideas appear out of the pressure of the necessity of discourse. Ideas, he says, come while speaking ("l'idée vient en parlant").[29] Although Kleist is by no means maintaining that language is somehow prior to thought ("dunkle Vorstellungen," he says, must precede the act of speaking and endow it with the capability of developing concepts),[30] he is quite forcefully asserting language's role in doing what Edward Said calls the "activity" of beginning.[31] "Beginnings," in Said's sense, are not so much discovered as *made*, and indeed Kleist himself uses the phrase "den Anfang machen" in describing the process.[32]

Granted all the well-known and much discussed differences between spoken and written discourse, it still seems reasonable to see in *Penthesilea* a particularly forceful application of "die allmähliche Verfertigung der Gedanken beim Schreiben" ("the gradual development of thoughts while writing"), to use Malcolm Pasley's revision of Kleist's title.[33] I propose this heuristically, not as an actual description of Kleist's method of composition or of the sequence of his ideas. However Kleist's own thought process developed, the *play* makes its beginning with figurative language that then becomes transformed into the very progress of the plot. This is not to say that Kleist in any sense wrote *ins Blaue hinein* ("off the top of his head"), as Friedrich Dürren-

---

28. See *Sämtliche Werke* 2:319–24.
29. *Sämtliche Werke* 2:319.
30. This "Vorstellung" is not, of course, anything like a formed concept; it is more like Gadamer's "Vorverständnis."
31. *Beginnings: Intention and Method* (New York: Basic Books, 1975), 19.
32. *Sämtliche Werke* 2:320.
33. "Der Schreibakt und das Geschriebene," in *Franz Kafka: Themen und Probleme*, ed. Claude David (Göttingen: Vandenhoeck und Ruprecht, 1980), 15.

matt claimed to do;[34] the "dunkle Vorstellung" of the concluding maenadic frenzy was probably present from the start of Kleist's conception. It is rather to recognize that rhetoric is a central part of what makes the play go, not merely a decorative adjunct to it. *Penthesilea* is without doubt a mimesis in the Aristotelian sense: it is the imitation of a human action, Penthesilea's failed effort to integrate herself into her society. But that effort is itself rhetorical, since it is an attempt to bring facts into conformity with figures by acting out the literal meaning of tropes. The play therefore depends also on logomimesis, the imitation on the level of plot of structures existing on the level of rhetoric, the microstructure of discourse. And while it would certainly be limiting, as well as false, to see rhetoric as the *end* or even the subject matter of Kleist's act of composition, it would be an oversight not to recognize in rhetoric its beginning.

While Penthesilea's efforts to integrate herself into the social structure by strict adherence to the maternal word are not successful, they are by no means ineffectual. Her insistence on reading tropes as programs for action opens up a tropological uncertainty in the minds of the audience. This is not to say that the audience members as individuals are no longer able to distinguish between the literal and the figurative but rather that they recognize, in their capacity as a theatrical audience, the reality of their interchangeability for Penthesilea. The effectiveness of the play's final scene, where the queen kills herself with a trope, depends absolutely on our participation in a rhetorical moment. We have been shown again and again that Penthesilea is capable of pushing figurative language as far as possible in the direction of literal enactment, and so we are willing—most of us—to grant that inside the boundaries of her own mind and body she can wreak destruction with a metaphorical dagger. After the horrifying slaughter and devouring of Achilles, Penthesilea can no longer claim sovereign authority over the Amazons. She cannot make them believe that her act was socially and linguistically justified. In the psychosomatic space she does control, however, she is able to carry out her rhetorical principles with her characteristic fierce zeal, and we are compelled to credit

---

34. See Clayton Koelb, "The 'Einfall' in Dürrenmatt's Theory and Practice," *Deutsche Beiträge zur geistigen Überlieferung*, 7 (1972): 240–59.

and perhaps even admire that ability. We hear her give voice to a lethal figure, and we see her die. In her death, if in no other way, she has unquestionably turned a figure into a fact.

Facts into Figures: Büchner's *Danton's Death*

Kleist's play raises the question of the relation of figures to facts. It will not do to look upon Penthesilea as merely a particularly unattractive case of hysteria, as some have done; we must admit that extraordinary circumstances such as hers could lead a person to understand figures as facts, or as scenarios to be turned into facts. Having recognized this possibility, we might also want to consider the other side of the rhetorical coin, the case in which facts are treated as figures or as programs for acts of figuration.

The rhetorical beginning of Büchner's *Danton's Death* is unquestionably in the event that makes its conclusion, the decapitation of Georges Danton. This is, no doubt about it, a historical fact, something that exists outside language. For Büchner, however, this event functions in a remarkable way; for it is less as concluding event than as initiatory signifier that it has its real importance in Büchner's play. Whereas Danton's death functions in the history of his life simply as the final and absolute termination, in Büchner's enactment of the story it functions as a fertile source. The event of Danton's death, the sundering of his body by the guillotine, is *as rhetoric* present everywhere in the play in the form of a remarkable series of metaphors of physical and psychic dismemberment. Although Danton's actual death is only one particular moment in the play, Danton's death as figure is present everywhere in the text from the very beginning and is the subject of the drama referred to in the title. *Danton's Death* is the story of the rhetoric of Danton's death.

The separability of the parts of the human body and psyche is proposed by the figure with which Danton jokingly opens the play: "See the pretty lady, how cleverly she flips the cards! Indeed she knows what she's doing; they say she always holds the heart [*das coeur*] up to her husband and her diamond [*das carreau*] to others."[35] In this complex

35. I cite Büchner in English from *Danton's Death*, trans. Hedwig Rappolt (New York: TSL Press, 1980); and in German from *Sämtliche Werke und Briefe*, ed. Werner R. Lehmann (Hamburg: Christian Wegner Verlag, 1967), vol. 1. This passage is from

trope Danton is talking about three things at once: (1) playing card suits, with the implication that the lady in question does not play altogether by the rules; (2) body parts, wherein the lady's heart is contrasted to her genitals; and (3) emotions, implying that the lady gives her real or pretended love to her husband while reserving her sexual desires for others. The cards are the vehicle for the body parts, which in turn are the vehicle signifying emotions or actions, or both. By using the French words *coeur* and *carreau* in the midst of a German text intended for a German audience, Danton does more than indicate his nationality: he foregrounds these elements *as signifiers*, as if he were putting quotation marks around them. As foreign elements they are sundered from the rest of the sentence and thereby pushed to the center of attention. While "heart" and "diamond" (in their German equivalents) might slip easily into the flow of Danton's discourse, *coeur* and *carreau* stand forth as if cited in an effort to display their special properties. Any illusion of the immediacy of language is instantly put into question. These out-of-place, foreign words cannot just "mean what they say," because we have to make an effort to determine what it is that they might mean. The joke is that they might say several things, and they do in fact say them all at once.

Danton is telling us that the lady is duplicitous (in more ways than one), and he uses duplicitous language to say it. It is almost enough, as he says, to "make a person fall in love" with duplicity ("Ihr könntet einen noch in die Lüge verliebt machen").[36] But behind the joke and behind the "Lüge" resides the possibility, made explicit by Danton's turn of phrase, that human beings and human language can be cut up into pieces and distributed in different directions. It is not pleasant to consider the body of a woman in such a way as to allow her to literally give her heart to one person, her genitals to others, but that is what the trope, in its middle term, presents. This horrifying picture is wrapped up, as it were, by two less disturbing notions, the first that playing cards have different suits—hardly an idea to cause distress—and the second that love and sexual desire do not necessarily always go together—a disillusioned view, perhaps, but not especially shocking.

Danton's Death, 9; *Sämtliche Werke und Briefe*, 9. "Sieh die hübsche Dame, wie artig sie die Karten dreht! ja wahrhaftig sie versteht's, man sagt sie halte ihrem Manne immer das coeur und andern Leuten das carreau hin."

36. Ibid.

But the shadow of the guillotine falls across every aspect of this drama, and it makes its appearance already here in what is apparently nothing but a clever jest. In the world inhabited by Danton, all bodies are subject to dismemberment at any time and for practically any reason.

A little later in the scene, one of the ladies at the card table complains to Hérault that she cannot endure something he is doing with his thumb, apparently finding the gesture he makes offensive. Hérault replies to the effect that his thumb seems to have a will of its own, indeed a personality of its own ("Sehn Sie nur, das Ding hat eine ganz eigne Physiognomie"). Here again, the joke is based on the proposed separability of the thumb from the rest of the body and on the possibility of the fragmentation or multiplication of the personality. A human being has, or ought to have, but one "Physiognomie," legible in the features of the face; the thumb should not possess another.

In between these jokes, Danton invokes another metaphor of dismemberment to explain how difficult it is for people really to know each other: "We'd have to break open our skulls and pull each other's thoughts out of the brain fibers."[37] While this imagery must have had a certain immediacy for Büchner the medical student—the dissection of corpses was part of his professional experience—its appropriateness in this play derives from its relevance to the death Danton will suffer. But the same process that is horrifying and destructive when performed by the guillotine is, in metaphor, potentially happy and ameliorative when performed by a lover. If the living body really could be disassembled, Danton suggests, there might be some possibility of genuine communication and genuine love.

The working out of this notion of an ameliorative dismemberment will reach its culmination at the play's end, to be discussed later. Büchner does, however, produce an ironic and comic variation on the theme in the second scene of the first act, in which the minor character Simon berates his wife for acting as pander for their daughter. Simon, overcome by both his rage and his inebriation, finally becomes persuaded that the fault lies with neither his wife nor his daughter but with the aristocrats who let poor people starve and then exploit their need by purchasing sexual services from them. At the end of the scene

---

37. Ibid. "Wir müßten uns die Schädeldecken aufbrechen und die Gedanken einander aus den Hirnfasern zerren."

Simon, who suffers almost as much from his love of classically rhetorical bombast as from alcohol, begs his wife for forgiveness:

> Ha, can you forgive me, Portia? Did I strike you? It was not my hand, not my arm, it was my madness that did it.
> His madness is poor Hamlet's enemy.
> Then Hamlet did it not, Hamlet denies it.[38]

Simon would exculpate himself, with Shakespeare's help, by separating himself into two psychological entities, only one of which is genuinely him. It is a rhetorical strategy we all have used at one time or another for reasons similar to Simon's. We would all like to be able to claim that a virtuous right hand did not know what a villainous left hand was doing, to figuratively sunder that offending hand from our bodies. By divorcing himself from his madness, by denying that the hand and arm that beat his wife were his, Simon is able to extricate himself from the unhappy position in which he has placed himself.

Imagery like this, based on the principle of a divisible self, occurs throughout the play and seems to infect the language of almost the entire cast of characters. Robespierre confesses to himself in a soliloquy (1.6) that "I don't know which part of me is telling lies to the other."[39] St. Just indulges in a paradoxical rhetoric in which he uses a grisly irony to argue in favor of guillotining Danton and all his followers on the grounds that not to do so would be an act of dismemberment: "We must bury the great body with decorum, like priests, not like murderers. We must not dismember it, all its limbs must go down with it."[40] That St. Just has qualms about the metaphorical "zerstücken" ("tearing to pieces") of the body of the Dantonists is heavily ironic, of course, considering the means by which he intends to avoid such a "murder." Cutting apart many actual, living bodies is apparently far

---

38. *Danton's Death*, 17; *Sämtliche Werke und Briefe*, 16. "Ha, kannst du mir vergeben, Porcia? Schlug ich dich? Das war nicht meine Hand, war nicht mein Arm, mein Wahnsinn that es. / Sein Wahnsinn ist des armen Hamlet Feind. / Hamlet that's nicht, Hamlet verläugnet's."

39. *Danton's Death*, 31; *Sämtliche Werke und Briefe*, 28. "Ich weiß nicht, was in mir das Andere belügt."

40. *Danton's Death*, 32; *Sämtliche Werke und Briefe*, 29. "Wir müssen die große Leiche mit Anstand begraben, wie Priester, nicht wie Mörder. Wir dürfen sie nicht zerstücken, all ihre Glieder müssen mit hinunter."

preferable to cutting apart a single figurative one. St. Just produces another ironic trope, though this time the irony must be seen as unconscious, when he proposes at the end of act 2 that the "Revolution, like the daughters of Pelias, dismembers mankind to give it new birth."[41] This learned classical reference is meant to justify the unrestrained use of the guillotine as an instrument of social change: dismemberment is alleged here to be only temporary, since the social body will arise from the experience with renewed vigor. What St. Just fails to mention is that Pelias did not survive being cut to pieces. Medea tricked Pelias's daughters into the gruesome murder of their father by telling them that by this means he would be rejuvenated. St. Just is thus acting in the role of Medea here, advising the people to an act of dismemberment allegedly curative but actually hideously destructive. This attempt to transform literal dismemberment into figurative healing is successful with St. Just's audience, who respond to this trope with "long, sustained applause," according to the stage direction. The irony is lost on them.

St. Just's rhetoric serves notably to confront the play's audience with the literal reality that stands as vehicle for his high-minded figure. What is at issue, here as everywhere in the drama, is "Danton's death," the actual and irremediable physical division of an actual person. Just as the daughters of Pelias cannot revive their father, cannot transform their act of hurting into an act of healing, so does St. Just's rhetoric fail—with us, at least—to efface the bloody violence of his vehicle by the happy regeneration of his tenor. The guillotine as signifier cannot be completely suppressed or hidden by the ameliorative tropes into which it can be turned.

Danton himself cannot decide how to valorize the guillotine and the figures it generates. As the hero of the Revolution he is obliged to see something positive in the instrument of execution and the dismemberment it causes. In his defense before the revolutionary tribunal Danton boasts that "I nourished the young brood of the Revolution with the dismembered bodies of the aristocrats."[42] Danton thus proudly announces himself as a figurative bird of prey, whose parental duty it is

41. *Danton's Death*, 52; *Sämtliche Werke und Briefe*, 46. "Die Revolution ist wie die Töchter des Pelias; sie zerstückt die Menschheit um sie zu verjüngen."
42. *Danton's Death*, 61; *Sämtliche Werke und Briefe*, 54 "Ich habe . . . die junge Brut der Revolution mit den zerstückten Leibern der Aristokraten geäzt."

to take apart living human bodies.[43] The destruction of one set of bodies serves to produce nourishment for another. This is of course good if you belong to the eaters, not so good if you are one of the eaten. The enemies of the revolution are depicted as the latter, while Danton expects his audience to identify with the former. Given Danton's insecure position at the time he makes this speech, however, there must arise at least a suspicion that he is no longer the bird of prey but one of its victims. Danton's pride in his earlier role in the revolution is, as we know from other, less public scenes in the play, tinged with a good deal of regret. Danton must entertain the notion, even as he speaks his proud metaphor, that the voracious young brood is entirely capable of tearing apart and devouring the parent himself.

Both Danton and the world he inhabits are, in his own mind, already thoroughly dismembered long before any credible threat of execution hangs over his head. There seems to be an element in his character that would like to restore the *disjecta membra* of this world to some sort of unity. Lacroix portrays Danton as one who tries to put broken pieces back together again even in his notorious whoring:

> Just now he's looking for the Venus de Medici piece by piece among all the grisettes at the Palais Royal, he's doing mosaics, as he puts it; heaven knows with what part of the anatomy he's occupied at the moment. It's a pity that Nature cuts up beauty—as Medea did with her brother—and sinks it into the body by fragments.[44]

Lacroix introduces an allusion to Medea very similar to the one St. Just will use later in his persecution of the Dantonists. In this case the reference is to Medea's murder of her brother Apsyrtos, whom she

---

43. Cf. Hoffmann's Sandman who, in the nurse's version of the story, also takes apart human bodies and carries pieces (the eyes) "to the moon as food for his children" ("in den Halbmond zur Ätzung für seine Kinderchen"). The Sandman's children, like Danton's revolution, are figured as a brood of voracious young birds. I make the analogy not to suggest that Büchner was influenced by Hoffmann in using this figure but rather to stress the functional similarity between Danton's story of himself and the nurse's story of the Sandman. Hoffmann's story will be discussed in detail in chapter 4.

44. *Danton's Death*, 22; *Sämtliche Werke und Briefe*, 20–21. "Er sucht eben die mediceische Venus stückweise bey allen Grisetten des palais royal zusammen, er macht Mosaik, wie er sagt; der Himmel weiß bey welchem Glied er gerade ist. Es ist ein Jammer, daß die Natur die Schönheit, wie Medea ihren Bruder, zerstückelt und sie so in Fragmenten in die Körper gesenkt hat."

dismembered and tossed into the ocean, knowing that he (like Pelias) could never be put back together. But Danton, according to Lacroix, sees no virtue in what Medea-like nature has done and is concerned solely with restoring the lost wholeness in the body of Beauty.

Danton confirms Lacroix's description in the following scene (1.5) when he refers to one of the prostitutes of the Palais Royal as a "restored torso on which only the hips and feet are antique."[45] The figure implies that this woman is in effect the result of "doing mosaics," of putting fragments back together in a matrix. But even this recuperative erotic activity tends as much toward further disruption as toward the recovery of unity. Danton's attempt to encompass and comprehend beauty does not appear to be successful, for one thing, and for another, it tends to shatter the psyche making the attempt. Danton confesses his inability to take possession of even one woman's beauty in asking the apparently rhetorical question of Marion, "Why can't I contain your beauty completely within myself, enfold it completely?"[46] While it would not be difficult to read this passage as an expression of a sort of vagina or womb envy, a wish to play the female role and thus be divested of external sexual organs,[47] I prefer for the moment to stress mainly the element of partial failure. Danton's question implies that, while he might be able to grasp (*fassen*) *part* of Marion's beauty, he cannot grasp it completely. Though she is unquestionably a unitary whole, he is able to comprehend her only piecemeal. Marion presents herself in this scene as perhaps the most integrated character in the play. Except for some early adolescent feelings of being "double and then melted into one again" and her grief at the suicide of a lover, she considers herself an unbroken unit: "I am always only one." It is this perfect unity, this "uninterrupted yearning and grasping, one glow, one stream," that defeats Danton's efforts.[48] Her grasping (*Fassen*) defeats his.

45. *Danton's Death*, 26, *Sämtliche Werke und Briefe*, 23. "Ein restaurirter Torso, woran nur die Hüften und Füße antik sind."

46. *Danton's Death*, 24; *Sämtliche Werke und Briefe*, 22. "Warum kann ich deine Schönheit nicht ganz in mich fassen, sie nicht ganz umschließen?"

47. I deliberately refrain from using the term "castration" in order to keep this discussion separate from Freud's notions about the relation of figurative language to castration anxiety. I am concerned with the economy of joining and sundering that derives from the nature of rhetorical discourse. There is, for my purpose, no need to search for additional explanatory principles in psychic disruption.

48. *Danton's Death*, 23–24; *Sämtliche Werke und Briefe*, 21–22. "Als wäre ich doppelt und verschmölze dann wieder in Eins. . . . Ich bin immer nur Eins. Ein ununterbrochenes Sehnen und Fassen, eine Gluth, ein Strom."

At the same time, though, he makes it clear that a successful effort at embracing the wholeness of Marion's beauty would cost him his own unity: "I wish I were part of the ether so I could bathe you in my flood, so I could break on each wave of your beautiful body."[49] The image would first make the self, in its wholeness, into something no longer whole, a mere "part of the ether"; it then transforms the act of encompassing ("bathe you in my flood"—a conventional figure for male orgasm) into an act of self-disintegration ("mich . . . zu brechen," that is, "break *myself*"). Danton's rhetoric thus implies that, to the degree that he can comprehend Marion's beauty, he must take her apart, and that if an act of total comprehension were imaginable it would take him apart.

The rhetoric that sets forth this state of affairs also performs a remarkable turn along the way. In the very moment when Danton's image proposes that he, the encompassing fluid of the ether, will break over her, the crucial characteristic of this substance—that it moves as a wave—is transferred from him to her. The image presupposes that the "flood" that breaks on something (the shore? a reef?) could only be a wave, but in midstream the wave suddenly appears as the undulating curve of Marion's feminine shape, and it is this "wave" that the "flood" breaks upon. This language thus acts out its announced topic of disintegration. The figure of Danton as flood cannot even hold itself together long enough to complete the trope before the elements of the metaphor start to scatter, to migrate to other points of focus in the discourse. *She* can be an "uninterrupted stream," but he cannot.

Lacroix, who introduced the figure of Danton's whoring as the reunification of fragmented beauty, seems to share Danton's suspicion that this activity harbors substantial danger for the mosaic maker. He proposes that one who traffics with whores runs the risk of becoming "a modern Adonis" who "doesn't get mangled by a boar but by sows."[50] Although Lacroix differentiates the modern from the ancient Adonis in a number of ways (the site of the wound, the agent producing the wound, the type of flower emerging from the wound), both have in common the essential characteristic of being torn apart. The remainder of act 1, scene 5, substantiates Lacroix's fears that Danton

---

49. *Danton's Death*, 24; *Sämtliche Werke und Briefe*, 22. "Ich möchte ein Theil des Aethers seyn, um dich in meiner Fluth zu baden, um mich auf jeder Welle deines schönen Leibes zu brechen."

50. *Danton's Death*, 25–26; *Sämtliche Werke und Briefe*, 23. "Wird nicht von einem Eber, sondern von Säuen zerrissen."

will be a modern Adonis, though what the action demonstrates is psychic rather than physical disintegration. Although Danton and Lacroix receive news that Robespierre appears ready to move against the Dantonist moderates, Danton cannot keep his attention on the danger while his mind is still occupied with Marion, who is present throughout the scene. She is apparently monitoring the condition of Danton's lips, for she finally breaks into the conversation to remark that his lips have become cold. Danton realizes that she is a distraction, that she causes him to "lose time," but in the same breath he asserts that this loss is worthwhile and dismisses his friends with a promise to do something about Robespierre "tomorrow." Lacroix appropriately comments that "the demoiselle's thighs [will] guillotine you,"[51] his language leaving open the question whether this guillotining will take place in the future or is taking place now. (In German it is common to use the grammatical form of the present to signify the future.) In this context that grammatical ambiguity obliges us to read both literally and figuratively, and the audience must take both tenses as correct.

The energy behind this premise, that the guillotine and the dismemberment it effects are as much a part of the present as the future for Danton and his party, fuels the engine of the play's imaginative language. Danton declares his dismemberment with almost punctual regularity, though frequently only by the way, as part of an observation about the general state of mankind. He remarks, for example, that "we consist of two halves" ("wir . . . aus zwei Hälften bestehen"), putting his own feelings of self-division in a context of universal human suffering.[52] It is characteristic of Danton thus to ascribe his own feelings to a generalized "we" and implicitly to assert thereby his solidarity with humanity at large. All human beings are flawed, he thinks, but since "we won't be able to dig it [the flaw] out of each other's guts, why break our bodies open?"[53] If we believe Danton's earlier rhetoric, however, we already know what this flaw is: all human beings are in fact *already* "broken open," at least psychologically, in that we are not at one with ourselves.

Danton continues in just this same vein of imagery in act 2, scene 5, when Julie hears him talking (or actually shouting) to himself:

51. *Danton's Death*, 28; *Sämtliche Werke und Briefe*, 26. "Die Schenkel der Demoiselle guillotiniren dich."
52. *Danton's Death*, 35; *Sämtliche Werke und Briefe*, 31.
53. *Danton's Death*, 36; *Sämtliche Werke und Briefe*, 32. "Wir werden es einander nicht aus den Eingeweiden herauswühlen, was sollen wir uns drum die Leiber aufbrechen?"

JULIE: You called out something about ugly sins, and then you groaned:
September!
DANTON: Me, me? No, I did not say that, I barely thought it, those words
were only my innermost, very secret thoughts.
JULIE: You are trembling, Danton.
DANTON: And why should I not tremble when the walls are babbling?
When my body is so shattered that my thoughts, unsteady, restless, talk
with lips of stone? It is strange.[54]

Danton's rhetoric travels the distance from what is "heimlich" (his
innermost, secret thoughts) to what is "unheimlich" (strange, uncanny) in one quick stride. Since he refuses, or is unable, to acknowledge
that he has been talking to himself, Danton creates an uncanny metaphor in which the stone walls of the room are somehow able to take
possession of his secret thoughts and speak them forth. This could
happen, though, only if what he supposes are inside (his thoughts) are
not inside after all: the body containing those thoughts must have been
broken open ("zerschellt") so that they could wander out and speak
themselves by way of the stone walls. Here again Danton presents
himself as split apart, alienated from himself. Danton's terminal weari-
ness ("life is not worth the trouble it takes to keep it")[55] is intimately
bound up with his sense that the effort to keep ourselves together is,
from the outset, lost labor. Although he does not explain why, he
deeply believes that all human beings are, ab initio, torn asunder.
Everyone is in the process of suffering Danton's death.

It is such a notion as this that informs the poignant little song Lucille
sings at the end of act 2, scene 3:

Parting, oh parting, oh parting,
Whoever invented parting?[56]

54. *Danton's Death*, 45; *Sämtliche Werke und Briefe*, 40.
"J: Du sprachst von garstigen Sünden und dann stöhntest du: September!
D: Ich, ich? Nein, ich sprach nicht, das dacht ich kaum, das waren nur ganz leise
heimliche Gedanken.
J: Du zitterst Danton.
D: Und soll ich nicht zittern, wenn so die Wände plaudern? Wenn mein Leib so
zerschellt ist, daß meine Gedanken unstät, umirrend mit den Lippen der Steine reden?
Das ist seltsam."
55. *Danton's Death*, 37; *Sämtliche Werke und Briefe*, 33. "Das Leben ist nicht die Arbeit
werth, die man sich macht, es zu erhalten."
56. *Danton's Death*, 44; *Sämtliche Werke und Briefe*, 39. "Ach Scheiden, ach Scheiden,
ach Scheiden, / Wer hat sich das Scheiden erdacht?" I have altered the translation for the
sake of clarity.

Lucille is worried about the threat to her beloved Camille, anxious lest death should separate him from her. But some of her concern is directed at another kind of "Scheiden" ("parting"), the act that threatens to separate him from himself: "When I think that they might—your head!"[57] We know who invented this kind of parting, this mode of execution. We know his name, and we know the mechanism that still carries that name. And so, while in one sense the question posed by Lucille's song is "rhetorical" in the traditional sense, in another sense it is not. Lucille's question might be rhetorical in the complex sense proposed by Paul de Man: it might be the kind of language whose illocutionary status we cannot determine, the kind of language that stands between the literal and the figurative and is possibly both at the same time—the imaginative language of rhetorical construction. Taken literally, as a "genuine" question about physical parting, it has as its answer the same "literal" meaning possessed by all the various tropes of dismemberment in the play: Guillotine.

There is a curious and moving turn that takes place in the imagery of dismemberment at the play's close. Danton's last words are a response to an unnamed executioner who prevents Hérault from embracing Danton: "Do you want to be crueler than death? Can you prevent our heads from kissing each other in the bottom of the basket?"[58] These are two apparently rhetorical questions, evidently taken as such by the executioner, who does not reply. The first question introduces the possibility of something more "grausam" ("cruel, gruesome") than this quite gruesome form of death, suggesting that human beings—or possibly human institutions—are more zealous in pursuing the concept of "Scheiden" than death itself. Danton thus opens the possibility, it seems, of a reuniting of parted spirits in death.

The second question seriously undercuts (without eliminating) such a spiritual and romantic reading of the first. Indeed, to the degree that Danton's question is only "rhetorical," it asserts the possibility, even the necessity, of a *physical* reunion of the two friends in the basket. The individual bodies are torn asunder, but this enables the joining of the severed heads, their renewed physical contact, in a

57. *Danton's Death*, 43; *Sämtliche Werke und Briefe*, 38. "Wenn ich denke, daß sie dieß Haupt! —"

58. *Danton's Death*, 85; *Sämtliche Werke und Briefe*, 74. "Willst du grausamer seyn als der Tod? Kannst du verhindern, daß unsere Köpfe sich auf dem Boden des Korbes küssen?"

way not even the executioner would want to prevent. The image is a grotesque one, of course, particularly because it uses the word "kiss" in a context that hardly seems appropriate. This very last word that Danton utters, "küssen," is being used both figuratively and literally at the same time. Certainly the heads in the basket do "kiss" in the figurative sense of "touch each other," much in the way that a hammer tapping very lightly is said to "kiss" a nail. But this simple act of touching is by no means the point of Danton's rhetoric. The insatiably erotic Danton is one for whom kissing was an essential part of his life, actually and fundamentally part of his quest for some kind of unity. He did his "mosaics" in part with his lips. Kissing has been Danton's way of putting the world back together. In a paradoxical fashion, then, the very physical nature of Danton's image here, with its allusion to kissing as an erotic act, reauthorizes a reading of this last speech as an expression of a kind of spiritual hope. If the executioner cannot prevent the "kissing" of the heads, then perhaps death by dismemberment can bring about a spiritual bond that will be impossible to sever.

But all this presupposes that the question is purely rhetorical. The fact is, Danton does not *assert* that the executioner cannot prevent this kissing from taking place, he only *asks* if he can prevent it. The possibility remains open that Danton does not know whether the kiss is preventable and that he retains at least the suspicion that the answer to his question might be, "Yes, I can prevent it. This parting is complete and eternal." The executioner might be a good, rationalistic philosopher who can split apart the figurative from the literal as easily as he splits human bodies and who believes that one kind of kissing, the figurative, need not imply the other. Physical touching is not necessarily spiritual union.

The course of the play's rhetoric is more on Danton's side here than on the "gruesome" executioner's. The language of *Danton's Death* forces us again and again to find the literal and the figurative coexisting with equal force in a single utterance. Thus, while we cannot reject the possibility that Danton's question might be a genuine, answerable one, and that the answer might involve an insistence—as the tradition always insists—on the primacy of the signified over the signifier, the tenor over the vehicle, we cannot reject the opposite view either. Danton's question might be purely rhetorical and might therefore hold out hope for a literal "kissing" and thus a spiritual union. The value of the guillotine and all the tropes of dismemberment it engenders, the issue of whether it could ever bring about the promised social healing, remains to be determined. The play as a whole remains rhetorical in the sense developed in chapter 1: it refuses to say what it is doing but only does what it says. It is an act of rhetorical construction.

The Name of the Self:
Hawthorne's "Rappaccini's Daughter"

Personal names are perhaps the most intimate point of contact between historical facts and rhetorical figures. The name, from the viewpoint of the person bearing it, is in our culture a given fact of history, permanently inscribed before one becomes a fully functioning person. But because it is a piece of language, it is also capable of being "turned" by figuration away from the person it designates. Some personal names happen to be particularly open to interpretation and are thus capable of initiating a rhetorical moment. Certain writers have learned that it is possible to generate fiction out of the process of reading such names, particularly when they are attached to the authorial self. The given fact of the personal name becomes for these writers a metaphoric nexus out of which they can develop an entire fictional structure. This is exactly what happens in the case of Nathaniel Hawthorne's story "Rappaccini's Daughter."

This enigmatic tale is, as Nina Baym assessed it, "one of the richest stories in the [Hawthorne] canon," but its richness has been as much a problem for critics as a pleasure. Baym in fact suggests that it is "too rich, in the sense that it is susceptible of a number of partial explanations but seems to evade any single wholly satisfactory reading."[59] The problem arises of course as much from our desire to find that "single satisfactory reading" as from any defect in the story, but a problem it is, nonetheless. Although "Rappaccini's Daughter" would fit very comfortably among the works of Kafka, for example, an oeuvre characterized by overdetermination of meaning, it seems rather out of place when compared with Hawthorne's other fiction, a body of writing many critics have found answerable to a "single satisfactory reading." Like so many of Kafka's tales, "Rappaccini's Daughter" seems on the

---

59. *The Shape of Hawthorne's Career* (Ithaca: Cornell University Press, 1976), 107.

one hand to invite allegorical interpretation and on the other decisively to prevent it.

The analogy with Kafka is instructive. If Hawthorne's tale somehow looks like a blood relative of the fiction produced by that master of rhetorical construction, it suggests that one might profitably approach "Rappaccini's Daughter" in terms of its rhetorical structure. The goal of such a procedure would be not to discover the single wholly satisfactory reading that has eluded all others but to investigate the principles and practices that engender a work of fiction that both invites and prevents such a reading. While rhetorical construction necessarily brings with it a theory of reading, that theory cannot be construed as a strategy for discriminating correct from incorrect interpretations. The reading of "Rappaccini's Daughter" offered here thus aims to clarify how the story works, not to decide definitively what it means.

The first among a number of odd features of this tale is the manner of its presentation. Unlike the other tales and sketches in *Mosses from an Old Manse*, "Rappaccini's Daughter" is introduced to the reader as the work of a foreign writer and not that of the "Manse persona" himself. The story proper is preceded by a brief preface explaining that the tale is a translation from the works of a certain M. de l'Aubépine, a French writer whose reputation is as limited at home as it is abroad. Lest the reader fail to notice that "Aubépine" is the French word for "Hawthorne," the author of the preface supplies a list of M. de l'Aubépine's works, including "Contes deux fois racontés" ("Twice-Told Tales") and French versions of several of the *Old Manse* titles. In this way it is made clear that the author of "Rappaccini's Daughter" is a fictionalized version of Hawthorne, a kind of Continental specular double, a persona that can offer itself as both Hawthorne and not Hawthorne at the same time. In this way Hawthorne distances himself from his authorial efforts without denying them.

These efforts at distancing seem, however, to be more than a little unnecessary. Hawthorne had already produced in the "Manse persona" an authorial double carefully separated from Nathaniel Hawthorne by considerable irony. The *Old Manse* collection as a whole is offered, in the introductory sketch "The Old Manse," with considerable misgivings and elaborate apologies:

> The treasure of intellectual gold, which I hoped to find in our secluded dwelling, had never come to light. . . . All that I had to show, as a man of

letters, were these few tales and essays, which had blossomed out like flowers in the calm summer of my heart and mind. . . . With these idle weeds and withered blossoms, I have intermixed some that were produced long ago—old, faded things, reminding me of flowers pressed between the leaves of a book—and now offer the bouquet, such as it is, to any whom it may please. These fitfull sketches, with so little of external life about them, yet claiming no profundity of purpose,—so reserved, even while they sometimes seem too frank,—often but half in earnest, and never, even when most so, expressing satisfactorily the thoughts which they profess to image—such trifles, I truly feel, afford no solid basis for a literary reputation. (P. 34)[60]

The author then asks the reader to imagine that he is in the study in the Old Manse, where the author gives him the manuscript of these tales to peruse. In the same sentence, however, the author denies he would ever do what he has asked the reader to imagine him doing, because to do so in actuality would be "an act of personal inhospitality" so terrible that he could not carry it out "even to my worst enemy" (p. 35).

This extended, fictional act of self-effacement appears quite sufficient in itself. It would require little more comment were it not that its rhetorical features seem to ask for attention. Hawthorne has taken an old chestnut of a trope, the metaphor of "bouquet" for a collection of texts (fossilized in the word "anthology," Latin *florilegium*), and drawn it out into the matter of his argument. He twists the trope mightily, though, in that he carefully reverses the values traditionally associated with the concept of a bouquet. The figure of the "anthology" had arisen, after all, to foreground the notion that what he had selected was the best of what was available. The bouquet represents not any random selection of plants but the loveliest flowers to be found. Hawthorne's florilegium has a different look. It is made up of "idle weeds and withered blossoms" along with yet older material that has "faded" like "flowers pressed between the leaves of a book." This bouquet is not the best there is; it is simply all there is, and it will have to do.

Given the thoroughness with which the act of self-deprecation is carried out through the Manse persona, its repetition in the figure of M. de l'Aubépine must have some other purpose than to impress on

60. I cite Hawthorne from *Mosses from an Old Manse*, vol. 10 of *The Centenary Edition of the Works of Nathaniel Hawthorne*, ed. William Charvat et al. (Columbus: Ohio State University Press, 1974). Page numbers in the text refer to this edition.

the reader Hawthorne's ambivalence about himself and his work. But what else could it be doing? One thing it does, whether intended or not, is to draw attention to the name "Hawthorne" as signifier. That this name can be translated into French reminds us that it is, in addition to the author's personal name, an English common noun denoting a tree or shrub of the genus *Crataegus*. The presence of M. de l'Aubépine, in other words, reminds us of the potential for autonomasia in the name "Hawthorne." Such a reminder would be of little importance were it not that the story that follows acts out the gesture implied by the figure: as "Hawthorne" is the name of a person *and* the name of a plant, the story of Rappaccini's daughter Beatrice finds and fills with text the space between person and plant. The two incompatible readings of "Hawthorne" as figure produce a rhetorical moment that generates the tale.

Although there are not many characters in "Rappaccini's Daughter," one of the most important among them is in fact a plant. The young student Giovanni notices it upon first looking into Rappaccini's garden from the window of his room: "there was one shrub in particular, set in a marble vase in the midst of the pool, that bore a profusion of purple blossoms, each of which had the lustre and richness of a gem; and the whole together made a show so resplendent that it seemed enough to illuminate the garden, even had there been no sunshine" (p. 95). This plant, which Rappaccini later refers to as "our chief treasure" (p. 97), seems to be especially dangerous to everyone but Beatrice. Rappaccini is afraid to come close to it, even when wearing a protective mask, and Beatrice warns Giovanni away from it in the strongest terms, telling him that to touch it would be "fatal" (p. 114). Beatrice, on the other hand, is on what can only be called intimate terms with the plant. She calls it "sister," tends and grooms it, and even at one point "threw open her arms, as with a passionate ardor, and drew its branches into an intimate embrace; so intimate, that her features were hidden in its leafy bosom, and her glistening ringlets all intermingled with the flowers" (p. 102).

This close relationship between Beatrice and the plant seems in a way only to substantiate in the physical world a metaphor Giovanni introduces upon first hearing and seeing Beatrice. The sound of her voice makes him think of "deep hues of purple" and of "perfumes heavily delectable," and her appearance is compared to "the most splendid of flowers." In his eyes she possesses a particularly vivid "bloom," a "luxuriance" that makes her appear to be "another flower, the human sister of those vegetable ones" (pp. 96–97). The commonplace trope that compares a girl to a flower is so close to literally true here that the story and the trope become as intimately bound together as the girl and the plant. It is impossible to say whether the story performs a logomimesis, carrying out the script of the trope in the fantastic way we are familiar with in Kafka's stories, or whether the trope is simply an anticipation of the narrative whereby Giovanni fathoms the "inmost nature" of Beatrice before he actually learns anything about her.

One would surely be inclined to the latter, conventional explanation, implying that Hawthorne engages here in a kind of foreshadowing that is not especially subtle, were it not for another feature of the text that suggests the priority of the trope. The very appearance of a character named Beatrice is noteworthy in this connection, since the first paragraph of the narrative proper brings up the apparently insignificant matter of Giovanni's knowledge of "the great poem of his country," Dante's *Divine Comedy*. The house in which Giovanni takes lodgings in Padua—the lodgings that overlook Rappaccini's garden—belonged to a family with an ancestor "pictured by Dante as a partaker in the immortal agonies of his Inferno" (p. 93). The place into which Giovanni moves, then, is a place already belonging to poetry, already inscribed as it were into the *Divine Comedy*. Having taken up his dwelling in (a metonymy of) Dante's poem, he discovers there one of Dante's characters. This Beatrice, then, is introduced to the reader *as a text* before she appears as a person.

The flower trope has also been introduced earlier, again as text, in the metaphor of the volume as a bouquet. The collection of which "Rappaccini's Daughter" is a part is a bunch of "idle weeds and withered flowers" that hover on the border between life and death. This trope, too, enters into the story of Giovanni and Beatrice, where the withering of flowers plays an important and dramatic role. The first conversation between the two young people, the first stage in their courtship, concludes when Giovanni throws down to Beatrice a bouquet of flowers he has bought on the way home:

> She lifted the bouquet from the ground, and then as if inwardly ashamed at having stepped aside from her maidenly reserve to respond to a stranger's greeting, passed swiftly homeward through the garden. But, few as

the moments were, it seemed to Giovanni when she was on the point of vanishing beneath the sculptured portal, that his beautiful bouquet was already beginning to wither in her grasp. It was an idle thought; there could be no possibility of distinguishing a faded flower from a fresh one at so great a distance. (P. 104)

Later, after the couple has met a number of times and recognized their love for each other, Giovanni begins to worry about the effect their relationship might be having on him. He buys another bouquet, this one "still gemmed with the morning dew-drops," and after carrying it home with the idea of testing whether Beatrice withers flowers, he examines it: "A thrill of indefinable horror shot through his frame, on perceiving that those dewy flowers were already beginning to droop; they wore the aspect of things that had been fresh and lovely, yesterday" (p. 121).

Giovanni suggests by denial that he too could become a withered flower when he thinks to himself, "I am no flower to perish in her grasp!" (p. 121). Although indeed Giovanni himself does not droop and fade away, others do. The old lady Lisabetta who shows Giovanni the private entrance into Rappaccini's garden is repeatedly described as "withered" ("withered face," p. 108, and "withered guide," p. 109) and thus cannot help but remind the reader of both the flowers in the story and the flower that is the story. She, no less than Beatrice, is the figurative sister of the stories in the *Old Manse* volume.

Both the plants and the stories, as Beatrice's metaphorical sisters, have a legitimate claim to be "Rappaccini's daughter." The plant with the purple flowers has a particular right to this title, according to Beatrice: "At the hour when I first drew breath, this plant sprang from the soil, the offspring of his [Rappaccini's] science, of his intellect, while I was but his earthly child" (p. 125). The reader is urged by this formulation to consider the matter of "intellectual offspring," a figural commonplace for the relation between a text and its author. "Rappaccini's Daughter" as the name of a text is not Rappaccini's "daughter" so much as it is Hawthorne/Aubépine's, and this in turn leads us to consider the possible kinship between the father of Beatrice and the "father" of "Rappaccini's Daughter."

At first glance there is little enough to suggest a similarity. The coldly scientific Rappaccini has nothing in common temperamentally with the rather emotional author of "The Old Manse" or with the "voluminous" Aubépine, contributor to the *Revue Anti-Aristocratique* (the *Democratic Review*), a periodical associated with "the defense of liberal principles and popular rights" (p. 93). Rappaccini seems firmly committed to aristocratic values, wishing the "daughter of my pride and triumph" to be special, different from "ordinary women" and "endowed with marvelous gifts" (p. 127). There is, however, intriguing evidence connecting Rappaccini to the *Revue Anti-Aristocratique* and thus to the *Democratic Review*, site of the first publication of Hawthorne's story. As Kent Bales has pointed out, Hawthorne departs from the pattern he had established for himself in naming the editor of the *Revue* "the Comte de Bearhaven" rather than some transparently clear analogue of John O'Sullivan, editor of the *Democratic Review*. Bales argues that "Bearhaven" is an allusion to the famous Dutch physician Herman Boerhaven, who not only kept "the most extensive garden of medicinal plants in northern Europe" but also had a beautiful and much-courted daughter.[61] This suggests—though Bales does not draw out the implication—that there is an analogy between keeping a garden of medicinal plants and editing a literary journal and thus, more generally, between gardening and literary activity. One can scarcely doubt that this analogy is intentional, given the intense preoccupation with it demonstrated in the "Old Manse" frame sketch. Not only does the Manse persona call his own work a collection of flowers, but he even describes the remnants of the old library he discovers in the garret of the Old Manse in terms of withered plants: "Nothing, strange to say, retained any sap" (p. 20). The similarity between texts and plants is asserted again and again.

Rappaccini shares with John O'Sullivan/Comte de Bearhaven the guardianship of the flowers of discourse, and he seems to share something with Hawthorne/Aubépine as well. Burton R. Pollin has alerted us that Hawthorne not only married a woman skilled in foreign languages but himself studied Italian briefly as a young man.[62] We have to take seriously the possibility that Hawthorne did not create the Italian background of his story just for exotic color but was "deliberately playing upon Italian language, literature, and history."[63] If we look at the name "Rappaccini" from this perspective, we find a curious situation. It seems to be taken for granted by Hawthorne scholars that

61. Kent Bales, "Names and the Root of Evil in 'Rappaccini's Daughter,'" *Nathaniel Hawthorne Journal* (1978): 175–78.
62. "'Rappaccini's Daughter'—Sources and Names," *Names* 14, no. 1 (1966): 30–35.
63. Bales, "Names and the Root of Evil," n. 1.

"Rappaccini" derives from *"rapace"* ("rapacious"), and indeed Bales characterizes him as "rapacious Rappaccini." In the sense that the father of Beatrice is greedy for knowledge, the epithet is justified, but in other ways Rappaccini does not seem particularly rapacious at all. His principal concern seems not so much with gathering wealth and power for himself as with making his daughter as invulnerable and happy as she is beautiful. The narrator describes him looking at Beatrice and Giovanni "as might an artist who should spend his life in achieving a picture or group of statuary, and finally be satisfied with his success" (p. 126). In bringing Beatrice and Giovanni together he has engaged at least as much in "reconciling" (*rappaciare*) as in being rapacious. Furthermore, if we are justified in supposing that Hawthorne's use of double consonants in the name "Rappaccini" is not significant—as we must believe if we derive the name from *rapace*—there are other Italian lexemes that might be equally relevant. One that comes immediately to mind is *rapa,* a word that might have caught the attention of a man named Hawthorne, since it can refer either literally to a plant (a turnip) or metaphorically to a person (a "stupid fool" or "blockhead"). He might also have noticed that the Italians use the phrase "non valere una rapa" to mean exactly the same thing as the (now obsolete) English expression "not worth a haw." "Rapa" for Italians, like "haw" for Englishmen, was the common rhetorical emblem of a thing of no value. In a story in which the heroine considers herself the sister of a plant, we had better take seriously the possibility that her father, like herself, has a vegetable as well as a human nature.

It is also remarkable how Hawthorne took up in the "Old Manse" sketch the theme of the garden so prominent in "Rappaccini's Daughter." If one harbored any doubt that the author of the story of Beatrice saw himself as fundamentally similar to his character Rappaccini, it would take only a glance at the section of "The Old Manse" dealing with the garden to dispel them. The "Hawthorne" projected there as the Manse persona is also an avid gardener, visiting his plot several times a day to "stand in deep contemplation over my vegetable progeny, with a love that nobody could share or conceive of, who had never taken part in the process of creation" (p. 14). He repeats this figure of the plant as progeny later with an ugly twist: "But, after all, the hugest pleasure is reserved, until these vegetable children of ours are smoking on the table, and we, like Saturn, make a meal of them" (p. 15). Such a perversion of nature is not the first to take place in and around the garden, for the plants are like people in a number of disquieting ways.

There is the Dutch cabbage "which swells to a monstrous circumference, until its ambitious heart often bursts asunder" (p. 15) and the various apple trees in the orchard, contorted into a "variety of grotesque shapes," one "harsh and crabbed," another "churlish and illiberal," all interspersed with trees characterized by "charity" and "benevolence" (p. 12). Such metaphors giving plants the characteristics of men would surely not seem out of place to Hawthorne, the man with the name of a plant.

Since Hawthorne and Rappaccini have so much in common (as they are presented in the *Old Manse* volume), we must entertain the possibility that the designation "Rappaccini's Daughter" is not only the literal title but the proper metaphorical description of the story of Beatrice. It is the literary offspring of another gardener, the figurative Rappaccini, the inhabitant of the Old Manse himself. The term "daughter" thus resonates with a variety of meanings. Beatrice, the plant with the purple flowers, and "Rappaccini's Daughter" itself can all be understood as daughters of the dedicated gardener. Even Giovanni is nearly brought into this metaphoric kinship, and Rappaccini almost succeeds in making him into a male version of Beatrice, another sibling of the deadly shrub. The "withered" Lisabetta, too, seems to be Rappaccini's creature and thus another of his many natural and unnatural "daughters." The word "daughter" keeps shuttling back and forth between the two poles disclosed by the rhetorical reading of the name "Hawthorne": literal and figurative, person and plant, animate and inanimate, self (Hawthorne) and other (Aubépine).

The name "Hawthorne" brings together other opposites as well. The plant is considered valuable both as an effective hedge maker and as an ornamental, and it is even a source of nourishment (though a last resort). At the same time it is the bearer of the haw, the "thing of no value." In addition, the plant is named in the English way by the juxtaposition of two of its prominent features: it possesses both haws and thorns, both that which can help (providing food in time of need) and that which can hurt. The uncertain, oscillating valorization of the hawthorn plant taints everything named "Hawthorne" and serves as a focus for an ambivalence about self and work evident in the author of the *Old Manse* collection. It certainly taints M. de l'Aubépine's artistic output, which the "translator" values enough to devote his energies to but not enough to praise outright. Everything positive that is said about him is surrounded by negatives and hedged about by qualifications to such a degree that the brief prefatory note devoted to introducing Aubépine could be taken as a model for the rhetoric of damning with faint praise. He is said to occupy "an unfortunate position" between the intellectual and popular writers of his day; he is "too remote, too shadowy and unsubstantial in his modes of development" for the popular audience, but at the same time too popular for the intellectuals:

> His writings, to do them justice, are not altogether destitute of fancy and originality; they might have won him greater reputation but for an inveterate love of allegory, which is apt to invest his plots and characters with the aspect of scenery and people in the clouds, and to steal away the human warmth out of his conceptions. . . . Occasionally, a breath of nature, a rain-drop of pathos and tenderness, or a gleam of humor, will find its way into the midst of his fantastic imagery. . . . M. de l'Aubépine's productions, if the reader chance to take them in precisely the proper point of view, may amuse a leisure hour as well as those of a brighter man; if otherwise, they can hardly fail to look excessively like nonsense. (Pp. 91–92]

The "translator" finds that he has "a certain personal affection and sympathy, though by no means admiration," for the object of his labors (pp. 92–93) and thus in the very act of introducing him "favorably" to his new audience brings up a host of reasons why they should not so receive him.

This same ambivalence finds another focus in the fictional plant doctor, Rappaccini. Where Aubépine had been the object of affection and sympathy, though not admiration, Rappaccini elicits admiration in the absence of affection and sympathy. The attitude of Professor Baglioni toward his colleague and rival seems a distillation of this ambivalence. On the one hand, Baglioni gives the impression that Rappaccini is "an awful man indeed," one who would "sacrifice human life" for the sake of his experiments (pp. 99–100), and Baglioni wants nothing more than to "thwart" and embarrass him. On the other: "let us confess the truth of him, he is a wonderful man!—a wonderful man indeed!" (p. 120). As with Aubépine, the reader is told that Rappaccini's successes are "probably the work of chance," but that his failures are strictly his own responsibility (p. 100). As he is presented to the reader directly in the two brief episodes in which he makes an appearance, Rappaccini makes a contradictory impression.

Giovanni sees in his face the traces of "intellect and cultivation [!]" but reads there as well the impossibility of "much warmth of heart" (p. 95). What the reader sees, however, is a person of considerable passion, both intellectual and more strictly emotional. He is deeply concerned not only with the welfare of his garden but also with the happiness of his daughter. In his final appearance he is presented as both benevolent and malevolent, both benignly paternal and frighteningly sexually potent at the same time:

> He paused—his bent form grew erect with conscious power, he spread out his hands over them, in the attitude of a father imploring a blessing upon his children. But those were the same hands that had strewn poison into the stream of their lives! (Pp. 126–27)

This same ambivalence infects everything Rappaccini touches, including particularly his garden and his daughter(s). The garden is a thing of wonder, with the great beauty and variety of its plants, but it is also mortally perilous because of the poisonous perfumes its inhabitants exude. Even its centerpiece, the marble fountain, seems both full of life and at the same time already dead. The narrator describes it as "sculpted with rare art" but also as "so wofully shattered that it was impossible to trace the original design from the chaos of remaining fragments" (p. 94). This description is really quite remarkable, for it asserts both that the fountain's design had been reduced to a chaos so complete that it was now impossible to find and that the "rare art" that directed its carving is perfectly evident to the casual observer like Giovanni. The young man has the impression that the fountain is an "immortal spirit" that had in an earlier age been embodied in marble but is now "scattered . . . on the soil" (pp. 94–95) in the form of Beatrice's sisters, the plants.

Beatrice herself is certainly the focus of much if not most of the tale's highly energized ambivalence. She seems to be both perfectly pure and demonically impure at the same time and to such a degree that one has to begin to question the distinction between the pure and the impure. Hawthorne is able to set up such a complex situation by exploiting the gap between the literal and the figurative. If a person is literally poisonous, about to kill with her very breath, is she figuratively—that is morally—"poisonous" as well? For Giovanni no distinction seems possible between the two. The "dreadful peculiarities in her physical nature," he believes, "could not be supposed to exist without some corresponding monstrosity of soul" (p. 120). And yet there is absolutely no evidence that Beatrice is in any way morally tainted. Giovanni's earlier "confidence in Beatrice," the narrator explains, was based on "something truer and more real, than what we can see with the eyes," and he calls this "better evidence" about Beatrice's character. Although she is physically "shattered," she is still a human work of rare art. The narrator compares her to a "pure fountain" that had been "made visible in its transparency" to Giovanni, who fails to correctly judge this "ugly mystery" as the "earthly illusion" that it is (p. 122). When Giovanni finally explodes in rage at Beatrice and calls her a "poisonous thing" (p. 124), he is making a moral accusation that may very well be misdirected. Beatrice in her dying words completes the circle of literal and figurative readings of the word "poison" by asking Giovanni if there was not, "from the first, more poison in thy nature than in mine" (p. 127). Giovanni's very concern with the issue of Beatrice's physical poison may have been a symptom of his own moral poison. His physical contamination by Beatrice and the plants is perhaps, in his case, the (figuratively) proper outward manifestation of an inward taint. It is his situation, not hers, in which the literal facts of "physical nature" could be understood to match some "corresponding monstrosity of soul."

This is all conjecture, however. The story does not allow any definitive judgments about the absolute innocence or guilt of any of its characters. It simply puts into question, through them, the relationship between the pure and the impure, the literal and the figurative, and in this way too becomes caught up in the general moral ambivalence. What is true of Rappaccini's daughter Beatrice is also true of "Rappaccini's Daughter." Hawthorne/Aubépine's creation is subject to the same sorts of doubts Giovanni directs at Beatrice. The reservations that the "translator" has about Aubépine and his writings in general must apply, in the absence of any further explanation, to this story as well, which the reader is encouraged to approach without great enthusiasm.

Framed in the *Old Manse* collection, "Rappaccini's Daughter" is placed in a context that casts an ambivalent twilight on literature in general. The Manse persona describes in the opening sketch the garret library of his predecessor as both valuable and valueless. It contained a set of old volumes consisting mainly of "dreary trash," we are told, books of no literary value that possessed interest only because they "had been transmitted down through a series of consecrated hands, from the days of the mighty Puritan divines." Some of them contained "marginal observations, or interpolated pages closely covered with manuscript, in illegible short-hand, perhaps concealing matter of profound truth and wisdom" (p. 18). Like the fountain in Rappaccini's garden, the old books may contain "rare art" that is now reduced to chaos. The books are, as noted above, placed in the metaphorical garden, and some of them seem to have been tended by a Rappaccini-like gardener: a number of the "little old volumes impressed me as if they had been intended for very large ones, but had been unfortunately blighted, at an early stage of their growth" (p. 19). The owner of the Manse even hopes to find in all this withered literary shrubbery something like Beatrice's purple-flowered sister:

> I burrowed among these venerable books, in search of any living thought, which should burn like a coal of fire, or glow like an inextinguishable gem, beneath the dead trumpery that had long hidden it. But I found no such treasure; all was dead alike; and I could not but muse deeply and wonderingly upon the humiliating fact, that the works of man's intellect decay like those of his hands. Thought grows mouldy. (P. 19)

In spite of this deep disappointment, however, he confesses to retaining "a superstitious reverence for literature of all kinds" (p. 21).

A similar ambivalence runs like a current through the introductory contents of the *Old Manse* volume. They are the "idle weeds and withered blossoms" we are already familiar with. The reader is led to wonder if the story of Beatrice, subtitled in the "original" French "La Belle Empoisonneuse," is not to be suspected of being potentially more morally poisonous than the lady ever was. The benefits of literature, while insisted upon in the "Old Manse" sketch, are at the same time cast into such doubt that one has reason to despair of their existence. Hawthorne's suspicion of his own art seems at times to surpass even that of Thomas Mann, who frequently compared artistic activity to illness and criminality.

Has the author of tales like "Rappaccini's Daughter" provided his readers with nourishment that will sustain and strengthen them, or has he "thrown poison into the stream of their lives?" Although the *Old Manse* collection does not oblige us to come to the latter conclusion, it does require us to consider it. It encourages us to understand the entire literary enterprise as readable under two opposed value systems, as either strengthened by or tainted with a powerful rhetoricity. We would expect as a consequence that other stories in the *Old Manse* collection would be affected by such a potent force. How could the vigorous rhetoricity evident in "Rappaccini's Daughter" be contained within the bounds of a single tale? Our expectation is not disappointed, for several of the other *Old Manse* narratives display the characteristics of rhetorical construction. Two prominent examples, though neither so rich nor so arresting as the story of Beatrice and her father, are "Monsieur du Miroir" and "The Intelligence Office."

"Monsieur du Miroir" is certainly not one of Hawthorne's major works of fiction, but it has a special interest in this context because it shows him writing fiction that is essentially rhetorical in the mid-1830s, quite a few years before "Rappaccini's Daughter" and most of the other *Old Manse* stories were composed. It is also particularly relevant here because it continues to display Hawthorne's occupation with the subject of the self, again a self observed from a certain distance and with not a little suspicion. The title character is, of course, nothing other than the author's own reflection, whether seen in a mirror, a windowpane, a polished kettle, or a puddle in the street. This in itself is neither original nor even specially interesting, since the theme of the spectral double in all its variations had been thoroughly explored by romantic writers in Europe. What keeps the story from being a routine variation on a well-worn theme is Hawthorne's development of the space between the literal and figurative meanings of "reflection."

Hawthorne introduces some complexity into his story by a reversal of expectations. Although it is the mirror image whose "whole business is REFLECTION" (p. 171), it is the narrator—the one who in the literal sense is reflected—who engages in all the figurative "reflection" the story has to offer. Monsieur du Miroir is in fact introduced to the reader as "a subject of . . . grave reflection" (p. 159), thus actually suggesting that the image is the *object* of reflection as much as or more than it is a reflecting "subject." And indeed this turns out to be the case: the narrator describes himself as "reflecting upon" (p. 169) the actions of the image and upon their more profound significance, while Monsieur du Miroir is presented as superficial, insubstantial, and indeed "ridiculous" (p. 163). In his closing apostrophe to the image, the narrator expresses doubt as to the intellectual capabilities of Monsieur du

Miroir ("It may be doubted whether you are the wiser") and calls him a "mere spectre of human reason" (p. 171). The image thus does not reflect so much as it is reflected upon, and this in two senses: it is reflected upon (considered) by the narrator's mind, and it is reflected upon by (suffers the consequences of) the narrator's actions ("all which concerns myself will be reflected in its consequences upon him" [p. 167]). There is a perfect, rhetorical symmetry between the narrator and his image, just as there is a perfect, though reversed, symmetry in their visual forms. Monsieur du Miroir reflects but does not "reflect," whereas the narrator "reflects" but does not reflect. The story exists in the discovery and description of that situation.

"The Intelligence Office" displays continued rhetorical dexterity. The initial moment of the plot arises out of an ambiguity inherent in the rhetorically complex language used to describe the bureau mentioned in the title. The term "intelligence office" was regularly used in nineteenth-century English to mean an agency dispensing information, particularly about employment, but it could also refer as it does today to a government bureau charged with gathering sensitive and secret information. As it is initially described, this intelligence office appears to be a kind of mixture of the two functions. The office's clientele is highly varied:

> Now, it was a thriving mechanic, in quest of a tenement that should come within his moderate means of rent; now, a ruddy Irish girl from the banks of Killarney, wandering from kitchen to kitchen of our land, while her heart hung in the peat-smoke of her native cottage; now, a single gentleman, looking for economical board; and now—for this establishment offered an epitome of worldly pursuits—it was a faded beauty inquiring for her lost bloom; or Peter Schlemihl for his lost shadow; or an author, of ten years' standing, for his vanished reputation; or a moody man for yesterday's sunshine. (P. 322)

The mechanic and the Irish kitchen maid are figures we would expect to find in an agency of this sort, concerned with finding employment, lodgings, or other assistance for servants. Webster's dictionary of 1864 defines "intelligence office" as "an office or place where information may be obtained, particularly respecting servants." The faded beauty, the author, and the moody man—not to mention the notoriously fictional Peter Schlemihl—are seeking "secret" information of the most spiritual sort. We have been moved from a literal to a figurative "intelligence office" in a very short space.

When the first client to be described declares that he has come seeking "a place," that again is what one would expect of a person patronizing such an office. But the narrative slips with Kafka-like suddenness into the figurative mode: "I want my place!—my place!—my true place in the world!—my proper sphere!—my thing to do, which nature intended me to perform when she fashioned me thus awry, and which I have vainly sought, all my lifetime!" (p. 325). The man we thought was seeking a job is revealed to be seeking philosophic or religious enlightenment. Hawthorne adds an additional rhetorical flourish: after the man leaves the office in despair at not being directed to his "place," the narrator adds that, "if he died of the disappointment, he was probably buried in the wrong tomb," because people such as he "are invariably out of place" (p. 323).

Several other applicants arrive on various errands, including for example a man who has lost a jewel, a pearl, indeed the "Pearl of Great Price," which the intelligence official finds but refuses to return. The "pearl" hovers between being a literal object and being a figurative spiritual quality. Finally there arrives a seeker of truth who compels the clerk to reveal the "naked reality" of his business: "My agency in worldly action . . . is merely delusive. . . . I am no minister of action, but the Recording Spirit!" (p. 336). Thus, what we originally thought was a secular agency dispensing intelligence is revealed to be a spiritual agency collecting it. The expression "intelligence office" initiates a rhetorical moment in exactly the way the name "Hawthorne" does in "Rappaccini's Daughter."

In that story the name of the self, read as rhetoric, provides both a focus and a method for generating complex fictional discourse out of the author's ambivalence. I do not wish to claim, however, that the name is the "origin" or cause of "Rappaccini's Daughter." Such origins and causes as are to be found must be discovered by others using different critical tools; as I indicated in the opening chapter, the study of rhetorical construction has nothing to contribute to that aspect of literary investigation, interesting and important though it may be. Rhetorical analysis can reveal much about how a text is made, but it can at best provide only hints about why it was made. This is not to say that linguistic structures cannot be causes of events in the world; it should be clear enough that I am arguing just the contrary. But it is to say that rhetorical analysis does not aim to determine some on-tologically privileged moment in the genesis of literary texts, and I do not wish to appear to make such a determination here. The readings presented in this book may discover circumstances in which linguistic structures are intimately bound up with extralinguistic actions and events, as in the case of Danton's death, but they cannot decide ques-tions of priority without recourse to a mode of analysis that lies outside rhetoric. This is only to make what ought to be a self-evident point, that the mode of reading exemplified here cannot explain everything. But that is a universal limitation on acts of reading: "Si ne le croyez, le fondement vous escappe."[64]

Hawthorne's sensitivity to his name provided him with both matter and method for the *Old Manse* collection. The matter is plant life, which seems to decorate, enhance, or infest much of the volume's discourse and to imprint its vegetable character on objects, activities, and even persons therein described. Given the book's evident and steady concern with the authorial self, signaled quite forthrightly at the outset in the "Old Manse" sketch and continued in artist tales like that of Rappaccini, it seems only reasonable to connect the preoccupation with vegetation with that self-concern, and thus with the name of the self, "Hawthorne." More important than the matter of the plants, however, is the rhetorical method implied by Hawthorne's use of his name. Such a name encourages, even almost requires, its possessor to become sensitive to the potential rhetorical complexity of discourse that may be read in two opposed senses at the same time. There is no other linguistic fact with anything like the affective power of the per-sonal name; it is that part of the linguistic universe that belongs most intimately to the self, and all its attributes seem to have the power to shape metonymically the character of the person to which it is at-tached. "Like his name, like him," goes an old saying, and even when the name does not demonstrably fit the person, it always threatens to do so. Examples of this abound, and one need only turn to Derrida's "Speculate—on 'Freud,'" to give just one recent example, to see it in action.

---

64. Stanley Fish and others would make the same point but in a contrary fashion. Fish might say that if you do not accept the limitation placed on acts of reading by the situatedness of all discourse, the "foundation" does not so much escape you as makes you its prisoner.

A proper name that is also a common noun and thus readily subject to autonomasia—a name like "Hawthorne" or "Kafka"—provides (or inflicts upon) its possessor a vivid personal experience of the rhetoricity of already-deconstructed language. The word that is on the one hand supposed to be the unique property of a human self is discovered to be a common token for something that would otherwise have no particular relation to that self. The common-noun meaning and the proper-noun meaning may be as disparate as you please, but the circumstance that a single signifier stands for both proposes a similarity, if not in fact a unity, of the two. The experience of the aporetic moment characteristic of rhetorical discourse becomes an almost daily experience for persons with such names. They know better than anyone the gap that exists between two divergent interpretations of the same utterance, for they have in a sense lived in that gap. For a verbal imagination like Nathaniel Hawthorne's, that gap becomes a space that can be filled with narrative. Hawthorne the writer finds a way to bridge the gap between "Hawthorne," the name of a man, and "Hawthorne," the name of a tree, by inventing a fictional situation in which it is no longer possible to distinguish readily between people and plants. He justifies the pharmakon character of his name by creating a story in which it becomes increasingly difficult to tell what is poisonous from what is beneficial. The story "Rappaccini's Daughter" is a perfect rhetorical analogue of the name of its author.

4 | *The Stuff of Rhetoric*

Living in disputed territory between two opposed forces is not necessarily safe, even when the opposition is between two modes of interpretation. Sometimes you get caught in the crossfire. Such an experience might seem at times like a great adventure, but, it remains risky even under the best of circumstances. Rhetorical construction opens up new spaces in which surprising adventures can take place, but it does so by moving into a dangerous area where destructive conflict constantly threatens. It is not surprising to find that inventions of reading often depict these dangerous adventures as the stuff of their narratives.

I turn now to a group of fictions that foreground the problematic, negative aspects of rhetoric and explore some of the disturbing implications of life in a world in which the literal and the figurative regularly confront each other. Even attempting to maintain a balance between literal and figurative can be dangerous, as Kafka suggests in his little story "The Bridge." The protagonist of Kafka's tale seeks both to embody the figurative meanings of "bridge" and to serve as an actual bridge across a chasm in a mountainous landscape. Unfortunately, the requirements of the two kinds of "bridge" are not always compatible; sometimes they are in deadly conflict; and finally the bridge loses its balance, hurtling into the abyss. The problem of the story, then, arises directly from a consideration of the circumstances of rhetorical reading.

Such a consideration also underlies Italo Calvino's far more lighthearted tale "The Dinosaurs" in his collection of *Cosmicomics*. Again, the problem is the confrontation of literal and figurative, this time arising not out of an attempt to balance the two but out of the unexpected, inappropriate, and altogether distressing survival of a literal dinosaur in a world in which "dinosaur" has only figurative meanings. The protagonist—the dinosaur, naturally—must learn how to survive in this new world. What he learns is that his survival depends entirely on his literal disappearance, on his merger with the new order of figurative reading. He has to quit being a dinosaur. He does so, realizing that figurative "dinosaurs" are potentially far more powerful and far more long-lived than the actual animals ever were.

But not everyone involved in the confrontation between literal and figurative is willing to acquiesce in this way. Nathanael, the hero of E. T. A. Hoffmann's tale "The Sandman," shapes the core of his identity on the principle that a literal reading is always preferable to a figurative one. This turns out to be a serious problem for everyone he comes in contact with; for him, it turns out to be fatal.

The Dismembered Metaphor: Hoffmann's "The Sandman"

At the close of "The Sandman," its hero is described as a person with a "lacerated soul" ("im Innern zerrissen"). The metaphor of internal dismemberment is a common one, and the phrase would pass without notice if it did not come at the end of this particular story. "The Sandman" so forcefully presents a fantasy of dismemberment or the anxiety of dismemberment that it has become, at least since Freud's essay on the uncanny, the central text for almost any discussion of "Zerrissenheit." Focusing on powerful images of bodies torn apart—the latest, the description of Nathanael's shattered head (*zerschmetterter Kopf*), occurs only two sentences earlier—the text does not allow the reader to accept the notion of being "im Innern zerrissen" as easily as one ordinarily might. In other circumstances we would read this as a metaphor of a troubled psyche and nothing more. In this case, however, the vehicle does not allow itself to be submerged by the tenor of the figure. The picture of Nathanael's corpse, quite "zerrissen" in its own right, is too fresh in the reader's mind, the physical reality of dismemberment too graphically present, to permit the signifier "zerrissen" to pass harmlessly out of the realm of the literal. The juxtaposition in the text of the description of Nathanael's shattered head and his dismembered psyche forces a question as to the relation between tenor and vehicle, between the literal and figurative readings authorized by rhetorical construction. Common usage suggests that we read the word "zerrissen" here as the vehicle in a metaphor of psychic disruption, but the context of the story, especially the immediate context, would authorize us to read it as a metonymic extension of the physical sunderings occurring throughout the tale. Where is the rhetoric, where the reality? Is the physical dismemberment presented by the body of the narrative to be seen as the figure for the reality of Nathanael's psychic trauma (as, for example, Freud would have it), or is that psychic trauma with its language of internal dismemberment a figure, a metonymic supplement brought into being by the power of the grisly reality just described?

Hoffmann's story is centrally concerned with this question, with spinning out the many possibilities inherent in a rhetoric of "Zerrissenheit." It makes its beginning out of this problem and finds its imaginative space in the area between the literal and the figurative. The very word "zerrissen," in its apparently figurative extension, is explicitly introduced at the commencement of the tale, in the very first paragraph. Nathanael excuses his tardiness in writing letters on the grounds of his "Zerrissenheit": "Alas, how could I write to you in the tormented frame of mind which has disrupted all my thoughts!"[1] At this early stage in the narration, though, the reader has no reason to pause over the commonplace expression "zerrissene Stimmung des Geistes"; it passes as an innocuous trope. So too does the related expression "pull myself together" ("fasse ich mich zusammen") by which Nathanael signifies his efforts to counteract the internal "Zerrissenheit" preventing his writing. This rhetoric of coming apart and pulling back together can work here only proleptically, anticipating the many scenes of dismemberment that will follow.

The reader is quickly introduced to one of these scenes, the explanation of the concept of the "Sandman" demanded by the young Nathanael, first from his mother and then from the nursemaid. The mother explains in a simple and direct way that there is no actual Sandman:

---

1. I cite Hoffmann in English from *Tales of E. T. A. Hoffmann*, ed. and trans. Leonard J. Kent and Elizabeth C. Knight (Chicago: University of Chicago Press, 1972); and in German from E. T. A . Hoffmann, *Novellen*, vol. 3 of *Gesammelte Werke*, ed. Nino Erné (Hamburg: Standard-Verlag, n.d.). This passage is from *Tales*, 93; *Novellen*, 117. "Ach, wie vermochte ich denn Euch zu schreiben in der zerrissenen Stimmung des Geistes, die mir bisher alle Gedanken verstörte!"

"When I tell you that the Sandman is coming, it only means that you are sleepy and can't keep your eyes open any longer, as though someone had sprinkled sand into them."[2] The Sandman, in other words, is a metaphor. But Nathanael cannot accept the notion that the Sandman is only the vehicle in a figure conveying sleepiness, just as the reader at the end of the story cannot simply take "zerrissen" as the vehicle in a figure conveying psychic disruption. At the end of the story, the reader's mind is too occupied with descriptions of actual dismemberment to accept the figure as nothing but figure, and here at the beginning Nathanael's mind is conditioned similarly by what he considers his experience of the "real" Sandman: "I had surely always heard him coming up the stairs."[3] Prejudiced as he is in favor of a more literal reading, it is no wonder that the nursemaid's picture of a monster Sandman, implausible as it might otherwise be ("I was old enough to realize that the nurse's tale of the Sandman . . . couldn't be altogether true"),[4] strikes Nathanael as intuitively correct:

> He is a wicked man who comes to children when they refuse to go to bed and throws handfuls of sand in their eyes till they bleed and pop out of their heads. Then he throws the eyes into a sack and takes them to the half-moon as food for his children, who sit in a nest and have crooked beaks like owls with which they pick up the eyes of human children who have been naughty.[5]

By accepting the nursemaid's version of the Sandman and rejecting his mother's, young Nathanael is exchanging one form of "Zerrissenheit" for another. For it is clear that the boy would far prefer a world in which his physical body is threatened with being torn apart by an actual, horrible Sandman to one in which meaning is forced so far apart from the apparent intuitive clarity of the signifier. The nurse-

---

2. *Tales*, 94; *Novellen*, 118. "Wenn ich sage, der Sandmann kommt, so will das nur heißen, ihr seid schläfrig und könnt die Augen nicht offen behalten, als hätte man euch Sand hineingestreut."

3. *Tales*, 94; *Novellen*, 119. "Ich hörte ihn ja immer die Treppe heraufkommen."

4. *Tales*, 95; *Novellen*, 119. "Schon alt genug war ich geworden, um einzusehen, daß das mit dem Sandmann . . . wohl nicht ganz seine Richtigkeit haben könne."

5. Ibid. "Das ist ein böser Mann, der kommt zu den Kindern, wenn sie nicht zu Bett gehen wollen, und wirft ihnen Hände voll Sand in die Augen, daß sie blutig zum Kopf herausspringen, die wirft er dann in den Sack und trägt sie in den Halbmond zur Atzung für seine Kinderchen; die sitzen dort im Nest und haben krumme Schnäbel wie die Eulen, damit picken sie der unartigen Menschenkindlein Augen auf."

maid's story preserves the notion that language means what it says, whereas the mother's explanation makes a rift between what is said ("The Sandman is coming") and what is meant ("There is no Sandman. You are sleepy."). It also proposes a gap between the boy's experience (hearing the "Sandman") and language ("There is no Sandman"). Nathanael chooses to preserve the unity of language both with itself and with the world of experience even though it means also accepting the threat of personal dismemberment. The latter seems somehow the lesser evil.

Of course, the mother's explanation of the Sandman as metaphor cannot be entirely erased from the child's mind. His desire to dispel lingering doubts about the reality of the Sandman motivates his wish to see what one might suppose he would never want to see, the "horrible Sandman" himself. This wish to "investigate the mystery" ("das Geheimnis zu erforschen") prompts him to hide in his father's room one night and to discover thereby that the Sandman, "the horrible Sandman, was the old lawyer Coppelius who frequently had dinner with us!"[6] This discovery would seem to solve Nathanael's difficulty: here was a real person who could plausibly fit the role of Sandman while at the same time banishing the bogeyman of the nurse's story. Nathanael relates that in this moment of discovery "the Sandman was no longer the hobgoblin of the nurse's tale, the one who brought the eyes of children for his brood to feed upon in the owl's nest in the half-moon."[7] But if that were so, Nathanael would have to reinterpret the nurse's story as itself somehow figurative and thus reinstate the linguistic rift he has labored so hard to deny. To validate his faith in the unity of words and meanings, Nathanael has to find a way to fit this new piece of information, that Coppelius "is" the Sandman, into the nurse's text.

Part of the solution to this difficulty lies ready to hand in the linguistic material of Coppelius's name. Since Nathanael, at the time he writes his letter, believes that Coppelius is identical to the Italian barometer dealer Giuseppe Coppola, it is evidently significant that the

6. *Tales*, 96; *Novellen*, 121. "Der fürchterliche Sandmann ist der alte Advokat Coppelius, der manchmal bei uns zu Mittage ißt!"

7. *Tales*, 97; *Novellen*, 122. "Der Sandmann war mir nicht mehr jener Popanz aus dem Ammenmärchen, der dem Eulennest im Halbmonde Kinderaugen zur Atzung holt."

Italian word "coppo" means "eye socket" (cf. Dante, *Inferno* 33). Since an eye socket is something that wants an eye, the bearer of the name Coppelius (or Coppola) would be at least linguistically equivalent to the nursemaid's Sandman. Nathanael's experience (real or imagined) then confirms this identification: Coppelius is presented as a kind of demon sorcerer at work on a project involving making eyes for automatons. His cry of "Give me eyes!" ("Augen her!") terrifies Nathanael into revealing his presence, and Coppelius threatens to carry out the nurse's script for the Sandman: "Pulling glowing grains from the fire with his naked hands, he was about to sprinkle them in my eyes."[8] Nathanael's father intervenes to save his son's eyes, but Coppelius acts out the role of the dismembering Sandman in another way: "He thereupon seized me so violently that my joints cracked, unscrewed my hands and feet, then put them back, now this way, now that way."[9]

The introduction of the theme of automatons in this scene—a theme that will play such an important role later in the story—serves to consolidate and reinforce the correctness of the nurse's picture of the Sandman. Since her story proposes the separability of body parts from the living body, its (nonfigural) interpretation requires some kind of framework for understanding human beings as assemblies of parts. Such a framework is readily available in the child's world in the form of the doll, a toy that often loses and regains eyes or limbs in the course of its lifetime. That Coppelius treats Nathanael like a doll, removing and rearranging his body parts, comes as a "logical" extension of the Sandman story, as does the implied scene of body part manufacture upon which Nathanael intrudes. The "Zerrissenheit" the child suffers at the hands of Coppelius is the price he pays for avoiding the dismemberment of the linguistic sign. It is a price he seems always ready to pay.

Other characters in the story, however, take up the role originally played by the mother, that of asserting that "there is no Sandman."[10] Nathanael's fiancée Klara advocates this view forcefully, proclaiming that "in my opinion all the fears and terrors of which you speak took

8. *Tales*, 98; *Novellen*, 123. "Und griff mit den Fäusten glutrote Körner aus der Flamme, die er mir in die Augen streuen wollte."
9. Ibid. "Und damit faßte er mich gewaltig, daß die Gelenke knackten, und schrob mir die Hände und die Füße und setzte sie bald hier, bald dort wieder ein."
10. *Tales*, 94; *Novellen*, 118. "Es gibt keinen Sandmann."

place only in your mind and had very little to do with the true, external world."[11] This realistic and down-to-earth position annoys Nathanael to such a degree that he begins to resent her and to suspect that she is devoid of all human emotion. When she refers to a poem he has written on the subject of Coppelius as a "mad, insane, stupid tale," he calls her a "damned, lifeless automaton."[12] The insult is a hyperbolic metaphor. Like the other figures in "The Sandman," however, this too become the locus of a confrontation between tenor and vehicle. It is clear enough that Nathanael utters the phrase with a figurative intent, that he does not mean to suggest that Klara is actually a mechanical artifact; but it is also clear that Nathanael's perspective on metaphor cannot allow the concrete vehicle to be obliterated by the intended meaning. If language has proclaimed Nathanael's beloved an automaton, then she must *really* be one. Nathanael's affections stray from Klara to Olympia, who turns out indeed to be (as far as the reader can determine) a wooden doll, an "Automat." When it is discovered that Professor Spalanzani has been passing off a mechanism as his daughter Olympia, the ladies and gentlemen of society are shocked and are not at all comforted by the explanation given by the professor of rhetoric that "it is all an allegory, an extended metaphor."[13] They, like the young Nathanael, can no longer accept the denial of the literal, the assertion that "there is no Sandman."

But if the existence of the "literal" *Automat* Olympia is a response to and validation of the vehicle of the metaphor applied to Klara, it is also in the event a validation of the view of the world that allows for the existence of a Sandman. Nathanael's preference for the literal over the figurative, for the vehicle over the tenor, implies the dismemberment of the self by the Sandman. Nathanael's way of thinking, carried to its logical end, envisions a world in which the self, in contemplating objects in the world, is always in danger of discovering that those objects are in fact parts torn out of that very self. This possibility, while in one sense deeply disturbing, is in another also highly attrac-

11. *Tales*, 101; *Novellen*, 126. "Wie ich meine, alles Entsetzliche und Schreckliche, wovon Du sprichst, nur in Deinem Innern vorging, die wahre, wirkliche Außenwelt aber daran wohl wenig teilhatte."
12. *Tales*, 110; *Novellen*, 137. "Das tolle — unsinnige — wahnsinnige Märchen. . . . lebloses, verdammtes Automat!"
13. *Tales*, 123; *Novellen*, 150. "Das ganze ist eine Allegorie — eine fortgeführte Metapher!"

tive: it holds out the hope that the world is not filled with alien objects but also contains elements actually belonging to the self.

The figure of Olympia actualizes both the buoyant delight in self-recognition and the abject despair at the discovery of one's personal dismemberment. At first only the former comes into play. Nathanael is enchanted with the recognition that in this creature he can find a reflection of himself: "You deep soul [*Gemüt*], in which my whole being is reflected," he tells her.[14] And to Siegmund he confesses, "I discover myself [*mein Selbst*] again only in Olympia's love."[15] The reader will certainly detect in these pronouncements a certain irony: to some degree the self that Nathanael discovers in Olympia is indeed nothing more than his own voice, his own interpretation of her silences. But in another sense she does double Nathanael's self, to the degree that we understand that self as the product of the elaborated myth of the Sandman, for she is always and only what he was in the memory/story/dream of his experience in his father's study: a collection of separable parts, something whose limbs can be "unscrewed." In particular one set of Olympia's parts, the eyes, are alleged by the narrative to belong to Nathanael: "The eyes—the eyes stolen from you!" confesses Spalanzani when Nathanael discovers the truth about Olympia.[16]

The discovery that Olympia is in fact a "lifeless doll" is what turns Nathanael's joy in self-recognition into horror. What had formerly seemed to be the reflection of living spirit in her now seems rather to be the reflection of her lifeless objecthood in him. Where before he has seen the two of them as parts of the same living organism, now he must see them both as pieces of one dismembered, dead body. When Nathanael calls upon the "wooden doll" ("Holzpüppchen") to "whirl around" ("dreh dich"), he is invoking himself as well as Olympia. More precisely, he is invoking the *trope* ("turn," "Wendung") by which language turns a person (Klara, Nathanael) into a wooden doll, a doll into a person. Such tropes, such "turned" phrases that insist on saying "Sandman" and "there is no Sandman" all at once, are the agents controlling Nathanael's existence: they are the things that make him what he is, but also the things that make his life impossible.

14. *Tales*, 115; *Novellen*, 144. "Du tiefes Gemüt, in dem sich mein ganzes Sein spiegelt."

15. *Tales*, 117; *Novellen*, 146. "Nur in Olimpias Liebe finde ich mein Selbst wieder."

16. *Tales*, 120; *Novellen*, 148. "Die Augen — die Augen dir gestohlen."

Nathanael's death itself (or at a minimum the madness that causes his death) is brought about by his last attempt to recover the literal level, the vehicle, from its metaphorical significance. The final scene takes place on a tower that Nathanael and Klara climb at her suggestion: "'Let us climb to the top once more and look at the distant mountains!' No sooner said than done."[17] After all that has happened in this story, with its emphasis on the movement from what is purely linguistic (*gesagt*) to what exists in reality (*getan*)—as for example the transformation of the pejorative epithet "Automat" into a genuine automaton—we are obliged to hesitate for an instant over this otherwise innocuous commonplace, "gesagt, getan." The common significance of this phrase, one that applies here also, stresses the speed with which a proposal is put into action. This is the aspect that is made explicit in the English expression "no sooner said than done." The German version, however, implies by juxtaposition the replacement of speech by action, the transformation of speech into action: what was "said" is now "done." Nathanael's story, especially the stories of his "madness," focuses attention precisely upon the process of turning something that is, ordinarily, only "gesagt"—"The Sandman is coming"—into a description of what is actually "getan." By introducing the scene at the top of the tower with the words "Gesagt, getan!" the narrator signals proleptically the return of the principle that allows the Sandman to exist and that makes Nathanael "mad."

Klara herself then, at the summit of the tower, provokes the return of the Sandman's perspective by calling Nathanael's attention to a "strange little grey bush" ("sonderbaren kleinen grauen Busch") that she says appears to be coming toward them. In doing so she conjures up a piece of language, a metaphor, that the narrator uses to describe Nathanael's preoccupation with Olympia. When he is prevented by a set of curtains from viewing Olympia throught the window,

Nathanael, in despair, driven by longing and an ardent passion, rushed out beyond the city gates. Olympia's image [*Gestalt*] hovered before him in the air, emerged from the bushes, and peered up at him with great and

17. *Tales*, 124; *Novellen*, 151. "'Steigen wir doch noch einmal herauf und schauen in das ferne Gebirge hinein!' Gesagt, getan!"

lustrous eyes from the shining brook. Klara's image [*Bild*] had completely faded from his soul.[18]

According to the narrator, then, bushes [*Gebüsch*] are things out of which Olympia's form [*Gestalt*] might emerge—though the narrator means this only figuratively. His trope is meant to tell us that, no matter what Nathanael actually experienced in the world, his thoughts were occupied with Olympia. The narrator's trope, though, also belongs somehow to Nathanael's consciousness—whether we understand this as a function of the narrator's "omniscience" or of the power of figurative language to infect every level of the story makes little difference—so that the mention of the bush immediately causes Nathanael to rediscover the Sandman's point of view ("er fand Coppolas Perspektiv") and to take up the spyglass. Taking up the spyglass in turn causes Nathanael to reenact the earlier psychic process by which Klara's image (*Bild*) was replaced by Olympia's form (*Gestalt*). When he accidentally looks at Klara through the "Perspektiv" ("spyglass/point of view") belonging to the Sandman, he sees Olympia, or more specifically the "turn" that makes the two women equivalent, and he once again goes mad. After trying to throw Klara off the tower, he jumps off himself and is "shattered" ("zerschmettert").

The transformatory power of Nathanael's perspective on figurative language is taken up by the narrative; it infects the story and its telling. If a perspective can bring about the metamorphosis of a living girl into a wooden doll (Klara into Olympia), then a "Perspektiv" ("spyglass") can bring about the reverse. To the same degree that Nathanael and his story force the reader to find the literal in the figurative, so too do they encourage us to find the figurative in the literal. When the narrator relates that Nathanael "egriff Coppolas Perspektiv,"[19] we know that the statement is to be read literally: Nathanael seized the spyglass he had bought from Coppola. But how, given the context, can we avoid hearing at the same time a figurative indication that Nathanael is here "taking up" the "point of view" belonging to the Sandman (in his

18. *Tales*, 113; *Novellen*, 141. "Olimpias Gestalt schwebte vor ihm her in den Lüften und trat aus dem Gebüsch und guckte ihn an mit großen, strahlenden Augen aus dem hellen Bach. Claras Bild war ganz aus seinem Innern gewichen."
19. *Tales*, 113; *Novellen*, 141. "Seized Coppola's spyglass."

incarnation as Coppola)? For, as we know, it is the (nurse's) Sandman whose point of view requires that there be no difference between human bodies and assemblies of parts. The word *Perspektiv* hovers undecidably between tenor and vehicle, between physical object and abstract idea.

Over and over again, the narrative presents figurative language in such a way as to put into question the unity of signifier and signified in the rhetorical sign. The possibility of literal reading intrudes upon the language used to describe even ordinary events. After a description in which we are asked to understand as literally true the phrase "he unscrewed my hands and feet," how can we fail to pause at a sentence saying, "The detestable and loathsome Coppelius stood before me with fiery eyes, laughing at me malevolently"?[20] Although the sentences immediately surrounding this one make it clear that this is a metaphor for young Nathanael's obsessive concern with the image (*Bild*) of Coppelius, the larger context makes one uncertain. A sentence of this form might very well be meant as literally true. When Klara writes to Nathanael that "the horrid barometer dealer Giuseppe Coppola followed my every step,"[21] our uncertainty must return. This is the down-to-earth Klara speaking, for whom metaphors are entirely figurative and for whom "there is no Sandman," so we can rest assured that she was not actually followed by anyone. But we need that contextual assurance.

Even the narrator's own discourse becomes suspect in this way. What does he mean when he says that "even at this moment Klara's face [*Bild*] is so vividly before me that I cannot avert my eyes"?[22] Can we really be absolutely confident that this is a metaphor, when just a few lines earlier, in Nathanael's second letter to Lothar, a character (Spalanzani) is described by reference to an actual picture in a Berlin pocket almanac? A few lines later Klara is described again in terms of pictures: she has "Magdalenenhaar," and her coloring is "Battonisch," while her eyes are compared to a "lake by Ruisdael." This language suggests that Klara is not so much a person as a "Bild," a picture (or a

---

20. *Tales*, 99; *Novellen*, 124. "Der verhaßte, abscheuliche Coppelius stand vor mir mit funkelnden Augen und lachte mich hämisch an."

21. *Tales*, 101; *Novellen*, 126. "Der fatale Wetterglashändler Giuseppe Coppola verfolgte mich auf Schritt und Tritt."

22. *Tales*, 106, *Novellen*, 132. "Aber in dem Augenblick steht Claras Bild so lebendig mir vor Augen, daß ich nicht wegschauen kann."

metaphor). Indeed, the narrator suggests in this same passage that the whole of his narration is a "picture [*Gebild*] to which I will endeavor to add ever more color as I continue with the story."[23] If "picture" is taken as a figure for the narrative "The Sandman," then we can reinterpret the narrator's sentence about Klara's "Bild" being before him as, in this new sense, almost literally true. The "image" of Klara *is* directly in front of the writer who writes that image.

The entire story becomes subject to the mutual contamination of literal and figurative language. It is as if language itself, which we think of as our servant and subject, had staged a rebellion and taken over the position of mastery. When the storyteller explains the problem he had in beginning his story and gives some examples of the alternative openings he rejected, he includes this one: "'Go to hell!' the student Nathanael cried, his eyes wild with rage and terror, when the barometer dealer Giuseppe Coppola—."[24] This opening was rejected because "I thought I noticed something humorous [*etwas Possierliches*] in Nathanael's wild look—but the story is not at all comic."[25] Does the narrator mean that *his description* of Nathanael's wild look had something comic about it? Or was that description so vivid that it came to life before him (like Klara's "Bild"), allowing him to discover far more information in that "wild look" than the words suggest? Did he reject this sentence because it was unsuccessful or because it was all too successful? Is the phrase "wild look" to be understood, in the second instance, as the figure of the discourse containing the first instance (a metonymy), or is it a reference to an actual wild look, indeed that very look mentioned in the previous sentence? Does this image promote or prevent the continuation of the narrative?

These same questions arise when we look again at the declaration that "even at this moment Klara's face is so vividly before me that I cannot avert my eyes." On the one hand, there seems to be the suggestion that this image of Klara is actually preventing the narrator from getting on with his story: "I could now confidently continue with my

23. *Tales*, 105; *Novellen*, 132. "Des Gebildes, in das ich nun erzählend immer mehr und mehr Farbe hineinzutragen mich bemühen werde."
24. *Tales*, 105; *Novellen*, 131. "'Scher' er sich zum Teufel,' rief, Wut und Entsetzen im wilden Blick, der Student Nathanael, als der Wetterglashändler Giuseppe Coppola'—"
25. *Tales*, 105; *Novellen*, 132. "Als ich in dem wilden Blick des Studenten Nathanael etwas Possierliches zu verspüren glaubte."

story, but even at this moment. . . ."[26] The continuation of the "story" ("Erzählung") is apparently interrupted by the narrator's effusive and highly figured description of Klara, or at any rate of that image of Klara that stands before the narrator's eyes. On the other hand, though, the story is itself a "Bild," one to which Klara certainly belongs; and the preoccupation with Klara's "Bild," far from hindering the progress of the "Erzählung," actually serves as its beginning, as its point of departure.

The reader is constantly pushed by the rhetoric of the story into the position of trying to adjudicate an undecidable confrontation between the literal and the figurative. Every time the reader makes a decision— "Yes, *this* is certainly a figure, while *that* has to be taken literally"—the text presents material that forces one to reverse the earlier ruling. The reader is thus in the middle of the story's action, construing that action, as I do, as a conflict between two modes of reading. This central position is exactly where the narrator expressly places both himself and his reader, though of course he does so figuratively. In the same passage I have been discussing—the point of transition between the epistolary opening and the narrator's continuation of the tale— Hoffmann's narrator tries to explain the technical problem he faced in beginning his story and his solution of it by means of the three letters. The problem, he says, is one that must be familiar to his reader, whom he asks—rhetorically, of course: "Have you, gentle reader, ever experienced anything that totally possessed your heart, your thoughts, and your senses to the exclusion of all else?"[27] The narrator then goes on to describe the difficulties one has in trying to communicate to others such an experience, which he describes as a "picture in your mind" ("das innere Gebilde"). Words are inadequate: "Yet, every word, everything within the realm of speech, seemed colorless, frigid, dead."[28] The solution to the problem could come only through the assistance of some kind of framing outline:

> If, like an audacious painter, you had initially sketched the outline of the picture within you in a few bold strokes, you would have easily been able

---

26. *Tales*, 106; *Novellen*, 132. "Nun könnte ich getröst in der Erzählung fortfahren."

27. *Tales*, 104; *Novellen*, 130. "Hast du, Geneigtester, wohl jemals etwas erlebt, das deine Brust, Sinn und Gedanken ganz und gar erfüllte, alles andere daraus verdrängend?"

28. *Tales*, 104; *Novellen*, 131. "Doch jedes Wort, alles was Rede vermag, schien dir farblos und frostig und tot."

to make the colors deeper and more intense until the multifarious crowd of living shapes swept your friends away and they saw themselves, as you see yourself, in the midst of the scene that had issued from your soul.[29]

The three letters which begin "The Sandman" are to be understood, we are told, "as the outline of the picture [den Umriß des Gebildes] to which I will endeavor to add ever more color as I continue the story."[30]

This metaphor (Bild) of the picture (Bild) proposes that the most desirable place for both teller and hearer of a story is "in the midst of the scene" ("mitten im Bilde"), where the word Bild is a manifest figure of narration and a literal expression of figuration. Whether or not the narrator succeeds in achieving the ideal of communication figured by the phrase "mitten im Bilde," he has certainly succeeded in putting both himself and his reader in the middle of his narration, since here, at the joint between the letters and the narrative proper, the attention of the story suddenly swerves away from Nathanael, Klara, and the others to the narrator and reader themselves. Nathanael's problems are for the moment forgotten while the text concentrates on the problem of the author, which he presents as also belonging to a hypothetical reader. This problem of author and reader is essentially rhetorical in the classical sense: that is, it is concerned with the adequacy of verbal expression, with how to make a verbal structure as vivid as the structure of experience. This experience belongs to an inner psychic realm (deine innere Glut), but it cannot be communicated unless it can be brought outside. The figure of the painting proposes that the transfer from inside to outside can be accomplished by making an outline or boundary (Umriß) around the internal picture (inneres Bild) and "throwing" this piece of inner experience "forth" (hinwerfen). The German idiom for making a sketch (einen Umriß hinwerfen) suggests both this act of throwing and another of making a tear (Riß) around something. The text foregrounds the notion of tearing (reißen) by using in the same sentence forms of the verbs umreißen and fortreißen containing

29. Tales, 104–5; Novellen, 131. "Hattest du aber wie ein kecker Maler erst mit einigen verwegenen Strichen den Umriß deines innern Bildes hingeworfen, so trugst du mit leichter Mühe immer glühender und glühender die Farben auf, und das lebendige Gewühl mannigfacher Gestalten riß die Freunde fort, und sie sahen wie du dich selbst mitten im Bilde, das aus deinem Gemüt hervorgegangen!"
30. Tales, 105; Novellen, 132. "Den Umriß des Gebildes, in das ich nun erzählend immer mehr und mehr Farbe hineinzutragen mich bemühen werde."

the morpheme *riß* (*Umriß, riß die Freunde fort*). The process of externalizing the inner picture, then, requires that the unity of the inner self be sundered.

That same process also obliges the narrator to sacrifice the unity of his text. In order to create the "Umriß" that he deems necessary for making his story of Nathanael a vivid and accurate depiction of his supposed experience, the narrator must resort to something that does not belong to his narration, the three letters: "There were no words I could find which were appropriate to describe, even in the most feeble way, the brilliant colors of my inner vision. I resolved not to begin at all" (perhaps better translated here as "I concluded not to begin at all").[31] The inadequacy of language—of his own language at any rate—forces the narrator to abdicate his office at the very outset of his story. He comes to a conclusion ("Ich beschloß") before he even begins—the conclusion that he must not begin at all but rather must leave the task of beginning to others. The very power he wishes to communicate, the "Farbenglanz des innern Bildes," is the thing that necessitates importing something not belonging to that "inneres Bild." The image described as residing within the self is somehow greater than the self that contains it. The narrator must have recourse to materials that are not narrated; that is, the story opens in the absence of the self whose experience it purports to depict. The body of the narrative is split apart (*zerrissen*) by the device, the outline (*Umriß*), that allows it to come into being.

The narrator's problem is, as Neil Hertz was perhaps the first to point out,[32] directly analogous to that of his hero Nathanael. Both are equally taken up with the problem of trying to preserve the integrity of inner experience, and both discover that this act of preservation calls for the dismemberment of the self. The matter of the plot and its narration thus form a solidarity that becomes at times almost impossible to disentangle. For just as the narrator wants to depict Nathanael, Klara, and so on, as vividly as possible, so does Nathanael want to give a lively image of his experience of Coppelius:

31. *Tales*, 105; *Novellen*, 132. "Mir kam keine Rede in den Sinn, die nur im mindesten etwas von dem Farbenglanz des innern Bildes abzuspiegeln schien. Ich beschloß, gar nicht anzufangen."

32. "Freud and the Sandman" in *Textual Strategies: Perspectives in Post-Structuralist Criticism*, ed. Josué V. Harari (Ithaca: Cornell University Press, 1979), 296–321.

Nathanael was forced to confess to himself that the ugly image [*Gestalt*] of Coppelius had faded in his imagination, and it often cost him a great deal of effort to present Coppelius with adequate vividness in his writing where he played the part of the sinister bogeyman. Finally it occurred to him to make his gloomy presentiment that Coppelius would destroy his happiness the subject of a poem.[33]

The same metaphor of painting, of filling in the vivid colors of a picture, that governed the narrator's presentation of his narrative problem figures in this presentation of Nathanael's waning power of imagination. In this case, though, storytelling is not so much the problem as the solution to the problem, for in writing Nathanael is overwhelmingly successful in restoring the image of Coppelius to its full power in his mind. He finds it so successful, in fact, that "when he read the poem aloud to himself, he was stricken with fear and wild horror and he cried out: 'whose horrible voice is that?'"[34]

Nathanael's story is like the narrator's in another way. The result of a successful narration, it was proposed, would be that the story would sweep the audience away ("riß die Freunde fort"). Nathanael the author succeeds in having just this effect on Nathanael the listener: "Nathanael was carried away inexorably by his poem."[35] The repetition of the verb *fortreißen* reinforces the imagery of "kolorieren" invoked before to characterize Nathanael's poem as a successful example of "sketching the outline of an internal image" ("den Umriß eines innern Bildes hinwerfen"). What formerly dwelled within him has been cast out, torn free from its original place, and now belongs completely to the world outside himself. The sentence that he himself uttered now seems to belong entirely to another, to demand the question, "Whose horrible voice is that?"

Nathanael finds his own narration of his version of the Sandman story so vivid that he takes it for reality, just as he had earlier taken the

---

33. *Tales*, 108; *Novellen*, 135. "Die Gestalt des häßlichen Coppelius war, wie Nathanael selbst es sich gestehen mußte, in seiner Fantasie erbleicht, und es kostete ihn oft Mühe, ihn in seinen Dichtungen, wo er als grauser Schicksalspopanz auftrat, recht lebendig zu kolorieren. Es kam ihm endlich ein, jene düstre Ahnung, daß Coppelius sein Liebesglück stören werde, zum Gegenstande eines Gedichts zu machen."

34. *Tales*, 109; *Novellen*, 136. "Als er jedoch nun endlich fertig worden und das Gedicht für sich laut las, da faßte ihn Grausen und wildes Entsetzen, und er schrie auf: 'Wessen grauenvolle Stimme ist das?'"

35. Ibid. "Den riß seine Dichtung unaufhaltsam fort."

nursemaid's version as correct. This story of which Nathanael is the author and audience takes on a certain life and power of its own, such that it begins to govern Nathanael's actions and thus to contaminate the narrator's story. One of the details Nathanael invents for his poem is the "Feuerkreis" ("circle of fire") into which Coppelius flings Nathanael and which takes him away from Klara, whirling "with the speed of a whirlwind" ("mit der Schnelligkeit des Sturmes"). This whirling circle of fire returns, first in the scene in Spalanzani's study where Nathanael discovers the professor and Coppola fighting over the doll he knew as Olympia, then at the very end of the tale, when Nathanael suddenly attacks Klara at the top of the tower. In both cases Nathanael, apparently overcome by his terror of the Sandman, suddenly begins to shout "Feuerkreis dreh dich" or "dreh dich Feuerkreis" and to behave in a violent, deranged manner. According to the narrator, Nathanael is indeed mad on both occasions, and in the first instance he describes in vivid metaphors the onset of this madness: "Then madness racked Nathanael with scorching claws, ripping to shreds his mind and senses."[36]

Once again Nathanael is made to experience "Zerrissenheit" at the hands of the Sandman, but again this dismemberment seems to be the price paid for an attempt to preserve unity. Nathanael here, just as earlier, attempts to make his experience conform to the text of the Sandman story, though this time it is his own version rather than that of the nurse that serves as the controlling text. The movement proposed by the earlier imagery of "den Umriß eines innern Bildes hinwerfen" is here reversed: what was formerly torn out of Nathanael's inner self now tears its way back in, creating a second "Riß" in the already severely ripped "Inneres" of the hero. The story tears him apart—his own story—both going and coming.

At the same time, the need to tell the story is performing a similar operation on both the narrator and his narration. The necessity of discourse ("I was most strongly compelled to tell you"),[37] requiring the internal to be made external, forces the creation of a "Riß" within the speaker. Such a person is, like Nathanael, "im Innern zerrissen."

---

36. *Tales*, 120; *Novellen*, 148–49. "Da packte ihn der Wahnsinn mit glühenden Krallen und fuhr sein Inneres hinein, Sinn und Gedanken zerreißend."
37. *Tales*, 105; *Novellen*, 131. "So trieb es mich denn gar gewaltig, von Nathanaels verhängnisvollem Leben zu dir zu sprechen."

The turn of the tale's attention away from Nathanael's problem to that of the author has not been much of a turn after all: the issue remains basically the same. Both author and character confront the dilemma of preserving the unity of experience-in-language and solve the problem by sacrificing the unity of the self. In both cases the "Bild" is preserved intact at the cost of allowing the self to be dismembered.

Both the character(s) identified with the Sandman and the story "The Sandman" participate fully in the problematic of unity and disunity. While the name belonging to Coppelius and Coppola seems on the one hand to suggest (by way of *coppo,* as mentioned above) the loss of eyes and thus a dismemberment, the same name also points, by way of *copula,* to an act of joining. To a German speaker, whose language contains the verb *koppeln,* this latter sense would in fact be more prominent. In his incarnation as Spalanzani (whose name might suggest *spalten* ("splitting") to a German speaker), the Sandman is in fact more concerned with joining than with sundering: not only does he put Olympia together out of lifeless parts, but he also encourages the joining of his "daughter" to Nathanael:

> Professor Spalanzani appeared to be most pleased by the intimacy which had developed between his daughter and Nathanael, and he gave Nathanael many unmistakable signs of his delight. When, at great length, Nathanael ventured to hint delicately at a possible marriage with Olympia, the professor's face broke into a smile and he said that he would allow his daughter to make a perfectly free choice.[38]

This act of "putting together" is at the same time, of course, a taking apart, since Nathanael's interest in Olympia so takes over his mind that he "had completely forgotten that there was in the world a Klara whom he once loved."[39] It is also in a very real sense superfluous; Spalanzani has already united Nathanael and Olympia in the most intimate way possible, since he claims to have assembled his automa-

---

38. *Tales,* 118–19; *Novellen,* 147. "Professor Spalanzani schien hoch erfreut über das Verhältnis seiner Tocher mit Nathanael; er gab diesem allerlei unzweideutige Zeichen seines Wohlwollens, und als es Nathanael endlich wagte, von ferne auf eine Verbindung mit Olimpia anzuspielen, lächelte dieser mit dem ganzen Gesicht und meinte, er werde seiner Tochter völlig freie Wahl lassen."

39. *Tales,* 118; *Novellen,* 146. "Nathanael hatte rein vergessen, daß es eine Clara in der Welt gebe, die er sonst geliebt."

ton/daughter using Nathanael's own eyes. The professor has already made them "one flesh" without benefit of clergy or of sexual intercourse. This sort of joining is, however, the most unsettling imaginable, particularly for Nathanael, since it is predicated on the possibility of the body's disassembly. The relationship between Olympia and Nathanael, as it stands revealed in Spalanzani's study, puts into question the opposition between joining and sundering: the proper word for it might be "cleave"—both "cleave together," as in the old wedding ceremony, and "cleave apart," as with a cleaver. The implications of this rhetorical construction are consoling and terrifying at the same time.

The body of the story, its formal presentation, is implicated in this same rhetorical process, since it must divide itself formally (between "letters" and "narrative") in order to preserve the integrity of the experience it purports to represent. At the same time, it questions the opposition between inside and outside, claiming as a guarantee for the authenticity of any experience its place "inside" the self, while acknowledging both the need to bring out the piece of inner experience, in a communicative act, and the impossibility of doing so successfully without the intervention of an agency whose origin is in fact "outside" (e.g., the opening letters). More important than these rhetorical maneuvers (though of course deeply interconnected with them) is the text's insistence on maintaining an opposition that both characters in the tale and readers of it would prefer to dissolve: that is, the opposition between tenor and vehicle. As readers, we have learned to understand the tenor of metaphorical language as by far more important than the vehicle. The vehicle exists, we learn, only for the sake of the tenor, as a kind of helping hand on our way to understanding. When we read that "Hector is a lion," we are supposed to think only about Hector's valor and strength and not about actual lions with all their nonhuman characteristics. Klara and Nathanael's mother are figures in the story who represent this position. Nathanael, on the other hand, wants to see the lion and hear its roar. For him "Hector" is the name of a lion, a creature with a mane and a tail, and "Sandman" is the name of a person who divides children from those they love and destroys their happiness.

Nathanael has something in common with Kleist's Penthesilea, for like her he defines himself in large measure by his insistence upon reading literally. To be sure, he does not announce this insistence to the world as candidly as does Penthesilea, but he does not have to. He inhabits a very different sort of world, one in which the boundary between literal and figurative is not so rigid. Penthesilea dwells in a society that firmly rejects her equation of kissing and biting (*Küsse/Bisse*) and allows her to carry out the full literal enactment of tropes only within the confines of her own mind and body. Nathanael on the other hand inhabits a world in which society is quite prepared to accept a mechanical doll as a human being and thus to ratify the equation of person and automaton proposed by the trope Nathanael uses against Klara. Nathanael's ·refusal to accept his mother's figurative interpretation of the Sandman does not go against the grain of his interpretive community. On the contrary, the universe he lives in seems prepared to accept, even to adjust itself physically, to the demands of a mode of reading in which the vehicles of metaphorical expressions efface their tenors.

The reader inhabits this same world, at least while reading the story, and finds it a very interesting but also intellectually uncomfortable place. Over and over again, the story's language puts the reader in a position of not being able to decide (at least for an instant) whether the sentences of "The Sandman" are to be read in the manner of Nathanael or Nathanael's mother. When we first begin the story, there is little question that we are expected to read tropes in just the way Nathanael's mother does: Nathanael's description of his spiritual condition as "zerrissen" encourages us, by the use of abstract terms like "Stimmung" and "Geist," to proceed directly and unimpeded from vehicle to tenor, from material signifier to psychic significance. By the story's close, however, we are no longer able to make such an easy choice. Nathanael's figurative and literal "Zerrissenheit" confront each other, and in that confrontation hangs suspended the essential issue of the story: "'Who is this nasty Sandman . . . ?' 'There is no Sandman.'"

The reader has to face up to the unresolvable uncertainty of rhetorical discourse and is left in a position quite different from that of the principal characters in the story. Klara, who tames the rhetoricity of figures by letting the tenor efface the vehicle, lives happily ever after. Nathanael, who sought to have the vehicle overwhelm the tenor, succumbs to the literal reading of the story's master trope and is shattered by the Sandman. The only figure within the fiction faced with a problem analogous to the reader's is the figure of the fiction itself, which struggles to present itself as unified and whole by an act of radical self-division. The story's characters all confront the problem of rhetorical language by trying in one way or another to eliminate it. If either tenor or vehicle could definitively suppress the other, figurative language would lose its rhetoricity. Only the narrative itself, which is in this case the figure of a character and not a genuine character, tries to accommodate itself to the absolute uncertainty of rhetorical reading. If the story itself, as figure, *were* a genuine character faced with the dilemma of reading its own rhetorical discourse, it would be able to dramatize the experience of its readers.

But that would be another story, and not one by E. T. A. Hoffmann. It might look rather more like Kafka's "The Bridge."

The Turn of the Trope: Kafka's "The Bridge"

The critical examination of figurative language that has been identified as an essential part of "The Metamorphosis"[40] and that reappears as a crucial issue in much of Kafka's fiction continues in a particularly dramatic form in the short parable "The Bridge."[41] The story explores the possibilities inherent in the metaphor of its opening sentence "I was a bridge" precisely in its character as metaphor. The concept of "bridge" already contains, as Kafka was well aware, much of the figurative content of the notion "metaphor" itself. The root meaning of *metaphor*, "carrying across," implies the concept of a bridge, the (verbal) thing that makes the connection from one thing to another. In the parable "Von den Gleichnissen," usually translated "On Parables" but equally correctly rendered by "On Metaphors," the exemplary metaphor cited is the injunction to "Go over" ("Gehe hinüber"). What one needs in order to "go over" is, of course, a bridge.

The bridge is thus, in itself, a strong figure of metaphoricity. This quality is doubled, as it were, in that this bridge figure participates in a further metaphor of the self as bridge. This doubling does not, however, result in an impulse to further abstraction. On the contrary, at the narrative level the story insists upon the concrete reality of the person as a human body (*Leib*) possessing feet, hands, teeth, and hair and

40. See Stanley Corngold, "Kafka's *Die Verwandlung*: Metamorphosis of the Metaphor," *Mosaic* 3, no. 4 (1970): 91–106.

41. *Complete Stories*, 411–12; *Sämtliche Erzählungen*, 284. Since the story is so short, I will not cite references for individual quotations.

wearing clothes. It also insists on the object quality of the bridge, to the degree that the first-person narrator (that is, the bridge) refers to him/herself in the third person when adverting to his/her bridge function: "The bridge was not yet traced on any map." The situation as the story develops it thus refuses any act of imagination that would synthesize the two sides of the metaphor. We have here not a person with bridge qualities or a bridge with human qualities but rather a pure rhetorical construction "bridging" the two.

An aspect of the metaphor of self as bridge explored in detail by Kafka's story is the possible consequence for the self of actually being used in this function by another. For, although the bridge links two sides of something, the bridge itself can never "go over." It takes another person to put this bridge function into practice. The requirement of this other is one of the first difficulties of being a bridge that the narrating subject faces. The bridge finds itself in a particularly untraveled spot, an "impassable height" ("unwegsame Höhe"), where no tourist is likely to "stray." That a metaphor should be thus placed in a position that is both "high" and difficult of access is quite in keeping with traditional notions of the proper functioning of metaphor. Figurative language of this kind is regularly associated with the "high" style of classical literature and the Bible and (at least since the Middle Ages) with texts or portions of texts that are stylistically or conceptually difficult. This is to say that the bridge's location, though poorly motivated at the level of the plot (Why build a bridge where nobody is likely to go?), is thoroughly and comprehensibly motivated at the level of discourse. As a piece of language, "I was a bridge" belongs exactly where it is.

The contrast between what is appropriate at the level of language and what is disturbing at the level of story makes itself felt again in the juxtaposition of the two sentences, "The tails of my coat fluttered at my sides. Far below brawled [*lärmte*] the icy trout stream." The narration presents these as two parts of the description of the landscape to which the bridge/self belongs. Syntactically, they do indeed belong together, both having the same basic structure (subject/modifier-verb-location) chiastically inverted (location-verb-modifier/subject) in the second sentence. As sentences, then, these two are mirror images of each other. In terms of the semantic level, however, the appropriateness of the justaposition vanishes, for the equation of a description of features of a person's dress with that of a portion of a wild, natural terrain is unsettling. The implied proposal that coattails and a trout stream belong to the same logical or semantic category jars the reader's sense of what is normal, thus already opening the question of the success of the metaphorical linking of person and bridge. It is as if, in the very moment of uttering the phrase "I was a bridge," the narrating subject begins to tear the figure apart by adverting to its least convincing details. By choosing to bring up the matter of the bridge's coattails (Why, after all, should it have coattails in the first place?), the text initiates substantial doubt about the propriety of its founding trope.

The deliberate incongruity of the figural equation of tailcoated person and bridge sets up the problem of the narrative as announced in the last sentence of the first paragraph: "Without falling, no bridge, once spanned, can cease to be a bridge." The sentence makes a point only in the context of the metaphor, since ordinary (nonfigural) bridges do not have the option of ceasing to be bridges. While it is true that ordinary bridges may have their bridge function interrupted or destroyed (the bridge may be blocked off, dismantled, and so on), such events are by no means always accompanied by the sudden, catastrophic collapse designated by Kafka's word "einstürzen." What would indeed collapse suddenly if this particular bridge ceased to be a bridge is the figure itself, though of course this "collapse" would be only metaphorical. In Kafka's fictions, we know well enough, the distinction between literal and metaphorical meanings itself tends to collapse. In any case, this person/bridge is under an obligation to wait ("ich mußte warten"), as bridges always wait, because its person aspect ("ich") is apparently also threatened with catastrophic disintegration should it ever lose or deny its bridge aspect. The collapse of the metaphor would also mean the destruction of the self. The story thus far does not provide any explanation why this is so, but it strongly indicates that it is.

What the bridge/person is waiting for is not stated in the text, but one assumes it is someone who will fulfill the bridge function by "going over." The story's second paragraph confirms this expectation by relating the approach of a traveler. Among the several peculiar features of this paragraph is the bridge/person's urge to active participation in bringing the traveler over. It calls (or imagines it calls, or figuratively "calls") the approaching traveler, "To me, to me" and prepares for his arrival by calling upon itself to "straighten yourself" ("strecke dich") and to do something else, translated as "make ready" but also readable as "put yourself into position" ("setze dich in Stand"). The active verbs *strecken* and *setzen*, followed then by another, *halten* ("hold"), are applicable to only one side of the metaphor, to the conscious subject, the "ich" who narrates. While an ordinary bridge might well be said to *hold* someone, it does not (except metaphorically) stretch itself out or put itself into position. The bridge/person then goes even further in its desire for active participation in the process of "going over": it proposes to "steady the steps" of the traveler (actually, Kafka's term is "even them out"—*ausgleichen*) and, if it should come down to it, to "show what you are made of" ("gib dich zu erkennen") and "hurl" ("schleudre") him across to the other side. Of particular interest here is the phrase "gib dich zu erkennen," for what the bridge/person dreams of doing would indeed be a self-revelation, a demonstration that it is at least as much a human consciousness as it is a bridge. By becoming an active participant in the process of "going over," it would betray itself as not simply a bridge but something else, something "like a mountain god," or at least more like a mountain god than an ordinary bridge.

Kafka's story sets up certain difficulties that effectively prevent our deciding what is tenor and what is vehicle in the metaphor "I was a bridge." In the first place, the figure does not belong to any context that might help determine which of the two, person or bridge, could be viewed as the topic of the discourse. A standard metaphor such as "Hector is a lion" presumably belongs in a context in which it is clear that the issue under discussion is Hector, and this context allows us to determine that, since lions are not otherwise germane, this lion must be introduced as an explanatory supplement to the central topic of Hector. Kafka's figure—and this is one of Kafka's most characteristic strategies—is presented in isolation, as pure figure, the apparent supplement to a nonexistent discourse. The figure hangs over an abyss, not locatable, its absence from the map reflecting its atopic separation from any knowable context. Are we talking about bridges, which might from a certain point of view be better understood if projected into the human realm; or are we talking about persons, about their "connectedness" with things and with other people? Although interpreters generally make the latter assumption—all literature supposedly reflecting the human condition—only the broadest possible context, the alleged function of literature as an institution in this society, sanctions the choice.

Also militating against any secure identification of tenor and vehicle is the foregrounding of elements of each side of the figure that are not easily read as common to both. One reason we are able with confidence to single out the lion's qualities of courage, strength, and ferocity as relevant to the metaphorical description of Hector is that the figure does not draw our attention to things like the mane and tail. If it did, if the locution were formulated as "Hector is the maned and tailed creature, a lion," our interpretation of it would become more difficult. And if one were to go further, to say for example that "Hector, that person with ears and spaces between his toes, is that maned and tailed creature, a lion," the metaphor becomes almost unreadable—at least in terms of a tenor-and-vehicle conception of its functioning. Kafka, by telling us that the bridge/person has a "Rock" with "Schöße," that the stream in the valley contains trout, and so on, gives information that tends to prevent rather than assist identification of tenor and vehicle. The details of the narrative landscape are consistent in that they all apply perfectly well to either a person or a bridge; but many of them— most of them—will not allow themselves to be applied to both.

The story does not seem to give any assistance to the narrator in its announced goal of declaring itself. To the degree that we are traditional readers—and all of us must be, necessarily, to some exent traditional, or reading would not be possible—we urgently wish to decide whether we are dealing with a bridge that is like a person or a person that is like a bridge. The equation of bridge and person, one that privileges neither side, appears radically unstable from the point of view of traditional rhetorical theory, though it is proposed by the narrator as the very definition of stability. As the narration reaches its climax, we discover that indeed there has been a reversal of values, that the process of imposing a hierarchy of tenor over vehicle is in this case a process of destruction.

The climactic act of turning, which the narrative presents as the immediate cause of the bridge's collapse, is thus only the final moment of a process of self-de(con)struction that begins in the very moment when the narrator announces itself. We realize that the opening statement, "Ich *war* eine Brücke," announces the pastness of the condition it asserts.[42] Of course we read this initially as simply an ordinary use of the narrative past, in which the tense carries no implication of completedness. The end of the story, however, shows that the use of the past was in that case also readable as a regular past, since the narrator is

42. I am grateful to Steven R. Huff for bringing this to my attention.

no longer a bridge at the conclusion. The process of the narration works, from the very beginning, to undermine the trope that makes the story possible.

The fatal turn at the climax is still the most emphatic act of privileging the human over the bridge aspect of the narrator and is thus the proper moment of collapse. It is, moreover, an act that radically denies not only the equality of the two sides of the metaphor but also the process of troping itself. The word "trope" and its German analogue "Wendung" are both metaphorical terms that designate rhetorical processes as a kind of turning, a deflection of language from one sort of meaning (literal) to another (figurative). Thus the bridge/person, an "Überlegung" that is both an object and a thought process, is already a "Wendung" in that it is a figure of speech. For such a "turn" to turn again ("Brücke dreht sich um!") is to undo itself, to reverse the process of figuration that brought it into existence. The turning of the trope is self-de(con)structing on another level in that the action described insists on the literal reading of the metaphor that both describes and is rhetoric: the figurative turn, the "Wendung" of "ich war eine Brücke," engages in an actual turn that negates the basis of the metaphor.

The temporal reversal makes the story's end not only a turn but a return to its beginning. The destruction of the bridge/person is already included in the rhetoric of the narrative, signaled, as discussed above, by the use of the past tense. The last sentence of the story even doubles back beyond this point, however, referring to a scene of peaceful contemplation that existed before the story began ("die mich immer so friedlich aus dem rasenden Wasser angestarrt hatten" ["which had always gazed up at me so peacefully from the rushing water"]). The last word of the story is a pluperfect verb, a reaching toward a past beyond the past that is the time before the narration, a time when the narrator was not the contemplator but the object of contemplation. It was also a time when the problematic equation of human and object traits could be ascribed not to the bridge but to the pebbles in the brook, which somehow had acquired the human ability to gaze peacefully out of the raging torrent while yet retaining their character as rocks. But even this metaphor is shattered by the bridge's collapse, because the rocks can greet the falling body only as rocks, as sharp objects that pierce and tear apart, not as eyes that contemplate in peace. The desire to see ("ich drehte mich um, ihn zu sehen") destroys the condition that made it possible to be seen ("die mich . . . angestarrt hatten"). The insistence upon acting as subject (person) destroys the balance that let the bridge be also a passive object. All the metaphors lie in ruins.

Kafka's bridge figure serves to remind us how difficult is the act of balancing required to keep a rhetorical construction from toppling. Kafka sees the threat to this balance coming from the traditional impulse to read metaphors so as to privilege the figurative tenor over the literal vehicle. The threat comes not from the mode of reading employed by wild and crazy Nathanael but from that advocated by nice, down-to-earth Klara. This helps to explain perhaps why "The Sandman" retains its rhetorical balance despite Nathanael's dogged and dramatic insistence on the primacy of the literal. The orthodox mode of interpretation Klara uses is such a powerful influence on all our acts of reading that it will of itself upset the rhetorical balance unless checked by a very strong counterforce. It takes an extraordinary act of perseverance to keep the figurative from driving the literal into extinction. Sometimes, as we shall see shortly, even superhuman perseverance is not enough.

Literal Extinction: Calvino's "The Dinosaurs"

The Cosmicomics of Italo Calvino are a treasure chest of rhetorical invention to which one can profitably return again and again. Calvino not only carries out in a dazzlingly successful way the principles of rhetorical construction but also uses the opportunity his fiction creates to discuss, as explicitly as the imaginative mode of discourse permits, the sorts of rhetorical issues that make stories like these possible. That is only to say that the *Cosmicomics* often thematize their own poetic process and in saying so to repeat one of the most persistent clichés of contemporary letters. Calvino's touch is so light and his approach so novel and so open, however, that the now familiar gesture of writing about writing becomes, in his deft hands, fun and magical again. The whole project of the *Cosmicomics* is, after all, as its title indicates, to bring matters of cosmic weight into the realm of the lightheartedly comic. Calvino is very serious about making serious matters fun.

One of the serious matters he plays with is the one that forms the subject of my book, the confrontation of two conflicting alternative readings such as the literal and the figurative. Calvino has the kind of verbal imagination that recognizes both the generative power of such confrontations and the great fun to be had by letting that power loose upon itself. Calvino, always a storyteller above all, sees a story in the very principle of rhetorical construction. What if we could stage a confrontation between literal and figurative meanings in which the confrontation is a real conflict, in which real blows are exchanged between actual characters? This idea comes to fruition in the story "The Dinosaurs," in which the immortal Qfwfq, incarnated as the last of the dinosaurs, finds himself in a world in which he is the last literal signifier of a signified now in a state of rapid figurative evolution.

In "The Dinosaurs," as in all the tales of the *Cosmicomics*, the narrative proper is preceded by a headnote setting forth the scientific theory on which the story is putatively based. As I have argued at length elsewhere,[43] these headnotes only appear to have a scientific character; actually they are simply pieces of language taken from a scientific source and mounted like exotic specimens in Calvino's imaginary notebook. In the case of the headnote to "The Dinosaurs," Calvino's total lack of interest in the scientific purpose or adequacy of the text cited is quite explicit. The headnote explains, matter-of-factly:

> The causes of the rapid extinction of the Dinosaur remain mysterious; the species had evolved and grown throughout the Triassic and the Jurassic, and for 150 million years the Dinosaur had been the undisputed master of the continents. Perhaps the species was unable to adapt to the great changes of climate and vegetation which took place in the Cretaceous period. But at its end all the Dinosaurs were dead.[44]

The narrative proper, though, begins with a significant modification of this scientific pronouncement: "All except me,—*Qfwfq corrected*—because, for a certain period, I was also a Dinosaur: about fifty million years, I'd say."[45] The narration forces an immediate choice: either the

43. *The Incredulous Reader* (Ithaca: Cornell University Press, 1984), chap. 8.

44. I cite Calvino in English from *Cosmicomics*, trans. William Weaver (New York: Harcourt Brace Jovanovich, 1976); and in Italian from *Le Cosmicomiche* (Turin: Einaudi, 1965). This passage is from *Cosmicomics*, 97; *Cosmicomiche*, 115. "Misteriose restano le cause della rapida estinzione dei Dinosauri, che si erano evoluti e ingranditi per tutto il Triassico e Giurassico e per 150 milioni d'anni erano stati gli incontrastati dominatori dei continenti. Forse furono incapaci di adattarsi ai grandi cambiamenti di clima e di vegetazione che ebbero luogo nel Cretaceo. Alla fine di quell'epoca erano tutti morti."

45. Ibid. "Tutti tranne me,—*precisò Qfwfq*,—perchè anch'io, per un certo periodo, sono stato dinosauro: diciamo per una cinquantina di milioni d'anni."

headnote or the narrator Qfwfq must be wrong. Not only does Qfwfq deny the validity of the generalization made in the headnote's final sentence, he tramples over the very principles that underlie scientific thought. By asserting that he was a dinosaur for "about fifty million years" Qfwfq denies the basis in empirical reality underlying such thought. What could it mean, to "be" a dinosaur for fifty million years? Calvino's language exploits an ambiguity: Qfwfq says "sono stato dinosauro," which does indeed mean "I was a dinosaur" but also suggests strongly the generic aspect of his affiliation. He says "sono stato dinosauro" the way one would say "sono stato avvocato" ("I was a lawyer"). Qfwfq seems to be saying both that he was a particular dinosaur and that he "professed dinosaurhood" for fifty million years. This suggests that "dinosaur" is being used to mean not just a certain reptilian creature but also a social function for which the concept "dinosaur" figuratively stands. A dinosaur is, according to a widespread Italian commonplace, a person of very great importance—"pezzo grosso," a "heavyweight"—as indeed Qfwfq turns out to be in the new society. But dinosaurs are also things that exist, for Qfwfq's new associates as for us, only as fossils, and the Italian word *fossile* has the figurative meaning of a thing or person that has become antiquated, has outlived its usefulness: "Is that old fossil still around?"

As the story develops, it becomes clear that Calvino is interested in precisely these figurative associations of dinosaurs/fossils and has brought up the scientific fact of the dinosaur's extinction only to set up the possibility of a situation in which there could be a dinosaur (a particular reptile) who was also a "dinosaur" (a "heavyweight," but also a "fossil"). The text of the headnote with its assertion that all the dinosaurs were extinct by the end of the Cretaceous period is interesting for Calvino only insofar as it creates, in the assertion that it is mostly right and a little wrong, the conditions for the narrative coalescence of the literal and figurative meanings of "dinosaur." While the value of scientific language is ordinarily understood to reside in its correspondence with the facts of the world, Calvino finds its value here in validating the facts of language: it substantiates the propriety of the equation in a single signifier of the related and yet opposed signifieds "a reptilian creature now extinct" and "something not yet extinct but well on the way."

The protagonist of the story, Qfwfq-as-dinosaur, embodies the literal meaning of a signifier whose literal meaning has essentially died out. He is a "fossil" in another figurative sense, a "word that has lost its meaning." And since no one now recognizes him as a dinosaur—no one knows what dinosaurs look like—he is able to observe what happens in the evolution of the figurative meanings that live on. Indeed, one could say that this story probes in a fictional mode the same sort of problems Jacques Derrida addressed in his reading of Shelley's *The Triumph of Life*, an essay called, appropriately enough, "Living On: Borderlines."[46] Calvino addresses the living on of "dinosaur" as a trace, which indeed achieves its real function and fertility only in the absence of the thing it names. Calvino ironically and comically adds the incongruous element of an impossible and disruptive *presence*, an actual dinosaur living on out of his time and participating in the dissemination of his own semiological substance. This can happen only in the context of a fiction, both the fiction of the dinosaur's presence (fashioned by Calvino) and the fiction of his absence (adhered to steadfastly by Calvino's characters, the "Nuovi" ("New Ones").

Much of the fun of "The Dinosaurs" arises from the problematic of "living on." Both the signifier "dinosaur" and this particular dinosaur have lived on, but they are no longer connected by a socially valid sign function. Qfwfq keeps expecting the word "dinosaur" to apply to him, and he discovers that in this new age it never does. When he first meets a group of the "New Ones," he runs away, thinking they will recognize him as one of the greatly feared dinosaurs. In fact, they only want to be friendly and are surprised that this odd creature should run off "as if you'd seen . . . a Dinosaur!"[47] The New Ones regularly make unintentionally ironic remarks in this vein, as when they reassure Qfwfq that "there hasn't been a Dinosaur seen here since the days of our grandfathers' grandfathers."[48] In the Italian this statement carries the hint of a further irony in that the locution that says "there hasn't been a Dinosaur seen here" ("Dinosauri . . . non se ne vedono") seems to define dinosaurs as things not seen. Ordinarily one would expect a comma, a question mark, or some other mark of punctuation to separate the word "Dinosauri," which is grammatically an absolute construction here, from the rest of the sentence: "Dinosauri? E dal tempo

46. In Harold Bloom, et al., *Deconstruction and Criticism* (New York: Seabury Press, 1979).
47. *Cosmicomics*, 98; *Cosmicomiche*, 116. "Avessi visto . . . un Dinosauro!"
48. *Cosmicomics*, 99; *Cosmicomiche*, 118. "Dinosauri è dal tempo dei nonni dei nostri nonni che non se ne vedono."

. . .” or something similar. But Calvino writes the sentence without this break, as if “Dinosauri” were, quite ungrammatically, the subject of the verb *è,* with an implied equation between the dinosaurs and “non se ne vedono” (“you don’t see any of them”). It is as if the New Ones were saying, “What dinosaurs are is things you don’t see,” which is in this context a very good description of the situation. What the New Ones do not and cannot see about Qfwfq is that he is a dinosaur, and it is precisely “since the days of our grandfathers’ grandfathers” (and not before) that this has been the case.

One of the comic-dramatic highlights of the story occurs when Qfwfq confronts the New One Zahn, who fears that this “Ugly One” would not be of much use in a fight. Qfwfq demonstrates his courage and pugnacity by calling out Zahn, and in the excitement of the fisticuffs one of the spectators cries out in encouragement, “Give it to him, Dinosaur!”[49] Qfwfq thinks for sure he has been discovered and only later realizes that “the cry ‘Dinosaur’ was a habit of theirs, to encourage the rivals in a fight, as if to say: ‘Go on, you’re the stronger one!’ ”[50] Their term “dinosaur,” even when applied to an actual dinosaur, no longer names a dinosaur; it has become a figure for a function (strength in battle) rather than the designator of a kind of reptile. Realizing this, Qfwfq also realizes that there is not necessarily any connection between this cry of “Dinosaur” and the dinosaur he is: “I wasn’t even sure whether they had shouted the word at me or at Zahn.”[51] Nothing could demonstrate more clearly the great gap between literal and figurative meaning.

If Qfwfq represents as a character the embarrassing and functionally irrelevant living on of a “dead” literal meaning, the character Fior di Felce (Fern-flower) represents the dynamic force of figuration. Almost all of Fern-flower’s discourse consists of reports of her dreams, which are all about dinosaurs. At first she dreams of being carried off by an enormous, terrifying dinosaur who wants to eat her, “but—isn’t this odd—I wasn’t the least frightened.”[52] Later she dreams of trying to catch the attention of a “Prince or a King of Dinosaurs,” but “he didn’t

49. *Cosmicomics,* 103; *Cosmicomiche,* 122. “Dài, forza, Dinosauro!”
50. Ibid. “L’apostrofe ‘Dinosauro’ era un loro modo di dire, per incoraggiare i contendenti in una gara, come un: ‘Dài che sei il più forte!”
51. Ibid. “Non era nemmeno chiaro se l’avessero gridato a me o a Zahn.”
52. *Cosmicomics,* 101; *Cosmicomiche,* 120. “Ma io, che strano, non ero mica spaventata.”

even deign to glance at me."[53]. Later these dreams of the dinosaur as a figure of power and majesty give way to something else: "There was this Dinosaur, very funny, all green; and everybody was teasing him and pulling his tail. . . . And I realized that, ridiculous as he was, he was the saddest of creatures."[54] The development of the images in Fern-flower's dreams corresponds to the evolution of the figurative significance of the word "dinosaur" among the New Ones. At first Qfwfq tries to find some relation between himself and these figures— an easy and pleasant task so long as the images were of ferocity, power, and dignity—but when the references become "jokes, in which the terrible monsters played ridiculous roles,"[55] he gives up. He is overcome by a feeling of "refusal to identify myself with the images"[56] of Fern-flower's dreams and of the newly popular jokes.

The enormousness of the gap between the word "dinosaur" and himself does not really come home to Qfwfq until the time one of the New Ones discovers the remains of a true dinosaur:

In the midst [of some rocks], lying as if asleep, his neck stretched by the widened interval of his vertebrae, his tail sown in a long serpentine, a giant Dinoaur's skeleton was lying. The chest cavity was arched like a sail, and when the wind struck the flat slabs of the ribs an invisible heart seemed to be beating within them still.

The New Ones ran down there, shouting gaily; facing the skull, they felt the empty eye sockets staring at them; they kept a few paces' distance, silently; then they turned and resumed their silly festiveness. If one of them had looked from the skeleton to me, as I stood there staring at it, he would have realized at once that we were identical. But nobody did this. Those bones, those claws, those murderous limbs spoke a language now become unintelligible; they no longer said anything to anyone, except that vague name which had remained unconnected with the experiences of the present.[57]

53. *Cosmicomics*, 194; *Cosmicomiche*, 123–24. "Un principe o un re dei Dinosauri . . . non mi degnava d'uno sguardo."
54. *Cosmicomics*, 107; *Cosmicomiche*, 127. "C'era un Dinosauro, buffo, verde verde, e tutti lo prendevano in giro, gli tiravano la coda . . . . E mi accorsi che, ridicolo com'era, era la più triste delle creature."
55. Ibid. "Barzellette, in cui i terribli mostri apparivano come personaggi ridicoli."
56. Ibid. "Una repulsione a identificarmi con le immagini."
57. *Cosmicomics*, 108–9; *Cosmicomiche*, 128–29. "In mezzo, disteso come se dormisse, col collo allungato dagli intervalli delle vertebre, la coda disseminata in una lunga linea serpentina, giaceva uno scheletro di Dinosauro gigantesco. La cassa toracica si arcuava

The language of the description of the skeleton is carefully wrought and particularly rhetorical. One is especially struck by the phrase "coda disseminata" ("tail sown"), which is particularly difficult to interpret literally. Calvino seems to be playing here on the vocabulary shared by these bones and a piece of music ("intervalli," "coda") to reinforce the notion that the dinosaur has become a signifier without any definite, fixed signified. More than that, "dinosaur" is a piece of music that is over, whose concluding notes ("coda") are now scattered on the wind ("disseminata") and present only in memory. What that music might have been is suggested by the gesture of the mouth, "as if in a last cry" ("come per un estremo grido").

We know, in a certain sense, what the "estremo grido" must have been, because the story has closely associated the "grido" ("cry") and its lexematic variants (*gridolino, gridò*) with one particular cry: "Dinosauro!" What the skeleton is saying in its disseminated music is nothing other than its own name. But now that name belongs to an "illegible language" that no longer speaks to the New Ones, or at least no longer speaks in such a way as to relate to the "experiences of the present," that is, a living dinosaur present among them. Qfwfq understands that the fate of the mute bones is directly analogous to the fate of the name: "they would follow the destiny of the name 'Dinosaur,' becoming an opaque sound without meaning."[58]

This epiphany of the bones is at the same time ironic, because though Qfwfq is correct in seeing that the word "dinosaur" was now "dead" in the sense he had known it and that it is now an "opaque" sign, it is not at all "without sense." What he does not see is that the death of the literal meaning of the word (which he represents and

---

come una vela e quando il vento batteva sui listelli piatti delle costole pareva che ancora le pulsasse dentro un cuore invisibile. Il cranio era girato in una posizione stravolta, a bocca aperta come per un estremo grido.

I Nuovi corsero fin lì vociando festosi: di fronte al cranio si sentirono fissati dalle occhiaie vuote; rimasero a qualche passo di distanza, silenziosi; poi si voltarono e ripresero la loro stolta baldoria. Sarebbe bastato che uno di loro passasse con lo sguardo dallo scheletro a me, mentr'ero fermo a contemplarlo, e si sarebbe accorto che eravamo identici. Ma nessuno lo fece. Quelle ossa, quelle zanne, quegli arti sterminatori, parlavano un linguaggio ormai illeggibile, non dicevano più nulla a nessuno, tranne quel vago nome rimasto senza legame con le esperienze del presente."

58. *Cosmicomics*, 109; *Cosmicomiche*, 129. "Avrebbero seguito il destino del nome 'Dinosauro' divenuto un opaco suono senza senso."

wishes to defend) opens the possibility of a new "dissemination" of figurative meanings. If we understand this dissemination in a Derridean sense (which, given Calvino's early interest in the *Tel Quel* critics, is not too great a leap), we can also see that the dinosaur Qfwfq is fighting a losing rearguard action against an inevitable loss of determinate meaning. He is the last of an extinct race of logocentrists who has a greater than usual stake in the defense of determinate meaning *because he is it*. He has an existential as well as a philosophical reason for wanting to stop the process of uncontrolled semiosis under way with respect to the word "dinosaur." He has a personal aversion to acknowledging the necessity of death, of absolute absence, that is a prerequisite for the fecundity of the trace.

Calvino's title, "I Dinosauri," recognizes the preeminence of the "coda disseminata" over the uniquely determined signified. Although the story pointedly takes as its subject a situation in which the world contains but one dinosaur, the protagonist Qfwfq, the title insists upon plurality. "The Dinosaurs" can refer either to the giant reptiles now dead or to the plurality of (figurative) "dinosaurs" engendered by the stories, dreams, and jokes of the New Ones. Paradoxically, it cannot refer to Qfwfq except to the degree that he merges with either or both of these groups—that is, to the degree that he himself becomes extinct (as he does, in a sense, at the end of the narrative) or somehow turns into a figure. As the tale draws to a close, Qfwfq comes to understand the intimate relationship between death and semiotic power:

> Now I knew that the more the Dinosaurs disappear, the more they extend their dominion . . . in the labyrinth of the survivors' thoughts. From the semidarkness of fears and doubts of the now ignorant generation, the Dinosaurs continued to extend their necks, to raise their taloned hoofs, and when the last shadow of their image had been erased, their name went on, superimposed on all meanings, perpetuating their presence in relations among living beings.[59]

---

59. *Cosmicomics*, 111; *Cosmicomiche* 132. "Ora sapevo che i Dinosauri quanto più scompaiono tanto più estendono il loro dominio . . . nell'intrico dei pensieri di chi resta. Dalla penombra delle paure e dei dubbi di generazioni ormai ignare, continuavano a protendere i loro colli, a sollevare le loro zampe artigliate, e quando l'ultima ombra della loro immagine s'era cancellata, il loro nome continuava a sovrapporsi a tutti i significati, a perpetuare la loro presenza nei rapporti tra gli esseri viventi."

This recognition that the power of dinosaur as trace is greater than that of the living reptiles has several logical consequences. First of all, Qfwfq reasons that even the existence of the name is still a kind of presence capable of having its own trace. The name "dinosaur" itself can be forgotten, erased ("cancellato"), leaving only the trace of the trace, so that all that is left of the dinosaurs merges "with the mute and anonymous molds of thought, through which they take on form and substance."[60] An actual dinosaur can fulfill the destiny of the race only by somehow ceasing to be a dinosaur, either by not recognizing himself as one or by somehow casting off all dinosaurian characteristics. When Qfwfq discovers that he has a son in consequence of a brief liaison with a female called the Half-breed (Mulata)—"a little Dinosaur, so perfect, so full of his own Dinosaur essence, and so unaware of what the word 'Dinosaur' meant"[61]—he is happy to learn that the creature calls himself "a New One" when asked who he is. Qfwfq, in answer to the little one's inquiry as to who *he* is, can only say that he is "Nobody," and then depart, take a train, get "lost in the crowd."[62] He slips off his identity as dinosaur and becomes just another one of us.

Qfwfq's acceptance of the extinction of the dinosaurs and of himself as dinosaur calls for contrast with the defiance shown by that other lone survivor of mass extinction, Bérenger in Ionesco's *Rhinoceros*. Calvino sets up the potential comparison himself in that the New Ones believe they have sighted a troop of dinosaurs in their vicinity, which Qfwfq discovers to be only a herd of rhinoceroses. Calvino's dinosaurs have thus been transformed, figuratively, into rhinos just as Ionesco's human race has transformed itself, literally, into a herd of these brutes, leaving only Qfwfq on the one hand and Bérenger on the other to stand up and defend a set of dinosaurian or human values. The question raises itself whether we are to understand Qfwfq's acceptance as the kind of capitulation that Bérenger so steadfastly resists.

The discussion just concluded should show, I think, both the similarities and the important differences between the two characters. At first Qfwfq indeed sees himself as a kind of Bérenger, insisting on the

60. *Cosmicomics*, 112; *Cosmicomiche*, 132. "Con gli stampi muti e anonimi del pensiero, attraverso i quali prendono forma e sostanza le cose pensate."

61. *Cosmicomics*, 112; *Cosmicomiche*, 133. "Un piccolo Dinosauro così perfetto, così pieno della propria essenza di dinosauro, e così ignaro di ciò che il nome Dinosauro significa."

62. Ibid. "Mi confusi con la folla."

meaning of his race as a set of noble ideals embodied in their presence. Qfwfq, however, undergoes an intellectual development in the course of the story through which he becomes convinced, rightly or wrongly, that his logocentric position has been misguided and that presence, the living on of the signified, is not necessary. Qfwfq remains ever committed to the central dinosaurian value, which is power; at the story's end, however, he understands the nature of semiotic power to be bound up with absence and extinction, and he gladly joins his fellows. Like Kafka's animal heroine Josephine the mouse, Qfwfq is able to "rise to the heights of redemption" by joining his brothers in oblivion.[63]

In this confrontation between the literal and the figurative, the literal finds it Darwinistically advantageous to his "species"—that is, to the system of signs clustered around the signifier "dinosaur"—to efface itself before the figurative. The "scientific" setting of the story, a chapter from the history of natural selection, becomes a paradoxically fitting figure for the mechanism of survival in extinction and indeed survival by means of extinction. The dinosaurs who were "masters" ("dominatori") in a figure of scientific discourse ("the undisputed master of the continents")[64] discover their true mastery in becoming, as Kafka's sage recommends, pure figures. Qfwfq the dinosaur has become the parable of the Dinosaurs and as parable potentially immortal, according to the literary topos claiming that, as long as the human race survives, "so long lives this, and this gives life to thee."

63. See Kafka, *Complete Stories*, 376.
64. *Cosmicomics*, 97; *Cosmicomiche*, 115. "Gli incontrastati dominatori dei continenti."

5 | Constructive Reading

Rhetorical construction, often enough a problem for the writers who employ it, can also work to solve both poetic and philosophical problems. Whether something is a problem or a solution often depends on your point of view. Inventions of reading such as "The Sandman" or "The Bridge" may look like inventions of the devil to the characters within them, but they are obviously a source of delight to readers and were a source of pride for their authors. The opposition between literal and figurative that creates a terrible problem for Nathanael solves a creative problem for Hoffmann: the construction of the story and the destruction of the protagonist are two sides of the same coin. Since rhetorical construction is a matter of reading, its valorization depends upon how one goes about reading this reading.

Texts from two very different writers, Goethe and Nietzsche, foreground the constructive side of rhetorical reading. Goethe's revision of Euripides' tragedy *Iphigenia in Tauris* both derives from and enacts a moral rereading of the ancient drama. Goethe was confronted with a text presenting a story he found attractive but representing a set of values that was in many ways opposed to his own. He found a way to preserve the story while at the same time altering the values: he made his drama into a great scene of reading in which the characters slowly and carefully reinterpret the meaning of the events in which they take part. They even reinterpret key texts deriving from the Euripidean material, including notably the oracle of Apollo charging Orestes to bring the "image of the sister" back to Greece. The result of these rereadings is to solve the compositional problem faced by Goethe and the moral dilemma faced by the play's characters.

Nietzsche faced a very different kind of problem, but his solution was remarkably similar. The problem of philosophy, as it is described in *The Gay Science,* is not so much to find answers to questions as to find interesting and important questions. The problem, in short, is to find the right problems. Nietzsche suggests that the familiar world around us contains a host of profound problems which we ordinarily fail to see principally because we recognize them as familiar. A central question for philosophy is thus how to see the familiar as a problem, and its answer lies in what Nietzsche calls "right reading." This "right" reading, which defamiliarizes the familiar, turns out to be a philosophical variant of rhetorical construction. Many of the aphorisms in *The Gay Science,* as well as the poems with which it begins, are inventions of reading.

Before turning to Goethe and Nietzsche, however, I want to return to Calvino's *Cosmicomics.* There we find a delightfully bittersweet demonstration of a rhetorical solution to a very physical sort of problem.

Rhetorical Space: Calvino's "All at One Point"

As I explained in the previous chapter, the story "The Dinosaurs" exists entirely in the space created by the distance between conflicting interpretations of the signifier "dinosaur." The confrontation between Qfwfq the dinosaur and the "dinosaurs" of the New Ones is productive of a discourse that operates between the literal and the figurative. Now, when I refer to the narrative potential thus engendered as "space" I am using a metaphor, and like all metaphors this one can be read as an aporia subject to deconstruction. If the thesis of this book is correct, even this rhetorical aporia would have the potential to generate a narrative exploring the "space" between the several conflicting readings discoverable in discourse about "space." It should come as no surprise that Calvino himself has provided this very narrative. The story is called "All at One Point" ("Tutto in un punto") and concerns the origin of the universe.

Like all the cosmicomic stories, "All at One Point" begins with a piece of paraphrased scientific discourse mounted as a headnote. This one explains: "Through the calculations begun by Edwin P. Hubble on the galaxies' velocity of recession, we can establish the moment when all the universe's matter was concentrated in a single point, before it began to expand in space."[1] From these conditions one could infer that at the instant before the big bang the physical universe had no dimensions and that the categories of "space" and "time" did not properly exist. This is the very thing that Qfwfq maintains as the crucial feature of the universe at that time: "Nobody knew then that there could be space. Or time either."[2] Of course, another implication of this hypothesis is that sentient beings could not have existed either, but this is of no consequence to Calvino. Here as elsewhere, he reads scientific theories lethetically, serenely ignoring the structures of thought to which they belong in order to plunder their language. The language that interests Calvino here is the word "space," or more specifically the phrase "there isn't any space" ("non c'è spazio"). It is interesting to Calvino the storyteller not primarily because of its scientific meaning but because of its everyday meaning, "there's no room." In the confrontation between the scientific and the ordinary meanings of the phrase "non c'è spazio" resides the energy necessary both to create the universe and to generate a story.

At the outset Qfwfq is forced to admit the inadequacy of figurative language and its necessity, thus immediately bringing the matter to the reader's attention. He explains that the concept of time was of no use to those living at the moment in question, since they were all "packed in like sardines" ("stando lì pigiati come acciughe"), but he then confesses that this phrase "pigiati come acciughe" is a "literary image" inadequate to a situation in which "there wasn't even space to pack us into."[3] The image is only "literary" in the sense that Qfwfq has made it so; it is as common a cliché in Italian as in English. But by pointing out its inadequacy, Qfwfq draws our attention to such commonplace figures and sensitizes us to their comic potential here. Thus, when only a few lines later he maintains that "when space doesn't exist, having

1. *Cosmicomics*, 43; *Cosmicomiche*, 55 (see chap. 4, n. 44). "Attraverso i calcoli iniziati da Edwin P. Hubble sulla velocità d'allontanamento delle galassie, si può stabilire il momento in cui tutta la materia dell'universo era concentrata in un punto solo, prima di cominciare a espandersi nello spazio."

2. Ibid. "Che ci potesse essere lo spazio, nessuno ancora lo sapeva. E il tempo, idem."

3. Ibid. "Non c'era spazio nemmeno per pigiarci."

somebody like Mr. Pber^t Pber^d underfoot all the time is the most irritating thing,"[4] we run headlong into another everyday trope which is of precisely the same order as "pigiate come acciughe." In both cases the inadequacy of the figures is ironic and funny because their shortcoming reverses the process of their formation. Both "packed in like sardines" and "being underfoot" are hyperbolic tropes when used in ordinary discourse. Sardines (or anchovies, *acciughe*) are packed far more tightly than the things to which they are ordinarily compared (e.g., people in the subway), and the space "underfoot" ("tra i piedi," literally "between one's feet") is much closer to one than the people or things we accuse of being there. In the case Qfwfq is narrating, however, this situation is reversed: these vehicles no longer overreach their tenors; on the contrary, they radically *understate* the case. The hyperbole of everyday discourse is unmasked ironically here as the driest imaginable understatement. They are the same words, and they are still tropes, but they have been turned upside down.

This is most true of all for the story's master trope, "lack of space." By imagining a human environment inside the pre-bang dimensionless point of matter, Calvino has established a context in which the phrase "we have no space" and similar hyperboles are literally true. Their hyperbolic function—which the discourse of the story maintains, even though its plot does not—is comically contrasted with the deadpan validity of their literal import. All of Qfwfq's spatial tropes slide out of control on the sheer ice of the outrageous context. When he speaks of the "narrow-minded attitude" ("mentalità ristretta") of the inhabitants of this primordial universe, and then cites as its cause the "environment in which we had been reared," he is using the word "ristretta" ("narrow") both literally and figuratively at the same time. Indeed, he seems to be suggesting that figurative narrowness (of mind) is the logical, expectable result of physical narrowness, restriction of space. This equation of physical space and personal character is further strengthened by the word "ambiente" ("environment") used both here and a bit earlier in the story ("ambiente così piccolo").[5] Since "ambiente" can refer to either the physical or the human environment and thus to either "surroundings" or "society," Qfwfq's recourse to the "ambiente

---

4. Ibid. "Perchè quando non c'è spazio, aver sempre tra i piedi un antipatico come il signor Pber^t Pber^d è la cosa più seccante."
5. *Cosmicomiche*, 56.

piccolo" as an explanation for the pettiness of individuals has a compelling if somewhat circular authority. In any case, the narrowness of the attitudes of the population is not distinguished from the narrowness of the physical environment, since the literal and figurative seem suddenly to have collapsed together "all at one point."

This narrow-mindedness is responsible for creating what one would think could not be created in the situation given: distinctions. If everything and everyone is all together in a single point, it seems it would be impossible to distinguish one thing from another. Actually Qfwfq complains about this very fact, pointing out that "you weren't able to tell what was later to become part of astronomy (like the nebula of Andromeda) from what was assigned to geography (like the Vosges, for example) or to chemistry (like certain beryllium isotopes)."[6] While this is a narrow-minded way of expressing the problem, its importance reduced to the confusion of a schoolchild about the taxonomy of his homework assignments, it points to a problem that ought to be universal in this punctiform universe. But it is by no means universal. The inhabitants do make distinctions, especially social ones. Most, including the narrator, look down their noses (or would, if there were any space to look down) at the Z'zu family because they are "immigrants" and "even wanted to hang lines across our point to dry their washing."[7] Qfwfq acknowledges that such an attitude could only be "unfounded prejudice," given that "neither before nor after existed, nor any place to immigrate from."[8] These considerations do not prevent the discrimination against the Z'zus from continuing, in part because (as Qfwfq explains) some of those then living "insisted that the concept of 'immigrant' could be understood in the abstract, outside of space and time."[9] A kind of philosophical platonism is invented ad hoc, as it were, to justify the crudest form of social repression. What is most interesting about this circumstance for my purpose is that it

6. *Cosmicomics*, 44; *Cosmicomiche*, 56. "Non riuscivi a riconoscere quel che in seguito sarebbe andato a far parte dell'astronomia (come la nebulosa d'Andromeda) da quel che era destinato alla geografia (per esempio i Vosgi) o alla chimica (come certi isotopi del berillio)."

7. Ibid. "Pretendevano perfino di appendere delle corde attraverso il punto per stendere la biancheria."

8. *Cosmicomics*, 44; *Cosmicomiche* 56–57. "Non esisteva nè un prima nè un dopo nè un altrove da cui immigrare."

9. *Cosmicomics*, 44; *Cosmicomiche*, 57. "Chi sosteneva che il concetto di 'immigrato' poteva esser inteso allo stato puro, cioè indipendentemente dallo spazio e dal tempo."

follows the necessity of embracing figurative meaning when literal ones are not plausible. Qfwfq demonstrates the impossibility of actually "immigrating" in a universe without time and space, but such an impossibility has no effect at all on the metonymic meaning of "immigrant" as "socially inferior person." Like "dinosaur" after there are no longer any dinosaurs, "immigrant" functions in its figurative mode with perfect ease before there are any immigrants.

Negative implications of "lack of space" such as these are counterbalanced by one great positive feature of the punctiform universe: it makes possible, indeed requires, a form of perfect intimacy unknown in the world of space and time. When everyone in the world is "all at one point," there should be possible a kind of paradisical love that is both physical and spiritual at the same time. As Calvino was certainly well aware, Dante makes use of this very figure to explain the perfect love that binds all things together in paradise.[10] The pilgrim describes the Eternal Light of heaven:

> Nel suo profondo vidi che s'interna,
>   legato con amore in un volume,
>   ciò che per l'universo si squaderna:
> sustanze e accidenti e lor costume,
>   quasi conflati insieme, per tal modo
>   che ciò ch' i' dico è un semplice lume.
> La forma universal di questo nodo
>   credo ch' i' vidi, perchè più di largo,
>   dicendo questo, me sento ch' i' godo.
> Un punto solo m'è maggior letargo
>   che venticinque secoli alla 'mpresa,
>   che fè Nettuno ammirar l'ombra d'Argo.[11]

Everything there is exists in this "nodo" that is also referred to, by juxtaposition, if not direct apposition, as "un punto solo" wherein

10. For more on this topic, see Susan Noakes, "Dante's *Vista Nova: Paradiso* xxxiii, 136," *Quaderni d'Italianistica* 5, no. 2 (1984): 151–75.

11. Vv. 85–96. Trans. J. D. Sinclair, *Dante's Paradiso* (New York: Oxford University Press, 1961), 483: "In its depth I saw that it contained, bound by love in one volume, that which is scattered in leaves through the universe, substances and accidents and their relations as it were fused together in such a way that what I tell of is a simple light. I think I saw the universal form of this complex, because in telling of it I feel my joy expand. A single moment [point] makes for me deeper oblivion than five and twenty centuries upon the enterprise that made Neptune wonder at the shadow of the Argo."

everything is perfect ("e fuor di quella / è defettivo ciò ch'è lì perfetto" [vv. 104-5]).

This little phrase "un punto solo" appears very prominently in Calvino's headnote to "All at One Point": "tutta la materia dell'universo era concentrata in un punto solo." Although the presence of three common words in a particular order hardly constitutes evidence of a conscious allusion to Dante, there are other features of the passage from *Paradiso* 33 that suggest the connection. Dante's words "quasi conflati insieme" ("as it were fused together") describe the situation in Calvino's story as well as they do the pilgrim's vision. Furthermore, the terms in which Calvino develops his cosmicomic tale force us to consider the possibility of a deliberate intertextual play. In a sense, "All at One Point" is a comic reduction of Dante's entire *Commedia*, the microcosm of the whole moral universe, into an inconceivable physical microcosm. The punctiform world Qfwfq describes is both heaven and hell at the same time. Its infernal aspect is, as in the *Commedia*, what we see first: the unpleasantness of Mr. Pber^t Pber^d, the complaining of the cleaning woman, the general pettiness typified by the universal prejudice against the Z'zus. It is a Sartrean sort of hell, conforming to his definition at the end of the play *No Exit*, "L'enfer, c'est les autres" ("Hell is other people"). There follows a description of the purgatorial world of the present, in which those who remember the days before the bang can only wait, with greater or lesser hope, for the time when the universe will contract again into the single point: "This story that the universe . . . will be condensed again has never convinced me," Qfwfq says. "And yet many of us are counting only on that, continually making plans for the time when we'll be back there again."[12] Only after all of this are we introduced to the most powerful element in the story, the absolute bliss of punctiform love.

Although the serpent (in the form—in one interpretation—of the Z'zus themselves, with their hissing name, or—in another—of the prejudice against them) has already entered Calvino's "single point," the pre-bang world described by Qfwfq still has a substantial element of Dante's paradise. We see it most clearly in the relationship of adoration that exists between the voluptuous Mrs. Ph(i)Nk$_0$ and everyone

12. *Cosmicomics*, 45; *Cosmicomiche*, 57. "La teoria che l'universo . . . tornerà a condensarsi. . . non mi ha mai persuaso. Eppure tanti di noi non fan conto che su quello, continuano a far progetti per quando si sarà di nuovo tutti lì."

else. It is as if all the narrow-mindedness that is focused on the Z'zus vanishes instantly when the object of consideration is Mrs. Ph(i)Nk$_0$: "And then, all of a sudden, the pettiness is put aside, and we feel uplifted, filled with a blissful, generous emotion."[13] Because of the punctiform nature of the universe, and thus of everyone in the universe, Mrs. Ph(i)Nk$_0$ is able to gather in herself that mythically powerful combination of promiscuity and virginity that characterizes many female divinities. No one objects to the fact that she "went to bed with her friend, Mr. DeXuaeaux," in part because "it was inevitable that she should be in bed also with each of us."[14] She is the object of a "contemplation" that is both "depraved" ("vizioso") and "chaste" ("casta") because she is at the same time both promiscuously mingled with everyone and virginally pure and impenetrable.

The coalescence of lover and beloved, wherein each both surrounds and is surrounded by the other, is a kind of edenic bliss. "In short: what more could I ask?" Qfwfq exclaims.[15] The catastrophic and irremediable annihilation of this Eden comes about not because of the mean-spiritedness engendered by the Z'zu family but because of the generous, loving inclinations of Mrs. Ph(i)Nk$_0$. She wants to make some "tagliatelle" for her friends, but her wish is thwarted by that one universal fact of life: lack of space. "Oh, if I only had some space," she says, "how I'd like to make some noodles for you boys!"[16]

And in that moment we all thought of the space that her round arms would occupy, moving backward and forward with the rolling pin over the dough . . . we thought of the space that the flour would occupy, and the wheat for the flour, and the fields to raise the wheat . . . of the space it would take for the Sun to arrive with its rays, to ripen the wheat; of the space for the Sun to condense from the clouds of stellar gases and burn; of the quantities of stars and galaxies and galactic masses in flight through space which would be needed to hold suspended every galaxy, every

13. Ibid. "E allora di colpo le meschinità vengono lasciate da parte, e ci si sente sollevati come in una commozione beata e generosa."
14. *Cosmicomics*, 46; *Cosmicomiche*, 58. "Che andasse a letto col suo amico, il signor De XuaeauX, era noto. . . . era inevitabile che lei fosse a letto anche con ognuno di noi."
15. *Cosmicomics*, 46; *Cosmicomiche*, 59. "Insomma, cosa potevo chiedere di più?"
16. Ibid. "Ragazzi, avessi un po' di spazio, come mi piacerebbe farvi le tagliatelle!" I have modified William Weaver's translation here, because he unaccountably renders "spazio" here as "room," thus spoiling the joke.

nebula, every sun, every planet, and at the same time we thought of it, this space was inevitably being formed.[17]

In the movement from Mrs. Ph(i)Nk$_0$'s wish for space (as room to operate in) to the thought of space (as the three physical dimensions), the entire universe comes into being. The world's founding utterance is here translated from the masculine imperative subjunctive "Fiat lux" to a feminine contrafactual subjunctive "avessi. . . ." The inaugural word is "made flesh" by the narrator's first thought, which fills the very first imaginable space with Mrs. Ph(i)Nk$_0$'s round arms and, immediately thereafter, her bosom.

The expansive joy Dante describes in *Paradiso* 33 becomes here the actual expansion of the universe, which in its punctiform configuration was not big enough to contain Mrs. Ph(i)Nk$_0$'s love, "a true outburst of general love" ("un vero slancio d'amore generale"). Just as her figurative "space" becomes physical space, so too does this figurative "slancio" ("impulse") become a physical rush, a "true" (that is, literal) outburst. The universe begins in a sudden release of rhetorical energy as figurative meanings instantly change into literal ones.

There is a price to be paid for this outburst of love. The creation of physical space also brings with it emotional and spiritual distance, a figurative "space" of another kind. Mrs. Ph(i)Nk$_0$ has with her wish unleashed the power of a terrible genie, for instead of "un po' di spazio" ("a little space") she gets a lot—far too much, in fact:

At the same time that Mrs. Ph(i)Nk$_0$ was uttering those words: ". . . ah, what noodles, boys!" the point that contained her and all of us was expanding in a halo of distance in light-years and light-centuries and billions of light-millennia, and we were being hurled to the four corners of the universe (Mr. Pber^t Pber^d all the way to Pavia), and she, dissolved into I don't know what kind of energy-light-heat, she . . . scattered

17. *Cosmicomics*, 46–47; *Cosmicomiche*, 59. "E in quel momento tutti pensammo allo spazio che avrebbero occupato le tonde braccia di lei muovendosi avanti e indietro con il mattarello sulla sfoglia di pasta . . . pensammo allo spazio che avrebbero occupato la farina, e il grano per fare la farina, e i campi per coltivare il grano . . . allo spazio che ci sarebbe voluto perchè il Sole arrivasse con i suoi raggi a maturare il grano; allo spazio perchè dalle nubi di gas stellari il Sole si condensasse e bruciasse; alle quantità di stelle e galassie e ammassi galattici in fuga nello spazio che ci sarebbero volute per tener sospesa ogni galassia ogni nebula ogni sole ogni pianeta, e nello stesso tempo del pensarlo questo spazio inarrestabilmente si formava."

thoughout the continents of the planets, kneading with floury, oil-shiny, generous arms, and she lost at that very moment, and we, mourning her loss.[18]

Calvino's story collapses the creation and the expulsion from Eden into one point. A universe whose origin is the most complete intimacy imaginable, the purest love, has become almost nothing but space, emptiness, distance. The generous Mrs. Ph(i)Nk$_0$ has said, as it turns out, just the wrong thing. Her desire to engage in *impastare* ("knead dough, make pasta") has turned instead into *impasticciare* ("make a hash out of something, bungle it"), not to mention *impacciare* ("hinder, encumber, get in the way"), as she hinders and bungles her own project of doing something nice for her loved ones. The rhetorical space she created, which in turn created her story, has become so vast that all the world's discourse is attenuated into nothing but the sound of mourning. She wanted to have space, but space instead has her. One has to wonder, then, whether Mrs. Ph(i)Nk$_0$'s apparently extraordinarily effective rhetoric has not done more harm than good. If the constructive reading of the word "space" has solved one problem, it has certainly created another. A universe that was by any standard too small is now by human standards far too big.

It would be wrong, of course, to lay too much stress on the mournful note sounded by the story's conclusion. While it is true that, like many of the cosmicomic tales, "All at One Point" chronicles a world in which love is forever thwarted by distance, the overall tone of the narrative is almost as light as space itself. Qfwfq's beatific vision of a Mrs. Ph(i)Nk$_0$ scattered (*sparsa*—another key word in Dante's *Comedy*) through the universe makes her a ludicrous sort of Beatrice, our attention focused not on her spiritual graces but on her "braccia unte e generose infarinate." Indeed, the very notion of a universe engendered (or destroyed, if one adopts Qfwfq's elegiac viewpoint) out of a sudden urge to make pasta is silly enough to keep even the most determinedly serious reader from going too far. And even if, in spite of the

---

18. *Cosmicomics*, 47; *Cosmicomiche*, 59–60. "Nello stesso tempo in cui la signora Ph(i)Nk$_0$ pronunciava quelle parole: — . . . le tagliatelle, ve', ragazzi!—il punto che conteneva lei e noi tutti s'espandeva in una raggera di distanze d'anni-luce e secoli-luce e miliardi di millenni-luce, e noi sbattuti ai quattro angoli dell'universo (il signor Pber^t Pber^d fino a Pavia), et lei dissolta in non so quale specie d'energia luce calore, lei . . . spars[a] per i continenti dei pianeti che impastano con le braccia unte e generose infarinate, e lei da quel momento perduta, e noi a rimpiangerla."

powerful comic undertow, the reader would like to venture into deeper waters of interpretation, there is always that one ultimate barrier: we do not have, never could have, enough *space*.

Changing Images: Goethe's *Iphigenia in Tauris*

Probably the best known work in the German language that solves problems by means of rhetorical reading is Goethe's *Iphigenia in Tauris* (*Iphigenia auf Tauris*, 1787). In Goethe's reworking of the Euripidean material, the impetus for the events of the plot comes from the human interpretation of a divine discourse that proves unexpectedly open to interpretation. The drama is set in motion by the efforts of Orestes and Pylades to conform to the command of Apollo to bring "the sister" back from Tauris; and it is resolved, somewhat notoriously, by the discovery that the sister in question must not have been Apollo's sister Diana but rather Orestes' sister Iphigenia. Unlike the Euripidean dea ex machina, however, this clever turn of language is anything but a sudden, unprepared, or supernatural event external to the terms in which the drama's problems were presented. Orestes' reinterpretation of the oracle is only one—the most explicit—of a whole set of such reinterpretations, through whose power one sort of world is turned into another. The surface of the plot, with its transformation of one sort of reading into another, conforms to the central goal of Goethe's project: the rhetorical transformation of the language of classical paganism into a language of Christian humanism.

That transformation takes place to a large extent within the domain charted by the concept of "sister" and related notions. Iphigenia's opening lament about the emptiness of her life among the Taurians focuses upon her inability to play the role of sister: "Alas for one who far from parents, brothers, / And sisters leads a lonely life!"[19] Her concern is reiterated in her prayer to Diana, whom she invokes as "Zeus's daughter," that both Agamemnon and she should be restored to their relatives; and again in her complaint to Arkas that she is "or-

---

19. Vv. 15–16. "Weh dem, der fern von Eltern und Geschwistern / Ein einsam Leben führt!" I cite Goethe's play in English from *Iphigenia in Tauris*, trans. Charles E. Passage (New York: Ungar, 1963). Quotations in German are from Goethe, *Werke* (Hamburg: Christian Wegner Verlag, 1952), vol. 5. References by verse number are to these editions.

phaned" ("verwaist") and that she never had the chance to become "attached to father, mother, brother, sisters" as normal children do (vv. 78–79). She thus laments the loss of something she never fully possessed. Her desire to take up her role in family relations is not so much a wish to recapture something lost as a desire to experience being something she never yet has been and may not fully know how to be.

On the other hand, it would not be inaccurate to say that Iphigenia's role in Tauris is precisely that of "Schwester," in a figurative sense. As priestess of Diana, she maintains a form of existence that Goethe's audience would readily associate with that of a "Schwester" in the sense of "nun." She leads a virginal life that is devoted entirely to the service of the divinity who saved her, and she is committed to the charitable project of rescuing and returning home errant strangers who land on Tauris's otherwise unfriendly shores. In this capacity she plays the role of nurse (also "Schwester") as well. Iphigenia's exile in Tauris can be seen, then, as both the loss and the gain of the sisterly role. That Iphigenia understands it, at the start of the play, only as a loss sets up one of the situations the action will serve to alter. Goethe constructs a situation productive of a classical dramatic irony in that the audience is in a position to understand more deeply than the character in the play the true state of affairs, which in this case is that Iphigenia is in a far better position to be sisterly than she realizes.

It is not inaccurate to say that Iphigenia holds the central position in this play precisely because of her intense interest in fulfilling her role as sister and, in anticipation of that fulfillment, understanding exactly what sisterly behavior would entail. Of course much more is implied by the notion of "sister" than Iphigenia realizes at first, but even at the play's beginning she knows that the central issue is the bond (*Band*) with others that she has never been able to develop: "an alien curse descended / Unfortunately upon me, severing me / From those I loved and rending that fair bond / In twain with iron fist."[20] The question of the "Band" becomes urgent forthwith, since King Thoas wishes to marry her and thereby establish closer ties ("ein näher Band") between the two of them. Iphigenia is firmly opposed to this proposal, but not for the reasons the king assumes. He imagines that she, woman through and through ("ganz ein Weib"), pays attention only to her

---

20. Vv. 82–85. "Leider faßte da / Ein fremder Fluch mich an und trennte mich / Von den Geliebten, riß das schöne Band / Mit ehrner Faust entzwei."

personal whims and knows the restraint of "no sacred bond" ("kein heilig Band") (v. 469). Iphigenia's concerns are in fact most urgently directed to what she understands to be the sacred bond linking her to her family in Greece, to which she longs to return. It is these familial bonds that prevent her from marrying Thoas in more ways than one, since she carries with her the curse of the house of Tantalus. Although Iphigenia's revelation of her family history does not deter Thoas in his proposal of marriage, it is a weighty demonstration of her commitment to the sacred bonds of blood relationship.

There is a rhetorical complication to Iphigenia's revelation, however, in that she must break one set of bonds in order to preserve another. Like the English "bond," the German *Band* can refer to various forms of physical and psychic restraint as well as to the ties of kinship, and Iphigenia has set this sort of restraint upon herself with regard to the story of her origin. To tell Thoas her family history and thereby declare her bonds of kinship, she must break the restraint she has set upon herself: "Unwillingly the tongue is loosened from / Its bonds of old."[21] This act of loosening one set of bonds in order to assert the binding power of another prefigures a second gesture in which Iphigenia does essentially the same thing. Act 3 opens with Iphigenia and Orestes, still unknown to each other, on the stage, she acting in the role of Diana's priestess, he a prisoner and an intended victim for Diana's altar. Her first gesture is to loose his bonds ("ich löse deine Bande" [v. 926]) and thereby initiate a conversation in which Orestes begins to suspect that she is "bound to [the house of Agamemnon] by closer ties" than simple friendship ("mit nähern Banden ihm verbunden" [v. 986]). In a further irony, Orestes' discovery of the priestess's burning interest in the affairs of Agamemnon's family prompts him to call for her to place restraints upon her heart ("So bändige dein Herz und halt es fest" [v. 988]), lest further news of the family's unhappiness be unendurable for her.

The issue of "bonds" is clearly a fundamental one in the play, since the prinicpal characters all find themselves bound in one fashion or another. In the case of Orestes and Pylades the bonds are physical: they are imprisoned and quite literally tied up. Iphigenia, too, though she is not tied up, suffers under a set of physical and social constraints that prevent her from returning to her homeland and to the set of bonds she

---

21. Vv. 300–301. "Vom alten Bande löset ungern sich / Die Zunge los."

desires. Even the goddess Diana is understood to be kept in bondage by the Taurians. But the play makes clear that "Band" may be read either positively or negatively, and the action of the drama moves toward an adjustment of understanding whereby the contradiction can be divested of its potential for harm. The contradiction is not canceled or resolved; rather, a way is found to exist somewhere between its two extremes. This adjustment takes place in the final scene when Orestes proclaims, that "Your harsh bonds are / Now stricken off, and you, O holy one, / Are now restored to your own people."[22] In the terms set up by Iphigenia at the beginning of the play, the return to "her own" is the reestablishment of a "lovely bond" ("schönes Band") broken when she was taken away from her family and homeland. The restoration of this "schönes Band" is at the same time the dissolution of the "strenge Bande" that held her—and Orestes, Pylades, and even Diana—captive. The plot of the drama has worked its way between the two readings of "Band," the one as "harsh," the other as "lovely."[23]

This is the same kind of adjustment that is made in our understanding of "sister," and indeed of other terms of family relation as well. Whereas the Greek value system that informs Euripides' drama places overwhelming importance on the blood bonds of kinship, Goethe cares as much or more for the notion of a family of mankind. As important as the brother-sister relation between Orestes and Iphigenia is for Goethe's drama, almost equally important is the brotherly relation between Orestes and Pylades. When Pylades makes up a tale to tell the priestess of Diana about who he and his companion are and why they have come to Tauris, he fictionalizes himself as Orestes' brother: "We are from Crete, and sons of King Adrastus: / I am the younger, Cephalus by name, / And he Laodamas, the eldest of / The house."[24] Pylades' story is not simply expedient; it images the real ties of affection and intimacy that link the two men. They did grow up together, after all, and Pylades conceives of his entire existence as so closely bound to Orestes' that "since childhood I have lived and only / Care to live with you and for your sake" (vv. 641-42). "My life began when I

22. Vv. 2117–19. "Die strengen Bande / Sind nun gelöst: du bist den Deinen wieder, / Du Heilige, geschenkt."

23. My investigation of Goethe's use of the word *Band,* and of other words discussed below, was greatly simplified by reference to Peter Schmidt, *Der Wortschatz von Goethes "Iphigenia"* (Frankfurt a.M.: Athenäum Verlag, 1970).

24. Vv. 824–27. "Aus Kreta sind wir, Söhne des Adrasts: / Ich bin der jüngste, Cephalus genannt, / Und er Laodamas, der älteste / Des Hauses."

began to love you," he says a few lines later (v. 654).[25] The internal bond of human affection is as strong as the external one of kinship, if not stronger.

As with "sister" and "brother," so too with "father": as powerful as the father–daughter bond between Agamemnon and Iphigenia is alleged to be throughout the play, the only such relationship the audience actually sees is a metaphorical one. Twice in the play Iphigenia utters exactly the same line, word for word, whereby she names Thoas "the king who has become my second father,"[26] and in her very last speech, it is this metaphorical fatherly relation upon which Iphigenia insists: "As valuable and dear / As my father was to me, so are you to me."[27] The play thus closes with a demonstration that figurative fatherhood, like figurative sisterhood and brotherhood, is at least as valuable as the literal thing. The action of the drama had begun with the latter at the center of attention but ended with our minds firmly on the former.

Such a process is typical of this play, which alerts us repeatedly to the possibility of multiple interpretation (or misinterpretation) of all kinds of language, even of divine discourse. The interpretation of divine will is a matter of urgent personal concern not just for Orestes but for all the characters in the drama. Thoas and Iphigenia have a substantial difference of opinion over just what it is that Diana requires of the faithful. According to the ancient custom of the Taurians, Diana insists upon blood, upon the sacrifice of all strangers who happen upon the shores of Tauris. Iphigenia was the first exception to this practice, and she has been able in her capacity as priestess of Diana to keep the custom in check. She argues that the practice had arisen out of misunderstanding: "He has misunderstood the heaven-dwellers / Who fancies them a-thirst for blood; he merely / Attributes his own cruel will to them."[28] Thoas, on the other hand, accuses Iphigenia of engaging in willful misprision: "It ill beseems us to interpret and / Distort the sacred usages to suit / Our minds by Reason's facile variations."[29]

25. "Da ich mit dir und deinetwillen nur / Seit meiner Kindheit leb' und leben mag. . . . Da fing mein Leben an, als ich dich liebte."
26. Vv. 1641, 2004. "Der König, der mein zweiter Vater ward."
27. Vv. 2155–56. "Wert und teuer, / Wie mir mein Vater war, so bist du's mir."
28. Vv. 523–25. "Der mißversteht die Himmlischen, der sie / Blutgierig wähnt: er dichtet ihnen nur / Die eignen grausamen Begierden an."
29. Vv. 528–30. "Es ziemt sich nicht für uns, den heiligen / Gebrauch mit leicht beweglicher Vernunft / Nach unserm Sinn zu deuten und zu lenken."

Thoas, a man who believes in straightforward "common sense," supposes that it is possible for understanding to take place directly, unmediated by any process of interpretation (*Deutung*). Pylades takes up a similar argument in the very next scene, less than a hundred lines later. He tells Orestes not to doubt the words of Apollo's oracle, which promised hope and comfort in the sister's sanctuary: "The words of gods are not ambiguous, / As downcast people in their gloom imagine."[30] The events of the drama demonstrate that the words of the gods may be unambiguous *in retrospect* but that they are very open to misconstruction by mortals before the passage of time clarifies matters. The situation in which Pylades makes this statement comes about precisely because the oracle *is* (from the human standpoint, at any rate) "doppelsinnig," that is, possessed of at least two different meanings.

If the words of the gods, and of men for that matter, were not capable of being read in more than one way, the action of *Iphigenia in Tauris* would be impossible. Goethe's conception of the play derives in no small part from his creative rereading of the oracle described in the prologue of Euripides' *Iphigenia in Tauris.* It is important to remember that, in Euripides' version, the gods really do want the statue returned to Greece, that Orestes and Iphigenia do steal it, and that it is only the last-minute intervention of Athena, the dea ex machina, that prevents Thoas and the Greeks from slaughtering each other over possession of it. Athena forces Thoas to let Orestes and Iphigenia take the statue of Artemis back to Athens, where she says it belongs, and the story ends happily—for the Greeks. Euripides' play is still strongly chauvinistic and in an important way cult centered. What happens to Thoas and the Taurians is relatively unimportant there, whereas what happens to the statue of Artemis is crucial. The return of Iphigenia to Greece is a fringe benefit, not the fundamental goal, of Orestes' mission to Tauris.

Goethe is able to make this pagan Greek material amenable to his German, humanistic value system precisely because its language is so often readable in more than one way. The divine oracles of classical antiquity were notoriously rhetorical. By long-standing custom they did not need to be clear so long as they could be construed as being true. The "wooden walls" really do save Athens, as the oracle predicted, but in a way no one had foreseen. Goethe is able to take a set of

30. Vv. 613–14. "Der Götter Worte sind nicht doppelsinnig, / Wie der Gedrückte sie im Unmut wähnt."

signifiers from the classical Greek world and submit them to a process whereby they gain new significations that overlie the original ones. The vehicles for the play's figures remain recognizably Greek, but their tenors undergo a radical revision. Orestes really does bring back the image of Diana, but in a way no one expected. The letter of the ancient, pagan language remains almost as it was, but its spirit undergoes a metamorphosis. This transformation does not erase the pagan meanings, but it does restrict their range of validity.

Pylades is not exactly wrong, however, in what he says about the language of the gods. His language too is open to rhetorical construction. His precise words were, "Der Götter Worte sind nicht doppelsinnig, / Wie der Gedrückte sie in Unmut wähnt." Of course the words of the gods are "doppelsinnig," but not in the way one who is "pressed" by an unhappy turn of events will construe them. Pylades is objecting to Orestes' newly voiced interpretation of the oracle at the opening of act 2:

> [Apollo] seemed to promise
> Aid and deliverance in the temple of
> His much-loved sister who rules over Tauris,
> In god-like words of hope and certainty.
> And now it is fulfilled that all distress
> Is to be ended wholly with my life.[31]

The words of the oracle, as cited, are open to this melancholy construction, particularly because of the principle of oracular infallibility. Since Orestes seems bound to die, his death must somehow be construed as the fulfillment of Apollo's words. But Pylades objects that it is still too soon for such an act of interpretation, since the outcome is by no means certain. He would still hope for rescue even at the moment when "the priestess lifts her hand to cut our locks / Of hair in sign of consecration."[32] Orestes' reading of the oracle *in malo* is in error not because it assumes the oracle to be ambiguous but because it leaps

---

31. Vv. 565–70. "Schien er Hilf' und Rettung / Im Tempel seiner vielgeliebten Schwester, / Die über Tauris herrscht, mit hoffnungsreichen, / Gewissen Götterworten zu versprechen; / Und nun erfüllet sich's, daß alle Not / Mit meinem Leben völlig enden soll."

32. Vv. 606–7. "Wenn die Priesterin / Schon, unsre Locken weihend abzuschneiden, / Die Hand erhebt."

too soon, and under pressure, to its gloomy conclusion. Pylades is particularly adept at the art of interpretation *in bono*. Not only is he sure that Apollo will save the two Greek travelers from death on Diana's altar, he also assumes that their capture and imprisonment are all part of some great divine plan:

> Not without
> Some cleverness I have linked up things past
> With things to come and have it all worked out.
> Perhaps the great work has been ripening
> This long while in the planning of the gods.
> Diana longs to quit this harsh shore of
> Barbarians and their blood-stained human victims.
> We were appointed for that noble purpose,
> It is enjoined on us, and we have strangely
> Been brought by fate already to this portal.[33]

Pylades is evidently quite proud of his hermeneutic skill in having thus "worked out" ("ausgelegt") the connection between the oracle and the unpromising fact of Orestes' and his imprisonment. Remarkably enough, Pylades' version of the story is exactly right—only not in the way he means. Pylades is still acting, as it were, in Euripides' version of the play; he thinks that the goddess really wants her statue moved back to Greece. Those who have read Goethe's play can, with hindsight, perceive that we need to understand "Diana" here as "die Schwester," to read the name of the goddess as a figure for the "divine" Iphigenia. (Pylades calls her "Göttliche" just a few lines later [v. 823]). If we make this slight adjustment in Pylades' interpretation of events, we can declare it to be perfectly accurate.

This adjustment in reading requires of us nothing different from what Orestes does at the play's end, that is, to substitute Iphigenia for Diana. The substitution is justified on several grounds, not the least of which is the frequent recurrence of turns of phrase that link Iphigenia

---

33. Vv. 730–39. "Ganz anders denk' ich, und nicht ungeschickt / Hab' ich das schon Geschehne mit dem Künft'gen / Verbunden und im stillen ausgelegt. / Vielleicht reift in der Götter Rat schon lange / Das große Werk. Diana sehnet sich / Von diesem rauhen Ufer der Barbaren / Und ihren blut'gen Menschenopfern weg. / Wir waren zu der schönen Tat bestimmt, / Uns wird sie auferlegt, und seltsam sind / Wir an der Pforte schon gezwungen hier."

with Diana in particular or with divinity in general. She is not only Diana's priestess but also Diana's consecrated sacrificial victim. It was Diana who required her death at Aulis and Diana who saved her. She sees herself and Orestes as the earthly doubles of Artemis and Apollo and so presents the case in her lovely prayer, "Geschwister, . . . rettet uns Geschwister" (vv. 1317–20). Not only Pylades (as mentioned above) but Orestes as well sees in her a version of divinity: he addresses her as "Heilige" ("holy one") in the speech in which he declares her to be the "Schwester" whose return is demanded by the gods.

These suggestions of the close relation—almost interchangeability— of Iphigenia and Diana are not simply a means to accentuate the special value of the heroine. They are rather a part of a larger project of reinterpreting the relation between human beings in general and the gods, wherein the great gap between mortals and divinities that is emphasized again and again in ancient literature is nearly closed. Once again Goethe takes a typical mode of classical discourse, the distinction between gods and men, and lets the action of his play propose a radically different interpretation of that discourse. The classical version of the gap between the divine and the human receives a powerful formulation in the famous "Song of the Fates" ("Parzenlied") that closes act 4. Iphigenia remembers that her nurse used to sing this song to her and her brother and sister, explaining that it was the song the Parcae had sung "When Tantalus fell from his golden chair; / They suffered for their noble friend; grim were / Their hearts, and full of dread the song they sang."[34] Indeed, the song is "full of dread" ("furchtbar"), since it insists on the limitless and arbitrarily used power of the gods and the helplessness of even the most exalted human beings, such as Tantalus. The melancholy power of the song is balanced, however, by its distance from the one who sings it. This is not Iphigenia's song, nor is it even her nurse's song; it is the song of the Parcae sung long ago in response to the curse Iphigenia (though she does not know it) is about to expiate. The whole thrust of Iphigenia's speech that introduces the "Parzenlied" is the desperate hope that the state of affairs described in the song will no longer obtain. The image of the gods that Iphigenia cherishes in her heart and wants to save ("rettet euer Bild in meiner Seele" [v. 1717]) is quite pointedly *not* the one expressed by the Song of

34. Vv. 1721–24. "Als Tantalus vom goldnen Stuhle fiel: / Sie litten mit dem edlen Freunde; grimming / War ihre Brust, und furchtbar ihr Gesang."

the Fates. The picture of the gods that she paints earlier in the play is
the one she wants to save; that is, the description given in the lyrical
conclusion of act 1:

> For the Immortals bear love unto
> The good and far-flung races of men,
> And they gladly lengthen fleeting
> Life for a mortal, willingly granting
> To him some small share of the cheering
> View of their own everlasting sky
> For a certain measure of time.[35]

These "races of men" ("der Menschen . . . Geschlechter") need
not stand in fear of the gods like the "race of man" ("Menschenge-
schlecht") of the Fates' song. In Iphigenia's version of the relationship,
mortals are given the chance to share in the enjoyment ("mitge-
nießend") of the gods' own realm ("ewiger Himmel"). The gap between the human and divine is in this view not so great at all.

Goethe's version of the story of Iphigenia and her family takes place
precisely in the space between the picture presented in the "Parzenlied"
and that of the closing lines of act 1. It would not be amiss to understand the curse of the house of Tantalus as residing as much in the
interpretation of the gods proposed by the song of the Parcae as in
Tantalus's sin of pride, and the expiation as occurring by means of
Iphigenia's reinterpretation. Iphigenia not only saves her brother by
being "divine" herself and thus a fitting replacement for the statue of
Diana, she saves as well by adhering to a concept of the gods that
greatly lessens their distance from men. She does in fact almost exactly
what Thoas accuses her of: she interprets "the sacred usages to suit" the
dictates of reason. She saves many luckless travelers by opposing the
custom of human sacrifice on the ground that Diana did not insist upon
Iphigenia's own death on the altar: "My service must mean more to her
than my death."[36] And what does that service consist of if not the
godlike act of lengthening fleeting life for a mortal?

---

35. Vv. 554–60. "Denn die Unsterblichen lieben der Menschen / Weit verbreitete
gute Geschlechter, / Und sie fristen das flüchtige Leben / Gerne dem Sterblichen,
wollen ihm gerne / Ihres eigenen, ewigen Himmels / Mitgenießendes fröhliches An-
schaun / Eine Weile gönnen und lassen."
36. V. 527. "Ihr war mein Dienst willkommner als mein Tod."

That Iphigenia is "godlike" ("Göttergleich") is explicitly stated by
Pylades on more than one occasion: he calls her "a godlike woman"
("ein göttergleiches Weib") and later inquires after her "godlike ances-
try" ("göttergleiche Herkunft") (vv. 772, 814). We would expect this,
given the pattern of imagery and the analogous terms (*Göttliche,
Heilige*) in which she is addressed elsewhere in the play. What is perhaps a little surprising—but crucial for the project of the drama's rhetoric—is that this quality of being "godlike" is attached to a large
number of other mortals. Iphigenia names her father as "the godlike
Agamemnon" (v. 45) and describes the Greek heroes at Troy as "images of the gods" ("Götterbilder") (v. 864). Orestes himself is linked to
Apollo in a manner similar to the way Iphigenia is linked to Diana: he
serves Apollo (through the oracle) just as she serves Artemis; and the
two of them imitate, as brother and sister (*Geschwister*), the divine
brother-sister pair. Orestes has a vision of his ancestors in which they
appear to be godlike, particularly Tantalus himself, who is referred to
as "der Göttergleiche" (vv. 1272, 1306).

The language by which Orestes describes the ancestors is particularly rich in rhetorical complexity: "How godlike and how like each other
/ They seem to move, these forms."[37] A more literal translation might
serve better for close examination: "The moving/changing forms seem
godlike and similar." The language does not make it clear whether the
figures are similar to each other or to the gods; indeed, some editions
print the line as "göttergleich und -ähnlich" to enforce the latter interpretation. The possibility cannot be ruled out that the forms are similar
both to each other and to the gods; perhaps what is godlike in them is
the very thing that makes them similar. The language also withholds a
decision whether the forms are simply moving around or are in the
process of some kind of transformation. The word "forms" ("Gestalten") also produces hesitation, since the notion of a form can be
valorized either negatively, as that which is merely external and acci-
dental, or positively, as that which is central and essential. The characteristic of being "göttergleich" is thus linked with similarity (either to
other men or to gods), alteration (either in position or in character),
and form (either as appearance or as essence).

All the possibilities of these "wandelnde Gestalten" who are "göttergleich und ähnlich" are actualized in the course of the play, becom-

---

37. Vv. 1272–73. "Göttergleich und ähnlich scheinen / Die wandelnden Gestalten."

ing especially prominent at its conclusion. Orestes' description, apt as it may be for the vision of his ancestors, is even more relevant to Iphigenia and himself. They are the figures in the play who are most often characterized as godlike, similar both to the Olympian siblings Apollo and Artemis and to each other in their sense of bearing the full weight of the heritage of the Tantalides. Most important, they change in the course of the play, and it is difficult to say whether the change takes place more crucially in the essence of their souls or in their character as meaning-bearing "Gestalten." One could argue that it makes no difference; that it is only as significant forms that these characters function in the first place; that any "character development" discernible in the course of the action is as much a matter of shifting meanings as of personal growth.

The multiple, often incompatible readings that can be generated by rhetorical discourse provide both the pathos and the resolution of the story. The pathos (in the Aristotelian sense of "tragic act") that constantly threatens to overtake Iphigenia and Orestes is summed up neatly in the problematic of the word blood (*Blut*) read as rhetoric. Clearly, the interesting thing for Goethe in the concept of "blood"—prominent enough in the play, though less so in the verse text than in the prose— is that it can be understood to signify either the result of violent conflict or the most intimate bonds of kinship. The story's origins in pagan antiquity assert themselves in the frequency with which the former meaning ("spilled blood") appears in the mouths of virtually every character. When Iphigenia speaks for example of the "day of blood" ("Tag des Bluts") (vv. 978-79), she refers to the murder of Agamemnon, and every character in the play uses such a trope at least once.

But it can be used in other ways as well. When Arkas reassures Iphigenia that "impetuous new blood does not / Incite the king,"[38] this blood stands for powerful emotion, as it does again for Iphigenia in act 3, scene 1, when she chides Orestes for being slow to recognize her:

> Orestes,
> My dear one, can you not hear what I say?
> Has the attendance of the gods of terror
> So caused the blood to dry up in your veins?[39]

38. Vv. 201-2. "Ein gewaltsam neues Blut / Treibt nicht den König."
39. Vv. 1159–61. "Orest, mein Teurer, kannst du nicht vernehmen? / Hat das Geleit der Schreckensgötter so / Das Blut in deinen Adern aufgetrocknet?"

We quickly realize, however, that this use of "Blut" contains yet a third kind of trope. Here blood is the fluid of the heart, the carrier of emotion, as in Arkas's description of the king, but it is also the physical emblem of the closest kinship. In this case it is blood's absence that is distressing, whereas in most of its other appearances its presence is terrible.

The tragic plight of Iphigenia and Orestes is the fate that drives these several tropes on blood into one single figure. Orestes makes it explicit in a celebrated passage of stichomythia in the same scene:

> IPHIGENIA: Did she spill her own blood in angry regret?
> ORESTES: No, but her own blood brought death to her.[40]

Blood as violence is brought into terrible unity with blood as kinship and blood as emotion. Clytemnestra's own "blood" is responsible for her spilled blood in two ways, for not only was she slain by her son Orestes, but she also brought herself down, in a sense, by giving in to the powerful feelings running in her blood, feelings of hatred for Agamemnon and love for Aegisthus. But it is of course the conflict between violence and kinship that creates the powerful rhetoricity of these lines, as it does in the rest of the play as well. The dismal irony of the situation presented in *Iphigenia in Tauris* (Euripides' version as well as Goethe's) is that this same pathos of blood threatens to characterize the relationship between Iphigenia and Orestes, since she is required by custom and by Thoas's decree to supervise the sacrificial slaying of her brother. It is as if the gods had determined that these two mortals should actualize in their story all potential interpretations of the complex rhetoricity of "blood."

In Goethe's version, Iphigenia's character is such that "blood" is the thing that she most desires and most detests. Her most cherished fear is that she will have to do as Thoas and the custom of the Taurians require and spill the blood of foreigners on the altar of Diana. Her prayer to Diana at the close of act 1 ("O withhold then my hands from blood" ["Enthalte von Blut meine Hände"]) is therefore both perfectly straightforward and deeply ironic at the same time. Her intention is unquestionably a sincere and uncomplicated concern about the rite of

---

40. Vv. 998–99, trans. mine. "IPH.: Vergoß sie reuig wütend selbst ihr Blut? / OR.: Nein, doch ihr eigen Blut gab ihr den Tod."

sacrifice that Thoas has just insisted be reintroduced and that she certainly believes never brings "blessing and peace" ("Segen und Ruhe"). But the prayer is full of dramatic irony, since the very next scene will find Iphigenia's own "blood," Orestes, placed in her hands (in the sanctuary of Diana) by Thoas. Iphigenia will quickly discover that her most urgent problem is to find means to separate "blood" from "blood," to keep her hand firmly on her blood kindred while at the same time keeping it free of the violence of blood sacrifice.

It is fitting that a problem so full of rhetorical complexity should find its solution in the manipulation of rhetoric. Iphigenia, in her unwillingness to "sacrifice so much as one false word"[41] in order to prevent the sacrifice of her brother, tells Thoas the whole truth about their situation and thereby puts the burden of sacrifice on him:

> O let your mercy, circled round about
> With joy and praises and thanksgiving shine
> Upon me like the holy light of the silent sacrificial flame.[42]

It is not simply the desire to ornament her discourse that causes Iphigenia to compare the act of grace she seeks from Thoas to the light of the sacrificial flame. She is here working out the rhetorical slide from one sort of "sacrifice" to another that makes possible the happy conclusion of Goethe's play. The gods have called for a sacrifice here, and they will get one. Iphigenia is proposing, however, that Thoas relent from requiring the literal act of blood sacrifice and instead offer up a figurative sacrifice of his own desire for "blood," that is, both his angry urge to slay the Greeks who have sought to deceive him and his deep desire ("gewaltsam neues Blut") to found a new family with Iphigenia as his spouse. Diana no longer requires "a bloody sacrifice" ("ein blutig Opfer") (v. 913); she requires a sacrifice of "blood" that is self-sacrifice ("Selbstopfer") on the part of Thoas. It is no wonder that he observes with characteristic understatement, "You ask a great deal in a little time."[43]

---

41. V. 1676. "Ein falsches Wort nicht einmal opfern."
42. Vv. 1983–85. "O laß die Gnade, wie das heil'ge Licht / Der stillen Opferflamme, mir, umkränzt / Von Lobgesang und Dank und Freude, lodern." I have altered the translation to make my point clearer.
43. V. 1988. "Du forderst viel in einer kurzen Zeit."

One could easily imagine that Thoas might find it too much and that he would assert his right to keep his priestess and his prisoners. But Goethe has reserved for the Scythian barbarian the play's most civilized gesture: Thoas allows all the Greeks to depart in peace, convinced by "the voice / Of truth and humanity" that he hears in Iphigenia and her brother. The last bone of contention is laid to rest when Orestes answers the king's objection that he cannot let the image of the goddess be taken away. "The image shall, O king, not cause us discord,"[44] he insists, and goes on to explain his previous misreading of the oracle's injunction. Orestes' formulation is doubly true because it has become evident that the "image" ("Bild"), both as statue and as figure of discourse, works at the end of the play to unite rather than divide the play's conflicting elements. Iphigenia is revealed to be not only the "sister" of the oracle but also the "Bild" as well, though of course to so understand her one must read the word figuratively (that is, "bildlich"). Orestes compares his sister to "a sacred image / Into which a city's fate is charmed / Unalterably by mystic words of gods."[45] By saying she is "like an image" ("gleich einem Bilde") he proclaims her to be the image of an image and perhaps thereby more rightfully the image whose return to Greece the gods desire.

This troping on "Bild" has been carefully prepared for throughout the play, where it is as often used in its extended, figurative sense of "type" or "idea" as in the narrower sense of "statue." Iphigenia, for example, when she first speaks to Orestes, refers to him and Pylades as "the images of heroes / Whom I had learned to reverence from childhood."[46] Obviously she is not comparing them to the statues of heroes but rather to the ideal of heroic excellence. Again, in one of the most famous lines in a play full of famous lines, Iphigenia calls upon the gods to "Save me and save your image in my soul."[47] Here as nowhere else it is made absolutely clear how Goethe has rhetorically shifted the issue of the divine "Bild" he inherited from Euripides. Orestes' arrival in Tauris precipitates a series of events that will save both the "sister" and the "image" of Diana, but neither in the expected sense. The "Bild" in need of salvation is not the statue of Diana but the idea of

---

44. V. 2107. "Das Bild, o König, soll uns nicht entzweien!"
45. Vv. 2127–29. "Gleich einem heil'gen Bilde, / Daran der Stadt unwandelbar Geschick / Durch ein geheimes Götterwort gebannt ist."
46. Vv. 945-46. "Das Bild der Helden, / Die ich von Eltern her verehren lernte."
47. Vv. 1716–17. "Rettet mich / Und rettet euer Bild in meiner Seele!"

divine justice and benevolence that Iphigenia harbors within her. It becomes her modesty that she does not realize that she herself is the human type of the divine qualities she prizes so highly.

The possibility for referential multiplicity that allows Orestes to misinterpret the oracle also allows the transformation of this pagan story of blood, bonds, sacrifice, and images into the most characteristic and compelling document of eighteenth-century Christian humanism. Euripides' drama, composed according to a value system not only different from but often downright opposed to the charity, openness, and self-restraint prized by Goethe, seems to offer little promise as the foundation for a work of Weimar classicism. But Goethe evidently considered the Greek play not so much an expression of Greek values as a repository of signifiers, a hoard of rhetorical discourse that could be read both in Euripides' way and in the radically different way Goethe directs it toward at the end of his play. The brilliance of Goethe's execution lies not so much in his new interpretations of the old concepts (blood, bond, etc.) as in his carefully writing his play in the space between the readings. He does not simply impose his new understanding of "divine image," for example, extirpating the old; he lets the action of the play move from one to the other, insisting only at the drama's conclusion on the primacy of the new, humanistic reading. *Iphigenia*, far from effacing the Greek character of its source, maintains it in such a way as to leave the overpowering impression that these Greeks, Goethe's charitable, free, open "Götterbilder," must be the real ones. It makes us imagine it to be an example of the cultural "tyranny of Greece over Germany," whereas in actuality it displays the dominance of Goethean values over Euripidean discourse.

The discovery of a rhetorical potential in the language of others solves problems both for the characters in the play and for their creator. The possibility for multiple meanings in words like "sister" and "image," embodied in the person of Iphigenia herself and given voice most strikingly in Orestes' climactic act of rereading, makes it possible for the Greeks and Thoas to avoid slaughtering each other and to part as friends. But it is this very same rhetoricity that allows Goethe to write his drama in the first place. What is for the persons in the play an authoritative discourse of the gods is for the author an authoritative text from the past, Euripides' *Iphigenia*. The action that saves Iphigenia and Orestes and that constitutes Goethe's drama can take place only by aggressively finding and exploiting rhetorical moments within that preexisting, powerful language. The conventional, accepted readings taken as a given by others (other writers, other characters) must be put into question, though not erased, by alternative readings with an equal claim to validity. Both Goethe and the Greeks he invented thus work to civilize a pagan discourse by means of rhetorical construction.

Nietzsche's Rhetoric of "Right Reading"

I have devoted all my discussion of rhetorical construction so far to belletristic fictions. That is where we most often find the kind of imaginative language that is my subject. Since my announced topic is the process of rhetorical reading as a form of literary invention, it only makes sense to seek the characteristic examples of this process among works that acknowledge through their fictionality their imaginative beginnings. Both historical and theoretical considerations, however, prompt one to the recognition that other forms of discourse can have a rhetorical basis. Among the practitioners of those other forms are several whose work displays the same kind of rhetorical techniques I have been describing in my discussions of Rabelais, Hawthorne, Goethe, and so on. Not surprisingly, one of the first nonfiction writers to come to mind as belonging to this group is Friedrich Nietzsche, a philosopher widely recognized as an imaginative rather than a systematic thinker. It is worth considering whether his imaginative practice does indeed work along the same lines as that of the masters of rhetorical construction already discussed.

There is a prima facie case to be made for Nietzsche's early and abiding interest in the rhetorical aspect of all discourse. Much of that case has already been made by Paul de Man in *Allegories of Reading* and has become widely known and frequently discussed. Because of de Man and others associated with the "new Nietzsche," coming mainly from France, many are now familiar with the formerly obscure little fragment "On Truth and Lie in an Extra-moral Sense" ("Über Wahrheit und Lüge im außermoralischen Sinn") and its relation to Nietzsche's lecture notes on rhetoric made in the early 1870s. From these documents we get a clear sense of Nietzsche's transition from philology to philosophy in the period from 1868 to 1876, when he was in effect working as both philosopher and professional philologist at the same time. Consideration of classical rhetoric as expounded by scholars such as Richard Volkmann and Gustav Gerber provided Nietzsche with important materials out of which to build a bridge between the study of language and the reexamination of some of philosophy's fundamental questions.

The self-deconstructing Nietzsche is a figure that has already become familiar in one form or another over the past decade, and it is not my intention to paint that portrait again. While self-deconstruction is an important feature of Nietzsche's rhetorical style, it is not the aspect I want to focus on now. I prefer to draw out a slightly different implication of the position taken in the lecture notes on rhetoric and in "On Truth and Lie" that stresses its inventive rather than its subversive function in Nietzsche's philosophical project. This is what one might call, following Gregory Ulmer's extension of Derrida's term, the "grammatological" rather than the deconstructive turn in Nietzsche.[48] If indeed all language (and thus all truth) is figurative and therefore subject to deconstruction, it offers the possibility of becoming an almost endlessly fertile source for philosophical thinking. If there is no distinction to be made between the figurative nature of even the most ordinary language and truth, then one way to think about "truth" in fresh ways would be to "let language do some thinking for us"[49] by interrogating the figures themselves.

Interrogating them, however, would not mean attempting to discriminate between their "true" and "false" significations. Since all significations are the result of troping, according to "On Truth and Lie," there is no way to carry out such a discrimination. It would have to mean accepting both the literal and the figurative meanings as belonging to the same order—both, of course, figurative. While one point of view would see this leveling as destroying the value of both, Nietzsche often works on the assumption that all available meanings are equally useful. Out of this assumption comes a strategy for writing (in this case, writing a kind of philosophy) that derives from reading. The writer reads an already deconstructed language and out of that reading forms a new discourse that actualizes both the literal and the figurative, both the assertion and its subversion. The discovery that all truth is

48. See Gregory Ulmer, *Applied Grammatology: Post(e)-Pedagogy from Jacques Derrida to Joseph Beuys* (Baltimore: Johns Hopkins University Press, 1985).
49. Ulmer, *Applied Grammatology*, 315.

nothing but figuration ceases to be an alarming or paralyzing problem for the philosopher; on the contrary, it opens up new space for investigation. Rhetoric, since Plato the thing philosophy has sought to purge from its midst, becomes the wellspring of philosophy.

The rhymes that open *The Gay Science* show Nietzsche attempting publicly to demonstrate the integration of a form of rhetorical or poetic invention into his philosophical discourse. He uses wordplay to explain the nature of his enterprise, as for example in the twenty-third poem in the group, "Interpretation":

> Leg ich mich aus, so leg ich mich hinein:
> Ich kann nicht selbst mein Interprete sein.
> Doch wer nur steigt auf seiner eignen Bahn,
> Trägt auch mein Bild zu hellerm Licht hinan.[50]

The equation between "sich auslegen" ("interpret oneself") and "sich hineinlegen" ("get oneself into trouble") is a paradoxical wordplay. Since *ein* (in) and *aus* (out) are semantic opposites, the assertion that "sich hineinlegen" and "sich auslegen" are parts of the same process might come as a surprise; but since the locutions are so similar phonologically (the parallel structure "Leg ich mich . . . leg ich mich . . ." emphasizes this), the author's surprising conclusion seems justified. If self-interpretation can only get the author into trouble, then, he must count on the reader to do the work of interpreting, even if that reader has no particular interest in advancing Nietzsche's project. It is interesting to compare this text with a slightly earlier version written in February 1882 and found in the *Nachlaß* (11[336]). The first line is the same, but the last three go in a somewhat different direction: "So mög ein Freund mein Interprete sein. / Und wenn er steigt auf seiner eignen Bahn, / Trägt er des Freundes Bild mit sich hinan."[51] In this version, written with a specific person in mind, Nietzsche presupposes that the

---

50. I cite *The Gay Science* in English from *The Gay Science*, trans. Walter Kaufmann (New York: Vintage Books, 1974); and in German from the *Kritische Gesamtausgabe* of Giorgio Colli and Mazzino Montinari (Berlin: de Gruyter, 1973), vol. 5,2. For everyone's convenience I will cite by aphorism (or poem) number rather than by page. (Note that the Colli/Montinari edition uses *ss* regularly instead of *ß*.) "Interpreting myself, I always read / Myself into my books. I clearly need / Some help. But all who climb on their own way / Carry my image, too, into the breaking day."

51. "So may a friend be my interpreter. / And should he climb on his own way, / He'll carry his friend's image onward with him." Translation mine.

interpreting other will be well disposed toward him. The relation between reader and author is that of friend and friend. This supposition is dropped from the published version. The context of the other poems of "Scherz, List und Rache" makes clear that Nietzsche does not expect an audience necessarily friendly to him or to his project, especially since the material presented is not always easy to take. Poem 54, for example, admits that *The Gay Science* will need a reader with "strong teeth and a strong stomach" ("ein gut Gebiss und einen guten Magen") to consume what Nietzsche has to offer.

Even the unsympathetic reader, the one whom Nietzsche himself has put off with his "hardness" ("Härte") and willingness to step on others to reach the heights (poem 26), will be a better interpreter of Nietzsche than Nietzsche himself. There is a certain charming modesty about this, but we quickly realize that there is in fact not the slightest trace of self-deprecation in what Nietzsche is proposing. The protagonist of the poem may not be the author himself, but it does turn out to be his image (*Bild*). The goal of interpretation is to get the author's image (in both senses of "picture" and "trope") into a clearer light, and it is proposed that the reader is better equipped for that task than the author—even indeed when the reader is climbing along "his own way" and not necessarily Nietzsche's. Read my metaphors in whatever way you will, Nietzsche seems to be saying, so long as you eep reading them. What is closest to me, my image, will emerge into clarity in the process.

This notion that the reader can do the author's business while in fact attending strictly to his own is a particularly postmodern concept that goes somewhat, but not entirely, against the grain of the traditional imagery of reading. The idea is traditional in that it still assumes that the reader's role is to take over a burden the author is no longer in a position to assume, but it departs from the tradition in supposing that readerly independence, not subservience, will aid the transfer of the burden. In the Platonic formulation of the principal Western orthodoxy of reading, the author is understood as the parent of the text (*pater logou*), both progenitor of and absolute authority over his offspring; the reader is a kind of foster parent responsible to the wishes and intentions of the "father of the discourse," subservient to him in all matters pertaining to the welfare of the precious child. The goal of this fostering care could properly be described by Nietzsche's words, to carry the "image" of the author into the clear light of productive interpretation. This very traditional goal, however, is paradoxically alleged by Nietzsche to be most likely of attainment when the reader steadfastly pursues his or her own path without worrying about what path the author might have chosen.

This same idea is presented in the seventh poem, "Vademecum—Vadetecum":

> Es lockt dich meine Art und Sprach,
> Du folgest mir, du gehst mir nach?
> Geh nur dir selber treulich nach:—
> So folgst du mir—gemach! gemach![52]

The poem is concerned with "folgen" and "nachgehen" in their figurative senses of "comply with" and "inquire into" and thus once again with the issue of interpretation. Again the assertion is made that the proper method of inquiry into Nietzsche's writing is faithful investigation of the reader's self and that this act of self-examination will be the best way to imitate and obey (*folgen*) Nietzsche himself. This advice is at once both surprising and expected. It is very traditional in that it takes the Socratic position that the beginning of wisdom is self-knowledge, that to "follow" the philosopher is not so much to learn his doctrines as to obey the Delphic injunction to "know thyself." It is unexpected—and deliberately so—at the beginning of a volume so full of advice, warnings, precepts, and other forms of guidance. Nietzsche acknowledges that he is offering here a kind of guidebook, a vademecum for the philosophically inclined, but in the moment of acknowledging it he turns it against itself. The advice he gives here is that the best way of taking his advice is not to take anyone's advice but your own. Nietzsche evidently loved the logical involution implied by this game.

The gesture made by the text's rhetoric once again authorizes radical reinterpretation as the most valid mode of reading. We can read "vademecum" as "vadetecum" and vice versa, just as we could read "sich auslegen" as "sich hineinlegen" in poem 25. Nietzsche is showing us a method for rhetorical reading but at the same time urging that we must ourselves take up this tool and not simply wait for him to do it

---

52. "Lured by my style and tendency, / you follow and come after me? / Follow your own self faithfully— / take time—and thus you follow me."

for us. It is Nietzsche's version of the traditional invitation, *tolle, lege,* but with the notion of "reading" substantially revised.

Nietzsche is prepared to defend the value of incessant rereading even in the extreme case of rereading his own earlier readings. The thirty-sixth poem, "Juvenilia" ("Jugendschriften") exemplifies the process:

> Meiner Weisheit A und O
> Klang mir hier: was hört' ich doch!
> Jetzo klingt mir's nicht mehr so,
> Nur das ew'ge Ah! und Oh!
> Meiner Jugend hör ich noch.[53]

The commonplace German expression "das A und das O" ("the alpha and the omega") is regularly used to mean the sum total of something, even the "be-all and end-all." The clear implication of the poem is that the author did at one time think the sum total of his wisdom was something grand, all-inclusive, and definitive. That interpretation comes under scrutiny when a now somewhat older Nietzsche looks back at his early writing and finds it "nicht mehr so," no longer what he once thought it was. The text is the same, but its meaning has radically changed. That change is cleverly exemplified in the rereading of the poem's own initial text, the phrase "A und O," now revealed as the semiarticulate cries of one whose feelings are more powerful than his means to express them. The transformation of "A und O" into "Ah! und Oh!" involves a dramatic change of signification with no change at all in the (oral) signifier. The change in the graphic signifier (the addition of -*h!*) is the mark of an alteration in perspective that both does and does not change the nature of the material interpreted. One could argue equally persuasively that there is no difference between the signifiers *A* and *Ah!* or *O* and *Oh!* and that there is a huge difference; that is, one could take the point of view of a phonologically oriented linguist like Saussure or a graphically oriented grammatologist like Derrida. The crucial thing here—which a Saussurian would be as quick to see as a Derridean—is the interplay of sameness and difference, in which the phonological sameness stands as a figure for a persisting, invariable text and graphic difference for the highly mutable act of reading.

53. "My youthful wisdom's A and O / I heard again. What did I hear? / Words not of wisdom but of woe / Only the endless Ah and Oh / Of youth lies heavy in my ear."

The referential malleability of particular instances of discourse stands everywhere in these poems as a figure for the metaphoricity, and thus infinite interpretability, of all language, even of the whole world. Rhetorical reading becomes a method that retains the traditional aim of philosophy, to get to the bottom of things ("den Grund") but does not suppose that it can achieve that aim by means of research ("Forschung"):

> Ein Forscher ich? Oh spart diess Wort!—
> Ich bin nur *schwer*—so manche Pfund'!
> Ich falle, falle immerfort
> Und endlich auf den Grund![54]

Walter Kaufmann makes a noble try at translating Nietzsche's wordplay by rendering the title "Der Gründliche" as "The Thorough Who Get to the Bottom of Things," but even this laudable effort actually obscures the rhetoric of the original. The point of the poem is that one can be "gründlich" in the sense of getting to the bottom of things *without* being "gründlich" in the sense of "thorough" or "rigorous"— without, that is, being a "Forscher." The title is revealed by the poem to be readable as both ironic and not ironic, since the denial of "Gründlichkeit" as a method is shown to in no way prevent achievement of the "Grund," the bottom of things.

The process of falling to the philosophical ground is illustrated with particular consistency in the poems of "Scherz, List und Rache" but is an important strategy in all of Nietzsche's writing. It is essentially a strategy of rhetorical reading, and it is plainly visible in a number of aphorisms in the main body of *The Gay Science*. Here the prose format makes no special pretension to literariness, but what we might think of as literary methods (because they are rhetorical) can be found as readily as in the rhymes. Nietzsche proceeds as if everyday language were a joyous *Wissenschaft* whose power can be unlocked by an innovative act of reading.

Consider, for example, aphorism 371 ("We incomprehensible ones"), which depends on the interplay of "verwechseln," "wechseln", and "wachsen": those who are incomprehensible are "misidentified" ("verwechselt") precisely because "we ourselves keep growing

---

54. Poem 44. "A seeker, I? Oh, please be still! / I'm merely *heavy*—weigh many a pound. / I fall, and I keep falling till / At last I reach the ground."

[*wachsen*], keep changing [*wechseln*], we shed our old bark, we shed our skins every spring."[55] The phonological relationship between the German words for "misidentify," "change," and "grow" is not exploited here because of any supposedly genuine connection between language and something we might want to call reality; it is on the contrary an explicitly rhetorical device, a trick, a caprice. It is a way of acknowledging that Nietzsche's "truth" is no more exempt from contamination by metaphor than anyone else's. More than that, it announces that Nietzsche's method of philosophical discovery is a form of rhetorical *inventio* that is quite content to plunder the storehouse of available signifiers for all the ideas it will yield up.

The authorial persona reads the mother tongue as if he were a Cratylist and believed in some deep and essential connection between signifier and signified; as if, that is, the phonological similarity between "wachsen" and "wechseln" reflected a similarity existing at some "deeper" level. But the Cratylism of such passages has to be understood as nothing more than a heuristic device, since we know from numerous declarations on the subject ("On Truth and Lie" among them) that Nietzsche was as skeptical as could be about language as a repository of truth. The truth that Nietzsche proposes to have found here is one of his own manufacture, arrived at by attending scrupulously to the *surface* of the linguistic sign. He embraces the relationships among signifiers not because he believes they reflect the relationships obtaining among things in themselves, but because that is all he has to work with. Fancies like the elaborate discourse on *wachsen/wechseln* can only be understood as belonging to the dance of a "knower" engaged in preserving the universality of dreaming. It is one of Nietzsche's ways to be, like the Greeks, "superficial—*out of profundity*" ("oberflächlich—*aus Tiefe*").[56]

Nietzsche's inclination toward superficiality, his interest in exploiting the resources of language understood as surface, is matched by an equally strong urge toward depth. Being one of the "masters of ceremony of existence" requires something other than the kind of thoughtless assurance that goes with superficiality as we normally un-

55. "Das macht, wir selbst wachsen, wir wechseln fortwährend, wir stossen alte Rinden ab, wir häuten uns mit jedem Frühjahre noch."

56. From the close of the preface to the second edition (*Gay Science*, 38; *Kritische Gesamtausgabe*, 20).

derstand it. To be superficial out of profundity means to engage with the great sea of signifiers and to read it actively. You cannot be superficial in Nietzsche's sense by letting others read for you, by quietly accepting conventional interpretations as self-evidently correct. To let convention stand as truth—that is the surest way to be superficial out of superficiality. The great virtue of the artist/philosopher Nietzsche values so highly is that he is always active, always making his own readings, even rereading in a different way what he had read before.

"Right reading" is thus an act whereby a particular human will engages the great, endlessly figurative body of language and makes its own sense of it. "The will to power *interprets*," and as Stanley Corngold points out, the Nietzschean self is nowhere more clearly in evidence than in its efforts at reading, including especially its attempts to read the self.[57] Interpretation is the interaction between language, a system of tropes received essentially fully formed and belonging to the community, and the will, the individual human self that is for Nietzsche not only *a* "generative concept"[58] but *the* generative concept par excellence. Everything of intellectual value arises out of this interaction, including that most fundamental of philosophical goods, knowledge. We see Nietzsche working on just this problem—in a typically rhetorical way—in aphorism 355 of *The Gay Science*, where he seeks to explain "the origin of our concept of 'knowledge'":

> I take this explanation from the street. I heard one of the common people say, "he knew me right away." Then I asked myself: What is it that the common people take for knowledge? What do they want when they want "knowledge"? Nothing more than this: Something strange is reduced to something familiar. And we philosophers—have we really meant *more* than this when we have spoken of knowledge?[59]

How much this passage depends on the process of reading the German language is in part revealed by the text's lack of any point in the

---

57. See *The Will to Power*, ed. Walter Kaufmann (New York: Random House, 1968), 342; and Stanley Corngold, *The Fate of the Self* (New York: Columbia University Press, 1986), 126.

58. Corngold, *Fate of the Self*, 126.

59. "Ich nehme diese Erklärung von der Gasse; ich hörte Jemanden aus dem Volke sagen 'er hat mich erkannt'—: dabei fragte ich mich: was versteht eigentlich das Volk unter Erkenntniss? was will es, wenn es 'Erkenntniss' will? Nichts weiter als dies: etwas Fremdes soll auf etwas *Bekanntes* zurückgeführt werden. Und wir Philosophen—haben wir unter Erkenntniss eigentlich *mehr* verstanden?"

English translation. Kaufmann was forced to employ a series of foot-
notes to alert the reader to the play on various expressions formed out
of the verb *kennen,* but to a reader with no German the crux of the
matter would still remain mysterious. That crux is of course that what
is known (*Erkenntnis*) is, for a German-speaker, only a variation on
what is familiar (*das Bekannte*). In English, the relationship between
knowledge and familiarity is entirely semantic, but in German it is
phonological and morphological as well, suggesting a stronger and
deeper affiliation. The verb *erkennen,* out of which is formed the term
German philosophers use for "knowledge" (*Erkenntnis*), has in its everyday usage the sense of "recognize." The sentence Kaufmann translates as "he knew me right away" can also be rendered as "he recognized me," with the attendant connotation of perceived familiarity
(*recognize* is *re-cognize,* that is, *know again*). Nietzsche analyzes the sentence "er hat mich erkannt" as meaning the equivalent of something
like "er hat das Bekannte an mir gesehen," an analysis that is perfectly
reasonable for such a sentence spoken on the street. From there Nietzsche reasons that the people of the "Volk" understand knowledge to be
the rediscovery of something already known rather than the discovery
of "new" facts or relationships.

In his commentary on this passage, Kaufmann suggests that Nietzsche may have been thinking primarily of Hegel in suggesting that
philosophers have often considered knowledge in this same way. It is
just as likely, though, that he was thinking of Plato and the very
ancient tradition that all knowledge is in fact nothing more than a recognition or remembering (as in the famous geometry lesson in the
Meno).[60] The truth (Greek *aletheia*) is that which is "un-forgotten."
Nietzsche goes on to level a critique at such philosophers for thinking
that the discovery of the familiar is the acquisition of knowledge ("was
bekannt ist, ist erkannt"). The critique goes in a peculiarly Nietzschean
direction, however, because Nietzsche is not entirely sure that "knowledge," in the sense of a fundamental grasping of something, really
exists. The error of philosophers might lie not so much in taking up
the common people's notion of knowledge as familiarity as in refor-
mulating it in the high-sounding terms of epistemology.

Nietzsche understands "knowing" (*erkennen*) in a rather different
way: for him it means "to see as a problem" ("als Problem zu sehen"),

60. *Meno* 81e ff.

and that is hardest to do with something that is familiar.[61] *Erkennen* would thus be most difficult in the case of *das Bekannte,* the familiar. Nietzsche implies, though he does not explicitly say, that the philosopher's task must in part be to take what is familiar and see it as a problem. How does one do that? How does one "defamiliarize" the familiar? I borrow the language of Russian formalism here, not to imply any kinship between that movement and Nietzsche's work, but to suggest the fundamentally literary and rhetorical dimensions of the issue. The process of making the familiar problematic is precisely the process we have seen again and again in Nietzsche's practice of rhetorical rereading. What could be more familiar to us than the language of daily life, expressions like "er hat mich erkannt" or "Grund" or "das A und das O"? It takes a special sort of imagination to see these commonplaces as problematic, an imagination that Nietzsche understands as belonging to both the poet and the philosopher. The mainstream of the Western intellectual tradition has tended to view this verbal mode of imagination as exclusively literary, however, and to regard as unorthodox those philosophers like Heidegger (particularly of the post-*Kehre* years), Derrida, and Nietzsche himself who embrace it openly. But philosophy, like literature, may not be in a position to free itself from the verbal imagination without suffering a crippling impoverishment. Nietzsche indicates exactly what form that impoverishment can take: the limitation of philosophical knowledge to a set of transformations of the unfamiliar into the familiar. Such a limitation, were it successful, would leave entirely to literature the most difficult and perhaps the most important intellectual task, that of seeing the familiar as a problem.

61. Aphorism 355. "Das Bekannte ist das Gewohnte; und das Gewohnte ist am schwersten zu 'erkennen,' das heisst als Problem zu sehen, das heisst als fremd, als fern, als 'ausser uns' zu sehn."

6 | *The Rhetoric of Ethical Engagement*

If rhetoric always allows for the possibility of a new reading under a new mode of interpretation, what happens to standards of proper conduct that are disseminated through discourse? Obviously one fundamental result of rhetorical reading will be to destabilize the interpretation of moral absolutes. As we have seen in the previous two chapters, the destabilizing power of rhetoric can work either to create or to eliminate problems. We will see in this chapter how rhetoric can work in similar ways to produce or solve moral difficulties as well.

Although the moral status of rhetorical discourse is an interesting and important issue, it is by no means the sole or even the principal moral topic treated by rhetorical fictions. No practitioner of rhetorical construction interested in ethical issues could fail to be concerned also with the ethics of his or her own practice, but it will not do to look only in the mirror. In the works of Flannery O'Connor, Hans Christian Andersen, and Giovanni Boccaccio discussed below, we will find the ethical status of rhetoric thematized to some extent, it is true: one could argue that "The River," "The Shadow," and the *Decameron* are all at least in part about the moral effects of rhetoricity itself. But these fictions are about other matters as well, moral issues of perhaps wider general interest. They are particularly concerned with the effect of intention on the moral quality of an action. It turns out that the resources of rhetorical construction can be applied with great effect to the presentation of this kind of ethical problem.

Boccaccio's *Decameron* shows its ethical concerns most clearly in the most unlikely place, the story of Alibech and Rustico who zealously "put the devil back into hell." This is certainly the most notorious tale among the hundred, the one most likely to bring down the wrath of those who consider themselves defenders of public morals. But the apparently immoral content proves to be the vehicle for a subtle consideration of the ethics of intention. The moral quality of what Alibech and Rustico do is different for each of them, even though they would seem to be engaging in the very same improper (if also very entertaining) behavior. And the moral content of his story, Boccaccio tells us, depends far more upon the quality of our reading than on the bare facts it relates.

Hans Christian Andersen also demonstrates a concern for the ethical quality of literature, though he appears far less optimistic than Boccaccio about the reader's ability to engage in therapeutic acts of interpretation. Andersen's story "The Shadow" puts into question the assumption that poetry is noble and uplifting, even when it is unquestionably engaged in seeking out and proclaiming the truth. Seeking the truth may be praiseworthy when it is carried out by philosophers, scientists, and poets who are themselves sensitive to ethical issues. When they are not —as the title character in "The Shadow" is not—poetic or philosophical truth-telling can be morally indistinguishable from tattling. The shadowy side of literature, Andersen suggests, is as inevitable as shadows in sunlight. The stronger the light and the more powerful the search for truth, the more dangerous can be the misapplication of the truth's discovery.

Flannery O'Connor looks at the ethics of rhetorical reading in a situation where the stakes are perhaps the highest possible. Not only is a human life at risk, but it is the life of a very young child. That child's life, including perhaps even his chance at eternal life, stands in the balance between two modes of reading.

The Rhetoric of Life and Death:
Flannery O'Connor's "The River"

Flannery O'Connor's story "The River," first published in 1955 as part of the collection *A Good Man Is Hard to Find*, has received less attention than many of her other works of fiction.[1] It amply rewards

1. An exception is the stimulating discussion of "The River" in Robert Magliola, *Derrida on the Mend* (West Lafayette, Ind.: Purdue University Press, 1984), 57-83.

careful reading, however, and it is arguably one of the most elegant constructions of the verbal imagination to be written since the death of Franz Kafka. The opening of the narrative is unprepossessing:

> The child stood glum and limp in the middle of the dark living room while his father pulled him into a plaid coat. His right arm was hung in the sleeve but the father buttoned the coat anyway and pushed him forward toward a pale spotted hand that stuck through the half-open door.
> "He ain't fixed right," a loud voice said from the hall.
> "Well then for Christ's sake fix him," the father muttered. (P. 144)[2]

There is nothing here to grab our attention in the manner of, say, the first sentence of "The Metamorphosis," with its arresting announcement of Gregor's transformation. Indeed, one could suppose that there is very little happening between these persons—a father, a child, a voice connected to a pale spotted hand—and that the reader is being introduced to a set of events on the whole trivial, everyday, and lacking in emotional or intellectual complexity. Such a supposition would be incorrect, though not mistaken. It would be incorrect because the rest of the story makes clear that a very complex and important action is initiated here. But it would not be mistaken, because there is no way for the reader to know on first reading, or even to suspect, that phrases like "He ain't fixed right" and "for Christ's sake fix him," which we interpret literally or figuratively according to well-worn conventions, carry in an unconventional literal or figurative reading the program of the plot. Nor could such a reader know that this very possibility of substituting an unexpectedly literal or figurative reading for the "normal" one is the engine that drives the action. It is a story that forces us to reexamine our mode of reading and, in many cases, casts doubt on our usual inattention to the literal level.

The narrator adopts a perspective that is in general far more accepting of the surface appearance of things than is that of the ordinary "informed" reader[3]—that is, a reader interpreting according to the

---

2. I cite "The River" from *Three by Flannery O'Connor* (New York: Signet [NAL], n.d.). Page numbers in the text refer to this edition.

3. This is Stanley Fish's term, first proposed in "Literature in the Reader: Affective Stylistics," 1970; reprinted in *Is There a Text in This Class?* (Cambridge: Harvard University Press, 1980), 22–67.

norms of our community. In the opening sentence, for example, the narrator adopts a point of view, a position for his or her imaginary eye, that is inside the room with the father and child. This imaginary eye cannot see what is out in the hall and therefore reports only the presence of "a pale spotted hand" in its field of vision. The narrator does not jump to the obvious conclusion that there is a person in the hall, not even when the imaginary ear associated with the imaginary eye hears "a loud voice" uttering certain words. The narrator is, to put it bluntly, very literal-minded about these matters. When we consider the moral content of what is happening, however, it is evident that the narrator is by no means so accepting. The addition of the modifier "anyway" to the report of the father's buttoning the child's coat suggests a disapproving attitude. Even the verbs "pulled" and "pushed" have a certain evaluative force in that they imply that the father is treating the child more like an object than a person. Even in these first few lines, we get the impression that the father is not much concerned about his child and that the narrator has a distaste for such fathers.

This combination of a certain literal-mindedness and a special ethical standpoint helps account for the particular rhetorical perspective that informs "The River" and indeed much of O'Connor's other fiction. Once we have read the entire story we have an even stronger sense of that perspective, and we are able to adjust to the unusual mode of reading that the narrator demands. We realize that "He ain't fixed right" is as much a figure, and thus a moral condemnation, as it is a literal description of the need to adjust the child's sleeve. We also realize that the father's thoughtless oath "for Christ's sake" is intended—by the narrator, not by him—to be taken absolutely literally: the child ought to be "fixed," his situation in life remedied, for the sake of Christ and what Christ stands for.

The program for the entire story will fit comfortably in this first brief exchange between the father, Mr. Ashfield, and the "voice," Mrs. Connin. All the important issues that the narrative will explore are present in this brief rhetorical moment. At issue is the need for little Harry Ashfield's situation to be fixed in a way that is in keeping with the example and teaching of Christ. This constitutes a kind of moral imperative that the reader is made aware of from the very first lines of the story. At the same time, the story both presents and represents a fundamental problem in carrying out this moral imperative: does "fixing" someone "for Christ's sake" come about through a literal or a figurative reading of the language of Christ and his ministers and evangelists? Further, can we understand someone as being fixed for Christ's sake only by a figurative reinterpretation of the literal facts the world presents to us, or are those literal facts themselves the structure of a process of repair in the spirit of Christ's sacrifice?

Over and over again the reader of "The River" is forced to rethink the relation between tenor and vehicle in the story's figurative language. In a tale so abounding in images as this one, the reading process becomes an almost continuous process of reassessment. The most casually uttered phrases resound with meanings very different from their conventional, and usually intended, significance. When Mrs. Connin asks why Mrs. Ashfield is sick and in need of an ice pack, Mr. Ashfield replies, "We don't know" (p. 145). The reader has every reason to think that, since it is Sunday morning and the Ashfields are regular party givers, Mrs. Ashfield has a hangover and Mr. Ashfield knows it. His answer is meant only to avoid having to discuss with the baby-sitter the reason for his wife's condition. From the ethical perspective the narrator has taken, however, there is reason to think that the Ashfields indeed do not know what is the "trouble" that afflicts them, since from that perspective the real trouble is not simply a hangover but an entire mode of living. Again, when little Harry's father sends him off with another carelessly uttered phrase, "Good-by, old man" (p. 145), he means only to affect a kind of sham comradeship with his son. The reader who knows the story, though, knows that in a very real sense the child is old beyond his years, having learned of necessity many of the ways of the wicked adult world. Furthermore, although the text explains that the child is only "four or five" years old, it also compares him to "an old sheep waiting to be let out" (p. 145). The narrator and Mr. Ashfield agree, then, on the appropriateness of calling Harry "old," but they would have us read the adjective in very different ways.

The narrator is very skillful in subtly directing the reader's perspective; that is, in employing the "rhetoric of fiction" in Wayne Booth's sense.[4] This gentle manipulation has as its goal a significant restructuring of our process of reading in a direction one might describe as Socratic. The point is not to convince readers to accept a particular

4. I refer of course to the main argument of Booth's *The Rhetoric of Fiction* (Chicago: University of Chicago Press, 1961).

proposition as true but rather to force them to question their own assumptions. An example of this sort of Socratic rhetoric involves the matter of the child's name. When Mrs. Connin asks him his name, Harry tells her it is "Bevel," a name he had just heard her mention as belonging to a preacher she wants to visit. Although O'Connor's narrator knows, and tells us, that the child's real name is Harry Ashfield, the new designation is accepted instantly and permanently. Even after Mrs. Connin is set straight by the boy's mother ("'His name is Harry,'" she said from the sofa. 'Whoever heard of anybody named Bevel?'" [p. 155]), the narrator goes right on referring to him as Bevel. What this suggests, of course, is that the narrator for some reason prefers "Bevel" to "Harry," apparently believing that "Bevel" is somehow a more proper name. The reader, noting both the explicit correctness of the name "Harry" and the narrator's quiet persistence in using "Bevel," is forced to wonder what grounds there might be for preferring the latter. The story provides one reason, in that the visit to the Reverend Bevel Summers results in the child's being baptized under the name Bevel. The narrator evidently feels that a person's name "in Christ"— even a name taken thoughtlessly—is a more fitting designation than that given on the birth certificate. The reader is also brought to wonder if the meaning of the common English word "bevel" is not indeed applicable to this child and his situation. A bevel is not straight, and little Harry is not straight in several ways. He does not tell the simple truth (as when he lies about his name), and he steals. The instrument called a "bevel" is adjustable, having an arm that can move into a wide range of positions; this "Bevel" needs to be adjustable as well, to make his way in worlds as different as those of his worldly, sophisticated, and dissolute parents and of the poor, uneducated, and pious Mrs. Connin. Because of this suggestion of a motivation for names ("Ashfield" and "Connin" are clearly also significant), the reader is again forced to reexamine the process of reading. The narrator seems to be both a Christian and a Cratylist, to use Gérard Genette's term,[5] while the Ashfields are secular Hermogenists. Since the Ashfields' moral position is weak, given our well-orchestrated disapproval of their treatment of their son, the Cratylist position gains credibility.

5. See "Valéry and the Poetics of Language," in *Textual Strategies*, ed. Josué V. Harari (Ithaca: Cornell University Press, 1979), 359–73.

This suggestion of a "fitness of signs," of a doctrine like the medieval "nomina sunt consequentia rerum," brings with it a reevaluation of the relation between literal and figurative. If a name adopted as casually as Harry adopts "Bevel" can be understood as determined by the facts of the world, then indeed all casual utterances might be so determined and might demand to be interrogated for meaning on a literal or figurative level that we would ordinarily dismiss. All the story's language, whether that of the characters or that of the narrator, makes such demands, and there is no way to be certain that, no matter how careful or attentive our first reading, one reading will be enough.

Another aspect of O'Connor's rhetoric of fiction is the way she coaxes the reader to reread certain phrases by repeating them several times. At her first appearance, for example, Mrs. Connin is described as "a speckled skeleton in a long pea-green coat and a felt helmet" (p. 144). To call someone a skeleton is common language for saying a person is very thin, and we suppose that this, and not much more, is what the narrator intends here. When a short time later we are told that, in her sleep, she "began to whistle and blow like a musical skeleton" (p. 146), the image must seem a bit more sinister. It is presented this time in the context of describing Mrs. Connin's mouth, in which there were "a few long scattered teeth" (p. 146), and is closer now to a more concrete figure of a death's-head. The trope now seems to have less to do with the person of Mrs. Connin, to which it is still attached, than with some other ominous feature of the story. When, a little later, the narrator says that the row of people walking to the river "looked like the skeleton of an old boat with two pointed ends, sailing slowly on the edge of the highway" (p. 149), the metaphor has become almost wholly detached from the figure of Mrs. Connin: she is only one of the people in the group, one of the "pointed ends" of the skeleton. The vehicle has almost come apart from the tenor with which the reader has associated it. This word "skeleton" is not just a colorful token standing for Mrs. Connin; it evidently has a much wider area of meaning, which it is our work as readers to discover. The closeness of death hovers not just about Mrs. Connin, we must suppose, but over all those walking along the highway to the river, including little Harry Ashfield.

The narrator's language is vivid and packed with details, but its figures do not necessarily work in the direction of helping us to visualize or "feel part of" the narrated action. Often, rather than making a scene more "real," the language of the storyteller tends to draw attention to itself and its artifice. A picture on a wall in Mrs. Connin's house displays "a man whose eyebrows dashed out of two bushes of hair and clashed in a heap on the bridge of his nose; the rest of his face stuck out like a bare cliff to fall from" (p. 147). The violence of the vehicle goes far beyond what we might understand as required by the tenor, which we learn is none other than Mr. Connin. Is Mr. Connin a violent man? We do not know; in fact, this description of his picture and Mrs. Connin's explanation that it "don't favor him any more" is everything we learn about him. Although the description of Mr. Connin conveys great danger, it is hard to identify the locus of that danger as either the man or his photograph. But a world in which a man's face may be described as "a bare cliff to fall from" must be a very dangerous place, no matter what the character of the man. Since the source of the violence of this discourse cannot be readily found in the subject of the discourse, it must be somewhere else; and if it is elsewhere, it must be powerful indeed to infect this apparently innocent description of a passive object.

Part of the danger of the world for Bevel/Harry Ashfield lies in the complicated relation of signifiers to signifieds. The child finds that he needs to intepret various sorts of signs but that the rules for making the needed interpretations are extremely difficult to pin down. The difficulty is brought home to him particularly when the Connin children offer to show him some pigs:

> Bevel had never seen a real pig but he had seen a pig in a book and knew they were small fat pink animals with curly tails and round grinning faces and bow ties. He leaned forward and pulled eagerly at the board.
>
> "Pull harder," the littlest boy said. "It's nice and rotten. Just life out thet nail [*sic*]."
>
> He eased a long reddish nail out of the soft wood.
>
> "Now you can lift up the board and put you face to the . . . " a quiet voice began.
>
> He had already done it and another face, gray, wet and sour, was pushing into his, knocking him down and back as it scraped out under the plank. Something snorted over him and charged back again, rolling him over and pushing him up from behind and then sending him forward, screaming through the yellow field, while it bounded behind. (P. 148)

The notion of "pig" undergoes a radical revision in the child's mind. Henceforth all pigs will be associated with this one and with the terrifying experience it inflicts on him. The newly discovered truth does not, however, solve all future problems connected with the interpretation of pigs. When Mrs. Connin shows him a book called *The Life of Jesus Christ for Readers under Twelve,* he sees a picture of "the carpenter driving a crowd of pigs out of a man. They were real pigs, gray and sour-looking, and Mrs. Connin said Jesus had driven them all out of this one man" (p. 150). In spite of the reassuring thought that these, at least, are "real pigs," their reality testifying to the truth of the representation of which they are a part, one cannot help but find in this incident a paradigm of misreading. First of all, Mrs. Connin has completely misunderstood either the picture or the incident in Mark, chapter 5, that it depicts, or both, since it is not pigs that are driven out of the man but "foul spirits" that take up residence in a nearby drove of pigs. Or perhaps she has not. Because we cannot discount the possibility that this passage is written in the "style indirect libre" and that the perceptions reported are all those of the child, perhaps it is he who misunderstands her explanation. In either case, the "reality" of these gray, sour-looking pigs vouches for the authenticity of an understanding that is, from the perspective of the evangelist at any rate, completely mistaken. It is certain that somebody has got something wrong here, but that somebody might include us. The passage not only introduces the topic of misreading, it implicates the reader in its own problematic. Any superiority we feel toward "Bevel" or Mrs. Connin ought not to survive the reading of this paragraph.

We must also entertain the possibility that the "real" story of the pigs from Mark, which appears here only in mangled form, might have greater relevance to the story than simply to put into question what it is that constitutes a "real" pig. The New Testament narrative describes a process whereby something evil is transferred from a human being into a group of pigs. It is this very process that "The River" has presented in the scene just discussed, though here the element of plurality is transferred from the pigs to the human beings. The Connin children's desire to do some physical harm to "Bevel" finds its expression in the action of the pig. The potential victim somehow senses the threat to him on the way to the hog pen: "Once he had been beaten up in the park by some strange boys when his sitter forgot him, but he hadn't known anything was going to happen until it was over" (pp.

147-48). The Connin boys would like to beat him up too, but they are prepared to use indirect means to satisfy the demon within them. When the expected and wished-for catastrophe takes place, the foul spirit in the boys is at least temporarily subdued: "Their stern faces didn't brighten any but they seemed to become less taut, as if some great need had been partly satisfied" (p. 148).

When we read the pig incident in "The River" in conjunction with the account of the exorcism in Mark, we realize that it is possible, particularly for a speaker of English, to see in the pigs a rhetorical equivalent of "foul spirits"—that is, of "swinish" behavior. O'Connor's story transforms the swinishness of the Connin boys into an actual swine, whose violent act substitutes for and satisfies their swinish desires. In the context of her sons' behavior, then, Mrs. Connin's naive misinterpretation of the literal meaning of the biblical account (or that of "Bevel") seems indistinguishable from a sophisticated and correct figurative reading. If the man from Gerasa's possession by demons is at all like the swinishness of the Connin boys (and the text suggests by juxtaposition that it must be), then it would be figuratively accurate to say that what Jesus was doing in the picture was "driving a crowd of pigs out of a man." This understanding of Mark, chapter 5, is literally naive and figuratively sophisticated at the same time, and it is so no matter what we suppose Mrs. Connin's intention to be and no matter if we suppose that this (mis)reading is the child's.

Intended meaning, whether literal of figurative, and narrative meaning often diverge dramatically in "The River." I have already alluded to Mr. Ashfield's "for Christ's sake" in the story's opening lines, but there are other, even more ironic examples. When the Ashfields discover the book (*The Life of Jesus Christ for Readers under Twelve*) that Harry has stolen, one of their guests examines it and, finding that it was published in 1832, declares, "That's valuable" (p. 156). The irony is of course that this man has absolutely no interest in what makes this book valuable for Christians (though he would surely describe himself as a Christian if pressed), or even in what makes it valuable for Harry. For him it is valuable only in that it is worth a certain amount of money. His statement, "That's valuable," is nevertheless correct in both senses. For Mrs. Connin, we have learned, the book is valuable because "every word of it [is] the gospel truth" (p. 149)—again, a statement whose truth exceeds or escapes the intention of the speaker. In this case we are amused, because Mrs. Connin is referring to the one object of which her description could be said to be literally correct, though we know that she is employing the word "gospel" as a figure. The further we read in O'Connor's story, the more we realize that "jokes" of this kind are not only jokes; they are a paradigmatic case of Goethe's "ernsthafte Witze" ("serious jokes").

Since very often the difference between a joke and a serious statement is the difference between a literal and a figurative intention, the issue of what is and is not a joke lies at the heart of the story's concern. Little Harry Ashfield has as much difficulty distinguishing "jokes" from straight discourse as he has determining what are "real" pigs. He knows enough to know that there are such things as jokes and that such forms of discourse require special interpretation:

> He had found out already this morning that he had been made by a carpenter named Jesus Christ. Before he had thought it had been a doctor named Sladewall, a fat man with a yellow mustache who gave him shots and thought his name was Herbert, but this must have been a joke. They joked a lot where he lived. If he had thought about it before, he would have thought Jesus Christ was a word like "oh" or "damn" or "God," or maybe somebody who had cheated them out of something sometime. (P. 149)

The reader knows enough about the Ashfields to know that Harry has made no mistake: at his house "Jesus Christ" is a word exactly like "damn" and never a reference to Harry's creator, always a figure of speech akin to a joke and never a literal reference. He is also correct in supposing that the story of his being made by Dr. Sladewall is a joke in the sense of being a euphemistic figure for his actual secular origin. His only mistake is supposing that if the one explanation was a figure, the other must not be one.

This discovery that not everyone "jokes" in the way his parents and their friends do paves the way for another crucial perception he has later, at the healing conducted by the Reverend Bevel Summers. At first he supposes that the whole gathering at the river is some kind of game, which he is willing to play along with:

> Bevel rolled his eyes in a comical way and thrust his face forward, close to the preacher's. "My name is Bevvvuuuuul," he said in a loud deep voice and let the tip of his tongue slide across his mouth.
> The preacher didn't smile. His boy face was rigid and his narrow gray

eyes reflected the almost colorless sky. . . . The grin had already disap-
peared from his face. He had the sudden feeling that this was not a joke.
Where he lived everything was a joke. From the preacher's face, he knew
immediately that nothing the preacher said or did was a joke. (P. 153)

In the child's mind, the alternative to "joke" is "literal truth," and he
thenceforth reads the preacher's words as literally as he is able. The
Reverend promises that, after he is baptized, the child will "go to the
Kingdom of Christ. You'll be washed in the river of suffering, son,
and you'll go by the deep river of life." The preacher asks the boy if he
wants these things. "'Yes,' the child said, and thought, I won't go back
to the apartment then, I'll go under the river" (p. 154). As if to authorize this literal reading of the figure of the river, the preacher indeed
"plunged his head into the water," and after holding it there for long
enough to say the words of baptism, he pulls the shocked child out and
tells him that now he "counts," whereas he "didn't even count before"
(p. 154).

Once again, the Reverend Summers has told a truth beyond his
intention. The child Bevel surely does not understand the spiritual
sense in which he now "counts" according to the Christian system of
belief, but he has experienced vividly the sort of "not counting" that
comes from not being valued by one's parents. Back home after his
baptism, after the Ashfields have learned that their son was baptized
and that the Reverend Summers prayed that Mrs. Ashfield be cured of
her "affliction," Harry learns again where he stands in his parents'
estimation. His mother is concerned over what her son might have said
about her and asks him directly, "What lies have you been telling
today, honey?" (p. 156). Of course, it is not any lies he may have told
that worry her; it is the truth about her hangover that upsets her. Her
word "lies" does not mean actual lies; it is a "joke," in the child's
terms, and it means something like "unflattering truth." There is no
concern or even interest expressed about what has happened to Harry.
All his mother cares about is the supposed affront to her personal
dignity. The distance between mother and child is frighteningly wide,
and the child perceives it in terms of his experience of baptism: "He
shut his eyes and heard her voice from a long way away, as if he were
under the river and she on top of it" (p. 156). The distance from above
the river to underneath it is the distance between a place where a child
christened "Bevel" does not count and one where he does.

But this is a figure. It is pretend, and the child is able to act out the pretense successfully for a short period as he drops off to sleep. When he gets up the next morning, though, to an apartment that is still dark even though "he didn't wake up early," circumstances bring home to him that he still dwells in a place where he does not count. His parents are still asleep; no one gets up to dress him or feed him. He has to forage about the apartment for food, settling on "two crackers spread with anchovy paste that he found on the coffee table . . . [and] some ginger ale left in a bottle" (p. 157). It is not until he notices that his shoes are still wet that he remembers the river and "all of a sudden . . . knew what he wanted to do" (p. 157). He gets a streetcar token and "half a package of Life Savers" from his mother's purse and leaves for the river (p. 158).

He is taking figurative Life Savers to a real body of water that is, from Bevel Summers's point of view, the figure of genuine salvation. But Bevel/Harry's point of view now matches so closely that of Bevel Summers that they are no more different than is a word meant figuratively from one meant literally. The form of the narration brings this home to us already during the baptism scene, in which the name Bevel is always used to refer to the child (whose name, of course, is not "really" Bevel) and never to the preacher. Sometimes the reader has to pause to make sure what the reference is. But what is the difference between "Bevel" and Bevel? Perhaps everything and perhaps nothing. The child assumes, perhaps childishly, that words which are not "jokes" say what they mean and that the promise given by the very earnest Bevel Summers is one that can be cashed in: "He intended not to fool with preachers any more but to baptize himself and to keep on going this time until he found the Kingdom of Christ in the river" (p. 159).

In the terms in which the story is delivered to us, we cannot be sure he does not find it. It is not necessary to know Flannery O'Connor's commitment to the Catholic faith to realize that the narrative is informed by a deeply Christian perspective that embraces the notion of the kingdom of Christ and its availability to such souls as Harry Ashfield's. It does not matter that the child has mistaken the figurative for the literal: it is a mistake that God can easily make good. As Boccaccio suggests in the *Decameron*, an omniscient and omnipotent God attends to the intentions of the faithful even in their moments of error. If God can accept prayers made in the name of a saint who was in fact no saint at all,[6] then he can also accept into his kingdom one who has entered through a false door. A God who has announced himself ready to "fix" people "for Christ's sake" would surely not carp over the distinction between the literal and the figurative. It is clear enough what the child wants and what he is fleeing from. The final sentences of the story make use of the physical resemblance between the ironically named Mr. Paradise and the pig who chased "Bevel" at the Connins to bring the point home: when Mr. Paradise tries to rescue him, the boy feels pursued by something malevolent. "Then he heard a shout and turned his head and saw something like a giant pig bounding after him" (p. 159). Mr. Paradise, the unbeliever who mocked the Reverend Summers and his "healing," represents a world of "foul spirits" that the child wants to escape. The attempts to rescue Harry are the very thing that allow him to drown, since at first the "River wouldn't have him." Only his fear of the pursuing "pig" spurs him on to push himself under again, "and this time, the waiting current caught him like a long gentle hand and pulled him swiftly forward and down" (p. 159).

No reader, however, even the most devout believer, can read the ending of this story and feel unalloyed joy at the outcome. Read literally, "The River" is a wrenchingly sad tale of neglect, overzealous piety, misdirected rhetoric, and misunderstanding. Much as we might detest the Ashfields for their selfishness and mistreatment of their child, the alternative offered here—death by drowning—hardly seems better. Even if we share the faith of Mrs. Connin, it is hard to find this "skeleton in a helmet" a sympathetic and credible witness to the benefits of faith. The Reverend Bevel Summers, for all his rhetorical skill, is not the most effective minister of the Word we have ever heard. And, for all his impiety and for all he looks like a pig, or a boulder, or "some ancient water monster" (p. 159), Mr. Paradise seems of all the characters in the story the one most genuinely concerned about the child's welfare. He, at least, tries to save him, while Mrs. Connin and the Reverend Summers have been single-mindedly concerned with "saving" him.

As the narrative strategy adopted by "The River" demonstrates, it is sometimes necessary to read literally and figuratively at the same time. Sometimes "for Christ's sake" is both an empty imprecation and a powerful allusion to the sacrifice of Jesus. Sometimes a pig is just a pig and at the same time the figure of a foul spirit. And sometimes it would

6. See the section on Boccaccio below in this chapter.

be best if a child could be saved as well as "saved." The religious point
of view that directs the narration should not be understood narrowly as
the simple advocacy of orthodoxy. We do not read better by simply
taking figures literally, as Harry Ashfield does. If the protagonist of
"The River" were an adult—or even an adolescent—instead of a small
child, we would in all likelihood consider the effort to find Christ's
kingdom beneath an earthly river a theological as well as a hermeneutic
error. "Bevel" is not guilty of the sin of suicide only because he does
not know what he is doing. The Christian perspective elaborated here
arises out of nothing so simple as the rejection of this life in favor of the
next.

O'Connor points the way toward a complex Christian hermeneutic
that has far more in common with the great verbal and theological
sophistication of Dante than with the simple evangelical Protestantism
of Bevel Summers. Dante elaborates in his *Commedia* a view of reading
that points toward God as the ultimate unifying hermeneutic intelligence. The earthly reader sees things broken up into pieces (as literal
and figurative, for example) that God sees as a great unity. We on earth
look at "scattered pages" ("pagine sparse") while the divine intelligence
sees a coherent book.[7] The reverent reader of O'Connor's fiction
would see in "The River" certainly not an occasion to shout "Hallelu-
jah" but rather the spur to consider the limitations of human reading.
The attentive secular reader will discover, analogously, a sober, intellectually and morally complex examination of the problem of interpretation.

What is central for my purpose is the way this story's plot is generated. The rhetorical moment—for reader as for protagonist—wherein
two conflicting alternative understandings of the same utterance confront each other opens up the space in which the story moves. If there
were no difference between saving and "saving," between what is done
for Christ's sake and "for Christ's sake," between pigs and "pigs,"
between fixing someone and "fixing" someone (as in "I'll fix you"),
this story would not exist. It is not style but plot itself that arises out of
rhetoric. There is a tale to be told here only because language pushes us
along a river that seems to divide with no clear indication of which
branch one ought to take. There is a narrative and an ethical space
created in the area between the two branches (between the river and the

7. On "pagine sparse," see Susan Noakes, "Dante's *Vista Nova: Paradiso* xxxiii,
136," *Quaderni d'Italianistica* 5, no. 2, (1984): 151–75.

"river," one might say) that indeed exists only because it is marked out by the two choices. The mapping of this imaginary land between the rivers is the particular task of rhetorical construction.

As O'Connor presents matters in her story, the uncertain moral status of a series of acts including the Reverend Summers's preaching and baptizing, Bevel's suicide, and Mr. Paradise's attempt to save the drowning boy is bound up with the kind of uncertainty faced in reading rhetorical discourse. The story is memorable because it questions the morality of acts whose moral character might not otherwise be open to question by forcing the reader to compare in each case the intention of an action with its effect. Both Reverend Summers, who puts Bevel into the river, and Mr. Paradise, who tries to pull him out, unquestionably intend to do the child good. But are the effects of their actions really beneficial? The rhetoricity of expressions like "fix him" or "save a person" mirrors exactly this moral undecidability. We cannot tell whether figurative "saving" (which the Reverend wants) is what Harry Ashfield needs, or if it is not rather physical saving (which Mr. Paradise wants). Our inability to decide at the story's conclusion whether good or ill has come to the boy finds its perfect expression in the difficulty we have in distinguishing between saving and "saving."

A story like O'Connor's "The River" makes eloquently clear that, while the issues it deals with arise out of language and the interpretation of language, the matters at stake are of enormous consequence in the world of our experience. Matters of rhetoric are intimately bound up with morals, even with matters of life and death (and of "life" and "death") for Harry Ashfield. Anyone who believes that rhetoric is empty and ineffectual because it is only words ("That's nothing but rhetoric!") should be required to study the case of the little boy called "Bevel."

The Shady Character of Literature:
H. C. Andersen's "The Shadow"

Among the many variations on the theme of "saving" and losing, one that enjoyed a great and lasting popularity during the nineteenth century was Adalbert von Chamisso's tale of the man who sold his shadow, *Peter Schlemihls wundersame Geschichte* (1814). The story was quickly translated into all the principal languages of Europe and became an instant classic. It was so well known in the English-speaking world that Hawthorne could mention the character Schlemihl in "The Intelligence Office" in 1844 (in a passage cited above in chapter 3) in the secure knowledge that virtually all his readers would recognize the reference. The name "Peter Schlemihl" became synonymous with the story's basic concept, so that it was nearly impossible to mention the notion of a story about a shadow without invoking the name of Chamisso's hero. It is a little surprising, then, that Hans Christian Andersen undertook in 1847 to write his own story about a man who parts company with his shadow.

Andersen knew very well that he was taking on a literary task that many of his readers would find, at best, curious. Even the "learned man," Andersen's central character, displays some embarrassment:

> It did annoy him, but not so much because his shadow was gone, as because he knew that there was a story about a man without a shadow which everyone in the cold countries knew; and if the learned man went there and told them his own story they would say he was merely imitating the other, and that he had no business to do. So he determined to say nothing at all about it, which was very sensible of him.[8]

The language used to convey the notion of "imitating" ("han gik og lignede efter"), as well as the mention of imitation itself, proposes the disquieting possibility that this story, "The Shadow" ("Skyggen"), is indeed the shadow of another story. The learned man's solution to his problem, one that the narrator declares to be reasonable, is to abstain altogether from telling the story. The shadow of the story of Peter Schlemihl would thus ensure its safety by not being told, by disappearing, as the learned man's shadow had just done.

The parallel between the fate of the story "The Shadow" and the fate of the shadow in the story thus introduced might prompt the reader to consider the rhetorical complexity of the word "skygge" every time it

---

8. I cite Andersen in English from Hans Andersen, *Forty-two Stories*, trans. M. R. James (London: Faber and Faber, 1930), and in Danish from H. C. Andersen, *Eventyr og Historier*, ed. Villy Sørensen (Copenhagen: Gyldendal, 1965). This passage is from *Stories*, 236; *Eventyr*, 185. "Og det aergrede ham, men ikke saa meget fordi at Skyggen var borte, men fordi han vidste, at der var en Historie til om en Mand uden Skygge, den kjendte jo alle Folk hjemme i de kolde Lande, og kom nu den laerde Mand der og fortalte sin, saa vilde de sige, at han gik og lignede efter, og det behøvede han ikke. Han vilde derfor slet ikke tale derom, og det var fornuftigt taenkt."

appears in the narrative from then on. Does it refer to the learned man's shadow or to the story in which the shadow figures? Such elaborate reflexive play is not to be casually ruled out here simply because Andersen presents his "eventyr" in the conventional guise of a naive fairy tale, or because the narrator occasionally adopts the pose of speaking to an audience of children (as in the opening sentences). The literary sophistication of these tales has long since been recognized. We might also want to remember that Andersen reports starting work on this story when he was staying in Naples, himself a "learned man" sojourning in one of the "hot countries." Since the learned man is elsewhere described as one who "wrote books about what there was of truth and goodness and beauty in the world,"[9] there can be little doubt that the learned man is a textual double of the author, already involved from the outset in a play of reflection.

When the scholar first discovers his loss, he cries out, "I haven't got any shadow!"[10] It is in the very next sentence, already quoted above, that he renounces the telling of his tale lest his countrymen understand it as an imitation of Chamisso's story. The scholar's cry demands to be read rhetorically, therefore, as the expression of dismay at the prospect of the loss of both the shadow and "The Shadow." His dismay is misplaced, as we might have suspected: his story is not so much lost as not yet begun, and the shadow proves itself to be—in one sense at least—replaceable.

The way the writer loses his shadow is rather different from the way Peter Schlemihl disposes of his. In Andersen's story the scholar finds himself particularly curious about the dwelling opposite his own. He cannot see inside it, but one night "he thought there was a marvelous light coming from the balcony opposite. All the flowers were shining like flames of the most lovely colours, and among the flowers stood a slender, graceful maiden; herself, too, shining, as it seemed."[11] The light is so bright it forces him to shut his eyes, and when he opens them again the girl and the wonderful light are gone. The flowers look normal once again, but there is some particularly delightful music

9. *Stories*, 237; *Eventyr*, 186. "Han skrev Bøger om hvad der var Sandt i Verden, og om hvad der var Godt og hvad der var Smukt."
10. *Stories*, 236; *Eventyr*, 185. "Jeg har jo ingen Skygge!"
11. *Stories*, 235; *Eventyr*, 184. "Han syntes at der kom en forunderlig Glands fra Gjenboens Altan, alle Blomsterne skinnede som Flammer, i de deiligste Farver, og midt imellem Blomsterne stod en slank, yndig Jomfru, det var som om ogsaa hun lyste."

playing within, and it still seems to the learned man as if that house contains some kind of magic world ("en Troldom"). Unable to find the proper entrance to this curious place, he can only wonder what goes on there and who lives there, till one evening a few days later he gets an idea:

> One evening the foreign scholar was sitting out on his balcony, and a lamp was hung in the room behind him, and so it very naturally happened that his shadow passed across to the wall opposite, and there it stayed, right opposite among the flowers on the balcony, and when the learned man moved the shadow moved, too—it always does.
>
> "I think my Shadow is the only living thing to be seen over there," said the learned man. "Look how snug it's sitting among the flowers, and the door's standing ajar. Now if the shadow was sharp enough to go in and look about and then come and tell me what it saw! Yes, you'd be some use then," he said in a joke. "Do, please, go in there! Do! Are you going?" With that he nodded to the shadow, and the shadow nodded back. "Well, go then, but don't stay away!"[12]

When the man turns away, so does his shadow, and the narrator reports that, had someone been there to observe carefully, that person would have seen the shadow slip through the door on the balcony into the magic world within.

The attentive reader knows what that world contains and hardly needs the shadow's later testimony that it is "Poesien" (that is, imaginative literature) who dwells there. Our knowledge adds a further ironic complexity to the scholar's lament, "I haven't got any shadow," since the fiction is suggesting that the world in which one would find "The Shadow," the world of literature, can be reached only by sending one's "shadow" forth into that world. Even a learned author like this

---

12. *Stories*, 236; *Eventyr*, 184–85. "En Aften sad den Fremmede ude paa sin Altan, inde i Stuen bag ved ham braendte Lyset, og saa var det jo ganske naturligt at Skyggen af ham gik over paa Gjenboens Vaeg; ja der sad den lige over for mellem Blomsterne paa Altanen; og naar den Fremmede rørte sig, saa rørte Skyggen sig ogsaa, for det gjør den.—

'Jeg tror min Skygge er det eneste Levende, man seer derovre!" sagde den laerde Mand. 'See hvor net den sidder mellem Blomsterne. Døren staar paa klem, nu skulde Skyggen vaere saa snild og gaae indenfor, see sig om, og saa komme og fortaelle mig hvad den havde seet! ja Du skulde gjøre Gavn!' sagde han i Spøg! 'Vaer saa god at traede indenfor! naa! gaaer Du?' og saa nikkede han til Skyggen og Skyggen nikkede igjen. 'Ja saa gaa, men bliv ikke borte!'"

could gain "The Shadow" only by losing the "shadow." Is the loss, then, so bad after all? In the moment in which the learned man seems to have parted company with himself he is closest to finding the thing he wants. So he does not, like Schlemihl, lament the loss of his shadow; he doesn't have to, since a new one grows back quickly, and since he settles down to writing his books, thereby entering by other means into the shadowy literary world where he has already sent the darker part of himself.

Everything should be quite all right. The story could end here with the learned author living happily ever after with his books and his new shadow and with the old shadow simply gone off into the "Troldom" of imagination, whence he might never return. Yet this is not the end of the story but only its beginning. Andersen's interest in the topos of the lost shadow is quite different from that of Chamisso, who uses it to fashion an allegorical cautionary tale about the indivisibility of the self. Although Peter does save his soul, he never regains the soul's secular image, his shadow. In the fictional world of Andersen's story, shadows are not such rare and valuable commodities: the learned man obtains a new shadow in very little time and with no effort. That fact, if nothing else, alerts us to the fundamental contrast between *Peter Schlemihl* and "The Shadow." Where Chamisso was concerned with the basic unity of the self, Andersen is concerned with its divisibility. That the scholar can send off his shadow and immediately get another one is, or ought to be, disturbing on a number of counts. What is the old shadow doing, and what would happen if it actually came back, as it has been instructed to do ("Don't stay away")?

The return of the shadow is the obligatory scene in this little drama, and it comes quickly, just a few sentences after we are told of the growth of the new shadow. The figure who arrives at the scholar's door is described not as a shadow, however, but as a person ("Menneske"), a man, indeed a "man of distinction."[13] When the "person" reveals his true identity, the learned man is quite overwhelmed. His first words are, "Well, well! I can't get over it" ("Nei, jeg kan ikke komme til mig selv"),[14] in this context an utterance of considerable rhetorical complexity. While the phrase "komme til sig selv" does indeed mean "get over it" in the sense of "return to one's (normal)

13. *Stories*, 237; *Eventyr*, 186. "En fornem Mand."
14. Ibid.

senses," the literal meaning of the scholar's words is, "No, I can't come to my self!" Given the situation, this literal meaning is at least as relevant as the more usual and ordinarily more correct figurative reading. It is a rhetorical denial of the very thing that seems to be happening, the arrival of self to self. The action of the story performs a logomimetic acting out of a literal meaning that, in the normal course of things, ought to be impossible. That "I" should meet "myself" is a simple matter for language, since grammar splits the self into several pronouns, but we do not expect that grammatical possibility to be thus transformed into practice.

Andersen exploits further grammatical possibilities in the ensuing conversation between this "I" and "myself." Though they are two halves of the same person, they are not necessarily equal. We naturally assume that the corporeal human being has greater importance than the accompanying shadow, and Andersen's language supports that assumption. In the initial conversations between the learned man and the returned shadow, the man calls the shadow by the familiar *Du* and the shadow addresses the man with the respectful *De*. The individual is revealed to be divisible not only into parts ("I" and "myself") but also into higher and lower, more and less valuable, of greater and lesser moral worth, or as we might say, more and less "substantial." The shadow speaks and acts like a former servant who has come up in the world but still feels obliged to behave deferentially to his old master. The shadow even offers to buy out his contract, as it were, to indemnify the new shadow for the work he has to do in the old one's place. The old shadow thus acts like one who, in spite of his material success in the world, rightly merits the *Du* form of address, while he treats the scholar as one to whom it is necessary to say *De*. It becomes clear in this scene, then, that the division of the self into "man" and "shadow" is the embodiment of the distinction not only or most importantly between subject and object (*jeg* and *mig*) but, more centrally, between "higher" and "lower" aspects of that self (*De* and *Du*). Both distinctions, however, derive their narrative character from a basis in the structure of language, and both are therefore essentially rhetorical constructions.

Andersen calls attention to another rhetorical complexity of ordinary language relevant to the peculiar situation of this man and his newly corporeal shadow: sometimes he fails to capitalize the formal second-person pronoun *De* (or *Dem*), in which case it become graph-

208 | *Inventions of Reading*

ically as well as phonetically indistinguishable from the third-person plural pronoun *de* (*dem*). (Like the German *Sie*, the Danish *De* is nothing other than the troping use of the third-person plural pronoun.) The shadow's language does not allow us to be absolutely certain whether he is addressing the scholar as a single, more highly placed individual or as some kind of collective unit. The latter possibility must be seriously entertained, since the man has already split himself up in order to produce the two participants in the conversation. Furthermore, the corporeal shadow is highly conscious that the scholar to whom he is talking consists—from the shadow's point of view—of two entities, a man and a (new) shadow, that shadow itself potentially another independent entity. When the shadow asks, then, whether he owes any money "till den eller dem" ("to it or to you"), his otherwise perfectly ordinary discourse brings home forcefully the power of self-multiplication that still resides in the learned man. There is, from the perspective of rhetoric and from the perspective of the story, no way to distinguish between the scholar's higher status (that which makes him *De*) and his potential for self-replication (that which makes him *de*).

One of the subtle ironies of the story is that the shadow is more aware than the man of the man's power and importance and of their connection to the ability to reproduce. The scholar thinks nothing of the fact that he has a new shadow while the wealthy old shadow has none. The shadow, on the other hand, seems very much concerned with the one remaining defect in his newfound independence. While telling of his adventures, the shadow takes care to place his feet "as firmly as he could on the arm of the learned man's shadow, which lay at his feet like a poodle dog; and this was either out of pride or perhaps in hopes of getting it to stick to him."[15] The shadow knows that he can achieve genuine independence only by somehow obtaining for himself the ability to cast a shadow, to produce copies of himself. His most urgent wish, therefore, is to become engaged. He is capable, he says, of producing more than one family, presumably because of his great wealth. But when he declares, "Jeg kan føde mere en een Familie,"[16] his language reveals the presence of another, perhaps deeper issue. The

---

15. *Stories*, 238–39; *Eventyr*, 187. "Og saa satte den sine Been med de lakerede Støvler saa haardt, den kunde, ned paa Aermet af den laerde Mands nye Skygge, der laa som en Puddelhund ved hans Fødder, og det var nu enten af Hovmod eller maaskee for at faae den til at haenge ved."

16. *Eventyr*, 187.

verb *føde* can mean both "feed, nourish, support" and "give birth to." Although the corporeal shadow cannot produce a shadow of his own, he dreams of generating multiple offspring.

The learned man is quite unaware that his shadow's ambitions represent a danger to him, unaware even that he is confronting an alienated portion of himself. In the sentence quoted above ("Jeg kan ikke komme til mig selv"), his rhetoric denies the possibility of what is happening. When he asks rhetorically a little later, "Well, and is it really you?"[17] he shows no awareness that the proper response might be, "Yes, it is really you." In spite of his apparent willingness to accept the independence of his former shadow, the scholar does not seem to have fully accepted the divisibility of the self or its implications. At a crucial point in the plot, when the man swears that he will not reveal the shadow's true identity to anyone, the scholar swears by, of all things, the indivisibility of the self: "I promise it, and one man, one word, you know," to which the shadow ironically replies, "One word, one shadow!"[18] In these circumstances such an oath should be meaningless. It is like a notorious scoundrel taking an oath upon his honor. The shadow seems to acknowledge this, since his reply is not so much self-deprecation as it is an undercutting of the grounds of the scholar's discourse. How can the integrity of the self stand as a guarantee for the integrity of discourse when the self is in fact participating in furthering the alienation of a part of that self? The learned man is promising, on the warranty of his being "one man," to assist in making himself into two men. The writer of books about the good, the true, and the beautiful ought to know this, but he does not. Only the shadow knows.

The shadow indeed makes the grandest of claims about his knowledge: "I have seen everything and I know everything."[19] It is by means of his extensive knowledge that the shadow has been able to advance so rapidly and so far in society. He has apparently made his way by means of blackmail. People, he says, "were terribly afraid of me, and they became amazingly fond of me."[20] Here again the shadow's story

17. *Stories*, 238; *Eventyr*, 186. "Nei, er det virkelig Dig!"
18. *Stories*, 239; *Eventyr*, 187. "Jeg lover det og en Mand et Ord." "Et Ord en Skygge!"
19. *Stories*, 239; *Eventyr*, 187. "Jeg har seet Alt og jeg veed Alt!"
20. *Stories*, 240; *Eventyr*, 189. "De bleve saa bange for mig! og de holdt saa overordentlig af mig!"

moves in the space between two readings, in this case of the phrase
"holdt af mig." There is no doubt that the shadow is using the verb
holde af and that the translation "became fond of me" is correct. But the
verb *afholde* means "to pay," and the suggestion is clear that the people
the shadow dealt with were in fact more likely to pay him than to be
genuinely fond of him. The reported "fondness" is actually indistinguishable from a series of payoffs: "The professors made me a professor, the tailors gave me new clothes. . . . The master of the mint
coined money for me, and the women said I was very good-look-
ing."[21] It is in this way, the shadow reports, that "I became the man I
am."[22]

This account of the shadow's adventures in the realm of poetry and
its aftermath has a number of unexpected features, the most remarkable of which is precisely the effect the experience has on the character
of the shadow, his becoming the man he is. Since it is evident to the
reader, if not to the learned man, that the shadow is a scoundrel, we
might find it somewhat surprising that a work of literature should
portray contact with literature as somehow contributing to the formation of his corrupt character. Literature is supposed to be good for us.
The traditional foundation for humanistic education was the belief that
contact with literary classics would make the students better citizens
and wiser, riper human beings. The shadow himself invokes this ideal
when he reports that he emerged from the house of poetry "mature"
("moden") and that he had learned there about his "innermost nature,"
his innate qualities ("mit Medfødte"), and his kinship with the world
of literature ("det Familieskab, jeg have med Poesien").[23] What process
has taken place that makes the onetime shadow of a man committed to
the "good, the true, and the beautiful" into a human being and a
criminal?

The language of the shadow's narrative leaves room for doubt
whether there really was any process of transformation at all. When he
first tries to explain what the realm of poetry is like, he tells the
scholar, "Had you been over there you would not have turned into a
man, but I did."[24] One has to wonder if James's translation is correct

21. Ibid. "Professorerne gjorde mig til Professor, Skraederne gav mig ny Klaeder . . . ;
Myntmesteren slog Mynt for mig, og Konerne sagde, jeg var saa kjøn"
22. Ibid. "Saa blev jeg den Mand jeg er."
23. *Stories*, 240; *Eventyr*, 188.
24. Ibid. "Havde De kommet derover, var de ikke blevet Menneske, men det blev
jeg."

here, because the verb *blive* can mean both "become" and "remain." The shadow could very well be saying, "If you had been there, you would not have *remained* a person, but I became one." This would be in a sense more logical: the metamorphic power of poetry is so great that it changes everything it touches; "you would not have stayed human, while I could not stay nonhuman." But this ambiguity cuts both ways. Perhaps poetry does not transform at all; perhaps it simply allows one to recognize and express what one already is. In that case the shadow's "men det blev jeg" would mean that he *remained* the person he had been all along—"saa blev jeg den Mand jeg er"—in a slightly different sense than we might have read otherwise.

"The Shadow" operates in the uncanny space between the two senses of "blive," between changing and remaining the same. We cannot be sure whether the separation of the shadow from the man initiates a moral transformation or simply the emergence of an "innate" moral defect. This very problem is opened up, though in a typically casual and humorous fashion, in the opening lines of the story, where we learn about the powers of the sun in southern climates: "In the hot countries the sun can burn properly. People become as brown as mahogany all over; in the very hottest countries they are even burnt into negroes."[25] What is announced as a process of transformation we know to be the regular state of things. The narrator says that the sun burns people into Negroes, but he knows that we will take this as a trope. Even the same ambiguous use of "blive" occurs here: "Folk blive ganske mahognibrune." Do they "become" that way, or do they "remain" that way all the time? There is nothing in the language itself that will help us decide.

The shadow's sojourn in the house of poetry brings about something that is both an alteration and no alteration at all. If he has changed, from shadow to person, he has also remained what he always was, a creature of twilight and moonshine. Andersen exploits the conventional association of shadows with darkness and of poetry with the moonlit dreams of nighttime to suggest a less conventional idea, that the realm of literature is a naturally comfortable place for the morally shadowy aspects of humanity. With this suggestion Andersen touches on a theme to be thoroughly explored by his admirer Thomas Mann, whose figurative linking of art and criminality became the basis for a

25. *Stories*, 234; *Eventyr*, 183. "I de hede Lande, der kan rigtignok Solen braende! Folk blive ganske mahognibrune; ja i de allerhedeste Lande braendes de til Negre."

number of stories and novels. "Tonio Kröger," "Death in Venice," *The Confessions of Felix Krull*, and *Doctor Faustus*, to name just the most prominent, ring the changes on this notion. In Mann's fiction, of course, the "shadowy" side of poetic art never becomes separated from the more admirable aspects of the artist's character and work; for Mann it had become impossible to separate the "pure" from the "impure"— as Serenus Zeitblom expresses it in the opening pages of *Doctor Faustus*—because they are obverse and reverse of the same coin. Andersen's fairy-tale approach is very different in its technique, but the misgivings "The Shadow" expresses about the poetic impulse move in a direction that Mann could and probably did find congenial. The criminal behavior in which the shadow engages is nothing more than a literal acting out of one of the stock metaphors of artistic insight: the poet "sees the secrets of the human soul" and then has the impertinence to make these secrets public. The learned man from the north displays at least the desire for this kind of poetic insight; his urgent wish to pry into things hidden prompts him to send forth his shadow into the house across the street and thereby initiate the process that looses his shadowy side upon the world and upon himself.

The shadow's sinister nature is not the revelation of some hitherto unseen defect in the scholar's character but rather the unrestrained development of aspects of that character that had been there all along. The shadow expresses it in a neat piece of rhetoric: "I, as you very well know, have trod in your footsteps from a child."[26] Andersen uses the fact that this utterance happens in this case to be literally true to support the truth of the figurative meaning. The shadow is the moral and intellectual image of the learned man, one who "takes after him" in every way. He possesses the same artistic impulses, the same ethically questionable desire to "see everything," that animates his master.

The shadow amplifies his thoughts on his "kinship with Poetry" in this way:

When I was with you I never thought about it, but, as you know, every time the sun rose and set I used to become amazingly large. In the moonlight, indeed, I was almost plainer to be seen than you yourself. At that time I did not comprehend my own nature, but in that ante-room [in

26. *Stories*, 237–38; *Eventyr*, 186. "Og jeg, det veed De nok, har fra Barnsbeen traadt i deres Fodspoer."

the house of Poetry] it became clear to me; I became [or remained] a man.[27]

Literature is often conventionally held to be effective in helping us understand ourselves, and here literature fulfills its conventional task, though with paradoxical results. By learning to comprehend his own nature *as a shadow*, the shadow also learns to understand himself as a human being. The thing that makes him human (and might perhaps have made him human all along, had he only known) is the realization, with the help of literature, that his nature is "shadowy." He need not remain a literal shadow as long as he recognizes that he is a figurative "shadow." The lesson he learns in the house of Poetry is, fittingly, a lesson in rhetoric.

It is of considerable interest in this connection that the announced change from shadow to human being does not bring about a complete metamorphosis, with a complete loss of all shadow characteristics and an instant acquisition of all human traits. On the contrary, the shadow remains in many ways a shadow still. As we know, he cannot cast any shadow of his own, but more than that, he continues to behave very much as a shadow might be expected to behave:

> I ran along the street in the moonlight. I stretched myself right up the wall (it tickles one in the back deliciously). I ran up; I ran down; I peeped through the topmost windows, into the rooms, on to the roof. I peeped where no one else could, and saw what nobody else saw, and what nobody was meant to see. . . . I saw . . . what no human being was allowed to know, but what everybody very much wants to know, that is their neighbors' wrongdoings.[28]

Even after he has recognized himself as human, he remains able to do things that are impossible for human beings.

27. *Stories*, 240; *Eventyr*, 188. "Ja den Gang jeg var hos Dem, taenkte jeg ikke over det, men altid, De veed det, naar Sol gik op og Sol gik ned, blev jeg saa underlig stor; i Maaneskin var jeg naesten ved at vaere tydeligere end De selv; jeg forstod ikke den Gang min Natur, i Forgemakket gik det op for mig! jeg blev Menneske!"

28. *Stories*, 240; *Eventyr*, 189. "Jeg løb om i Maaneskinnet paa Gaden; jeg gjorde mig lang op ad Muren, det killer saa deiligt i Ryggen! jeg løb op og jeg løb ned, kiggede ind af de høieste Vinduer, ind i Salen og paa Taget, jeg kiggede hvor Ingen kunde kigge og seg saae hvad ingen Andre saae, hvad Ingen skulde see! . . . Jeg saae . . . hvad ingen Mennesker maatte vide, men havd de Allesammen saa gjerne vilde vide, Ondt hos Naboen."

There is further blurring of the opposition between person and shadow in the description of the human qualities the shadow has after his alleged transformation. The narrator observes:

> It was indeed most remarkable to see how much of a man the Shadow was: all dressed out in the finest possible black broadcloth, with varnished boots and a hat that would shut up so that it was only crown and brim [*Pul og Skygge*], not to speak of what we know already, the seals, the gold chain, and the diamond rings. The Shadow was, in fact, extraordinarily well dressed, and this was just what made him a complete man.[29]

Bracketed by the insistence that the shadow has become "entirely" human is a description of features that tend to remind us that he is a shadow. The blackness of his appearance is stressed by repetition: He is "dressed in black" ("sortklaedt") in the best "black cloth" ("sorte Klaede"). Beyond this, though, is the narrator's careful description of the collapsible hat—black, of course—once so fashionable; it is capable of becoming (or remaining—"blive" again) nothing but "Pul og Skygge." In the very center of the description of these human elements we discover something that remains "skygge" (that is, both "hatbrim" and "shadow"). If the shadow and, possibly, the narrator believe that "clothes make the man" ("klaeder skaber folk"), as they apparently do with literal punctuality here, they must quietly gloss over the outrageous contamination of these "entirely" human clothes by the attributes of the signifier of "shadow." The reader, who cannot ignore the clever pun or the ironic logomimesis on the proverb "klaeder skaber folk," will realize that the "humanity" of the shadow is itself another trope, readable both literally and figuratively in the context of this fiction. We have to understand his humanity, that is, in a rhetorical way.

The relation between "person" and "shadow" is mediated by discourse. Once experience of poetry has led him to understand the nature of tropes, the shadow can manipulate his existence through the twi-

---

29. *Stories*, 238; *Eventyr*, 187. "Det var ellers virkelig ganske maerkvaerdigt hvormeget Menneske den var; ganske sortklaedt var den og i det allerfineste sorte Klaede, lakerede Støvler, og Hat der kunde smaekke sammen, saa at den blev bar Pul og Skyyge, ikke at tale om hvad vi allerede veed her var, Signeter, Guldhalskjaede og Diamantringe; jo, Skyggen var overordentlig godt klaedt paa, og det var just det, som gjorde at den var ganske et Menneske."

light between the literal and the figurative, taking on the character of
shadow and "shadow," person and "person" almost at his convenience. What the shadow has learned, to put it baldly, is that both
"person" and "shadow" are words and that their verbal character can
act as a kind of bridge between them. It is this very bridge that is made
explicit in the words of the climactic oath, "en Mand et Ord, et Ord en
Skygge." It is the "word" that both man and shadow have in common,
a rhetoric that allows the one to both merge with and part from the
other. The "word" is the nodal point in the story, the place where
things cross over. Rhetoric allows the interplay of conflicting meanings, aids their merging and crossing over. And this particular "word,"
this promisory formula, acts as the pivot for the plot. Its chiasmus is
the verbal image of the chiastic form of the plot, in which the positions
of man and shadow are at the end reversed from what they were at the
beginning. Almost as soon as the oath is sworn, the process of reversal
begins. The shadow, upon receipt of the scholar's promise that he will
not reveal the shadow's true identity, begins the tale of his adventures
in the antechamber of Poetry's dwelling. The scholar, eager to hear all
about it, urges the narrative forward, asking, "And what sawest thou
then?" ("Og hvad saae Du saa?").[30] This question prompts the shadow
to a second request: he wants the scholar to address him in the formal
mode as "De" on account of his new status, his "accomplishments,"
his "good position," not to mention his "very easy circumstances."[31]
The man readily agrees, and both are on the polite footing of "De"
with each other.

This condition of equality does not last long, however—not in
terms of narrative time, that is. The shadow departs for "a year and a
day" upon completion of his story, but on his return he finds the
learned man in the process of decline. No one pays any attention to his
writings about the good, the true, and the beautiful, and he falls into
despair. The shadow, on the other hand, prospers: "I'm getting fat,"
he says ("blive fed" also means "to get rich"), and suggests that the
scholar ought to take a trip with him, going "as my shadow." The
phrase "som Skygge" carries the suggestion that "shadow" is an office
or a position, like "secretary" or "butler." The man rejects this pro-

30. *Stories*, 239; *Eventyr*, 188.
31. Ibid. "De Kundskaber jeg har, . . . min gode Stilling, mine fortraeffelige Oms-
taendigheder."

posal as "absolute madness,"[32] but things continue to get worse for him. He gets sick; he becomes, as one might expect, only a shadow of his former self,[33] and people begin to tell him so: "You really look like a shadow," they say, and the learned man "shivered, for it was exactly what he was thinking."[34] What he had rejected as "madness" ("for galt") no longer seems out of the question, and he finally accepts the shadow's invitation. The Danes say "naar galt skal vaere" to mean "if the worst should happen," and that is just what is happening here to the poor learned man. The very worst, though, is yet to come.

The story now begins to act out in deadly earnest the implications of the expression "kun en skygge af sig selv," between the readings of which the whole story in a sense resides. But this is by no means the first time the narrative has suggested the possibility of human beings' turning into shadows. Actually, the opening paragraph already points in a joking way to the transformation of people into shadows. In the world of Andersen and his readers, people are normally white, while only their shadows are black. In the hot countries the learned man is visiting, however, people ("folk") turn brown, and indeed even black under the influence of the sun, the caster of shadows. Assuming the narrow ethnocentric norm of white skin for all creatures accepted as "people," the change of color is a fundamental way of dehumanizing. Persons of a darker color simply do not count; they are "shadows" in the social order. Individuals who might once have been "folk" are transformed into "Negroes," a category perhaps no longer coordinate with "folk" at all. Since Andersen's story deals so centrally with the social debasement of a man who is forced to become a shadow, it would be a mistake not to recognize the implied parallel between his situation and that of the "Negre" so briefly alluded to in the opening sentence.

It is not unreasonable to suppose that the commonplace notion that a person can become a "shadow of himself," as the expression has it, is the very thing Andersen set out to investigate in this tale, in all its moral complexity. The imaginative gesture that sets the plot in motion simply makes a slight alteration in a commonplace formula: in addition to "mennesket er en skygge af sig selv" ("the person is a shadow of

32. *Stories*, 241; *Eventyr*, 190. "Det er for galt."
33. The Danish phrase Andersen plays upon is "kun en skygge af sig selv."
34. *Stories*, 241; *Eventyr*, 190. "'De seer virkelig ud ligesom en Skygge!' sagde Folk til ham, og det gjøs i den laerde Mand, for han taenkte ved det."

himself") Andersen posits a chiastic reversal, "skyggen er et menneske af sig selv" ("the shadow is a person of himself"). The proverbial expression already presupposes the interchangeability of person and shadow, in that it says a person can "be" a shadow, so that it is no great step further to imagine a shadow can "be" a person.

The learned man's painful social and physical decline into shadow-hood is no more than was to be expected from the tale's beginning, and the remainder of the plot carries it out with rigorous thoroughness. Having convinced the scholar to address him as "De"—for not only is he now an individual of high social standing, but he too is plural by virtue of his possessing both shadowy and human aspects—the shadow proposes that he will henceforth address his former master as "Du." The scholar has suggested that, since the two of them are going to be traveling companions, they should say "Du" to each other. The shadow, however, confesses that he cannot bear to be called "Du" by the learned man, because it makes him feel "absolutely as if I were crushed down on the ground, as I was in my first situation with you."[35] The shadow's language slips between two meanings of "trykket til Jorden" and of "Stilling," a rhetorical complexity in this case quite well captured by the English translation. The shadow's former "situation" (that is, "physical position") was indeed one of being "crushed" (that is, "pressed down to the ground"), but now his memory of that "situation" (understood as "employment") makes him feel "crushed" (in the sense of "emotionally depressed"). In this circumstance the shadow can meet the scholar's proposal only halfway: the shadow will say "Du" to his former master, while the learned man says "De" to the shadow—a symmetrical reversal of the former situation.

The reversal continues to takes its course along a path that is fundamentally guided by rhetoric. The shadow and the learned man go to the baths to take the cure, and there they meet a princess from a foreign country. She is there to cure herself of the sickness of "seeing too well," a malady into which the shadow, who boasts to have "seen everything," could claim some insight. When the princess explains to the shadow that his real problem is not that he cannot grow a beard but rather that he cannot cast a shadow, he immediately pronounces her cured. He shows her his remarkable shadow—the learned man—and

35. *Stories*, 242; *Eventyr*, 190. "Jeg føler mig ligesom trykket til Jorden i min første Stilling hos Dem."

even allows this "shadow" to demonstrate to her its amazing wisdom. The princess feels herself falling in love with this person possessed of such an unusual shadow. He is also a very good dancer: "She was light, but he was lighter."[36] She is "light on her feet" ("let til bens"), but he is more so. Or perhaps he is merely "lighter" in that he possesses less weight; perhaps she who sees "too well" recognizes the morally weightless character of the shadow. In this story, all the meanings of *let* ("light") apply equally well to the shadow. As she falls in love, the princess reveals her feelings by gazing at the shadow "as if she would look right through him."[37] The trope describing the intensity of her loving gaze is in this case also literally possible, particularly for one who sees too well. Ironically, however, her ability to "look through him" ("see igennem ham") does not carry with it the ability to "see through him" ("skue gennem ham") and perceive his real nature. Or if it does, the princess suppresses the perception.

The completion of the reversal, wherein the shadow achieves the highest possible social station by marrying into a royal family, while the learned man is utterly effaced to the point of being rather casually executed, takes place when the learned man is more fully transformed into a "shadow of himself" than he or anyone else ever imagined possible. One of the rhetorical complexities of Andersen's story impossible to approximate in English derives from the fact that *skygge* comprises the semantic fields covered in English by both "shadow" and "shade." Like "shade" (and unlike "shadow"), the Danish *skygge* can also mean "ghost" or "spirit." Already implicit in the story's principal assumption—the interchangeability of "menneske" and "skygge"—is the move from the realm of the living to the realm of the dead. For the learned man to become a "skygge" in the fullest sense of the word, he must die. The final irony is that the learned man forces his own execution (his transformation into "skygge" in the sense of "ghost") by refusing to cooperate in the shadow's plan for him to play the role of "skygge" (in the sense of "shadow") permanently. He threatens instead to inform the princess of her new fiancé's true identity—thus breaking his word—and the shadow has him arrested. When she is informed by her beloved that his "shadow" has taken it into his head to insist that he is the man, his master the shadow, she herself

36. *Stories*, 243; *Eventyr*, 191. "Hun var let, men han var endnu lettere."
37. *Stories*, 243; *Eventyr*, 192. "Hun var faerdig at see lige igjennem ham."

suggests that "it is essential that he should be quite quietly put out of the way."[38] The learned man is executed on the day of the shadow's wedding to the princess.

There is no doubt that "The Shadow" operates on one level at least as a melancholy allegory of the relationship between an artist and his work of art. Andersen takes the traditional notion that an artist's works are his "offspring," capable of living on after he is dead, and turns upon it an almost Freudian suspicion. The more successful a work of art is, the more it puts its creator "in the shade." The very act of analysis I am engaged in is complicit with this idea. Throughout this discussion of Andersen's story, the name "Andersen" has functioned to designate simply the author of "The Shadow" and not a fully complex human being. From the perspective of literary criticism, "H. C. Andersen" is little more than a shadow cast by his stories. That Andersen cast in the role of protagonist a transparent double of himself adds to the grim irony of the parable. The last line of the story captures both the irony and the melancholy of the effacement of the creator by his creation in a rhetorical formulation: "Ham have de tage livet af."[39] The locution "tage livet af" means "to kill" somebody, and James quite reasonably translates the last phrase as "he had already been executed." Another meaning lurks here, however, that such a translation misses completely. Behind "tage livet af" can be heard another locution, "leve af," which means to "live off" or "take life from." The story's conclusion thus suggests that the shadow and the princess "took life from" the learned man in two senses: that they killed him, and that they owed their existence to him.

The power of the literary shadow to efface and outlive its origin is particularly frightening here, since this shadow is such a morally shady character. What is left of the learned man after his execution, what "lives on," is in a sense the worst part of him, the capacity to see into people's private lives and the willingness to make public what has been seen. But there is a positive side. Although the shadow has succeeded in wiping his master from the page, "The Shadow" has effectively displaced another progenitor, Chamisso's *Peter Schlemihl*. The defeat of the author, his absolute destruction in terms of the plot, is his great

38. *Stories*, 245; *Eventyr*, 193. "Det bliver nødvendigt at det bliver gjort af med ham i al Stilhed!"
39. *Eventyr*, 194.

victory in the oedipal struggle between precursor and ephebe. There can no longer be any question of the learned man's (or Andersen's) "merely imitating" the German story. *Schlemihl* might even seem to some rather tame and naive in comparison with the rhetorical and moral complexity of "The Shadow." One could argue that Andersen's story puts Chamisso's in the shade.

But that is not the point either of Andersen's tale or of my discussion of it. Andersen's goal was to explore the moral problematic of literary art as it is expressed by the word *skygge* understood as rhetoric. The artist's ability to create especially lifelike "shadows" of himself in his fictions, shadows possessed of the ability to outlive their maker, might very well derive from a desire for "the true, the good, and the beautiful," but its effect in the world can have a far different moral character. Art has a shady side that is at least as powerful as the uplifting and noble side so often depicted. Seeing into the secrets of the human heart and displaying them to the world may bring wealth and honors from society, but it may be the worst rather than the best motives that prompt people to "pay off" the revealer of these secrets. The community may in the end grant secular success only to those artists who forget about the true, the good, and the beautiful to concentrate on peeping in at their neighbors' windows. A more ethically sensitive artist might have to wait to be turned into another sort of "skygge," a ghost, in order to exercise any moral authority over the community. In any case, the author who produces "shadows" has no choice: in one sense or another he will himself turn into a "skygge."

The remarkable achievement of "The Shadow" is that Andersen was able to base his morally and artistically complex tale on the frame of a familiar and apparently worn-out formula for an allegorical fantasy: a man loses his shadow. He did so principally by attending to the narrative potential in the language in which (a Danish version of) that formula might be stated, that is, by writing in the spaces between readings of expressions like "komme til sig self" or of words like "blive" and "skygge." Its achievement resides fundamentally in the thoroughness of its rhetorical construction.

Rhetoric as Remedy: Boccaccio's *Decameron*

In the "Author's Epilogue" to the *Decameron*, Boccaccio defends himself proleptically against a number of charges that "though remain-

ing unspoken, may possibly have arisen in the minds of my readers."
These objections may be unspoken, but they are evidently not un-
heard, since the author has knowledge of them, as it were, in advance:

> There will perhaps be those among you who will say that in writing these
> stories I have taken too many liberties, in that I have sometimes caused
> ladies to say, and very often to hear, things which are not very suitable to
> be heard or said by virtuous women. This I deny, for no story is so
> unseemly as to prevent anyone from telling it, provided it is told in
> seemly language; and this I believe I may reasonably claim to have
> done.[40]

What is at stake is "onestà," a quality that can be described as integrity
or virtue in persons and seemliness, decency, or integrity (in another
sense) in texts. What is the relation, the author assumes his readers will
ask, between these tales that are so "unseemly" ("disonesta") and the
virtuous ladies ("oneste donne") who are supposed to to be their audience? How are we to reconcile the "onestà" of the one with the
evident "disonestà" of the other?

Boccaccio answers the question in two ways, one explicit in his
language and the other implicit in his rhetoric. His explicit claim is that
the onestà of the language in which the tale is told is in a sense more
important than the moral quality of the material being related. This
implies that the moral quality of the individual words, the "vocaboli"
used to tell the tale, exists independent of the matter of the story. But
how could this be? How could one tell an indecorous story with words
that are uncontaminated by this indecorousness? The answer is evident
to those who have just finished reading the hundred stories of the
Decameron: one speaks in figures. Sexual intercourse, for example, does
not involve putting a penis into a vagina; it is a matter of putting the
"devil into hell," or "scraping a tub," or hearing a "nightingale sing."
If the vehicle of the trope is "onesto," the tenor is somehow redeem-

---

40. I cite Boccaccio in English from *The Decameron*, trans. G. H. McWilliam (Harmondsworth: Penguin, 1972), and in Italian from *Decameron*, ed. Vittore Branca (Florence: Accademia della Crusca, 1976). This passage is from *Decameron* (McWilliam), 829;
Decameron (Branca), 717. "Saranno per avventura alcune di voi che diranno che io abbia
nello scriver queste novelle troppa licenzia usata, sì come in fare alcuna volta dire alle
donne e molto spesso ascoltare cose non assai convenienti né a dire né a ascoltare a
oneste donne. La qual cosa io nego, per ciò che niuna sì disonesta n'è, che, con onesti
vocaboli dicendola, si disdica a alcuno: il che qui mi pare assai convenevolmente bene
aver fatto."

able from its disonestà, and the story no longer would deny itself to anyone ("si disdica ad alcuno"). By using the word *disdire,* Boccaccio underlines this process of the removal of unseemliness, since that verb means not only "to deny" but also "to be unseemly." The story under discussion, unseemly in its content but decorous in its language, is actually alleged to no longer "make itself unseemly to anyone."

The other answer to the question of how to reconcile the virtue of ladies with the apparent lewdness of these tales is offered by the curious way Boccaccio has deployed his second sentence. In a very literal translation, that sentence begins, "The which thing I deny, because none of them [fem.] is so lacking virtue . . ." If we read these words in the way advocated by Stanley Fish,[41] we realize that the antecedent of "niuna" is deliberately ambiguous. After reading the first half of the sentence, we are more than likely to assume that the reference is to "donne" ("ladies"), the feminine noun most recently mentioned, and mentioned pointedly in connection with the issue of "onestà." It is not until we reach the word "dicendola," relatively near the end of the sentence, that we are forced to revise our assumption: this feminine object of the verb *dire* simply cannot be "donna," and the reader quickly scrambles back to "novella" as the proper antecedent. In the meantime, however—still keeping to the sort of rhetorical reading Fish proposed—the idea has been introduced in our minds that it is the virtue of the ladies themselves (ladies being the conventional trope in the *Decameron* for readers) that will prevent unseemliness from making an appearance. The issue might not be so much the manner of writing a potentially lewd tale as the manner of reading it. Boccaccio, after all, having introduced the question of writing ("scriver") at the opening of this paragraph, quickly turns our attention to hearing ("ascoltare") and thus to the process of reception. The author's rhetoric implies that, as beauty ("onestà" in a figurative usage) is in the eye of the beholder, so might virtue, seemliness, and integrity be in the ear of the hearer as well. It might be as much up to the reader as the author to ensure the propriety of stories told with "onesti vocaboli."

Confirmation that Boccaccio does indeed mean to suggest that the audience of discourse has a major responsibility in determining its

---

41. Or at any rate the way Fish used to read. See "The Reader in the Text: Affective Stylistics" and "Interpreting the Variorum," both reprinted in *Is There a Text in This Class?* (Cambridge: Harvard University Press, 1980).

moral character comes only a few sentences later. He adduces a number of "honest words" from everday speech, words like "foro" ("hole") and "caviglia" ("rod") or "mortar and pestle," as examples of potentially offensive language that people nonetheless are able to use without giving offense. "Like all other things in this world," Boccaccio concludes a bit later on, "stories, whatever their natures, may be harmful or useful, depending on the listener."[42] He even goes on to argue that the moral qualities of persons are essentially independent of the onestà, or lack of it, in the language they hear:

> No word, however pure, was ever wholesomely construed by a mind that was corrupt. And just as seemly language leaves no mark upon a mind that is corrupt, language that is less than seemly cannot sully a mind that is well ordered any more than mud will contaminate the rays of the sun, or earthly filth the beauties of the starry heavens.[43]

While there are such things as words "which are not so seemly" ("che tanto oneste non sono"), their disonestà is potentially less important than the quality of the mind that receives them, which may be either "corrupt" ("corrotta") or "ben disposta" (either "well ordered" or "well disposed").

But what does it mean to say that a well-disposed mind will not be "contaminated" even by language that is less than seemly? Does it mean that the virtuous person will simply ignore what has been heard, remain untouched by it as the sun remains untouched by the mud it shines upon? Evidently not, since this implies that it would be best for readers simply to ignore books like the *Decameron* that might be thought to contain "one or two trifling expressions that are too unbridled" for the most sensitive listeners.[44] No, Boccaccio apparently expects the reader with a mind "ben disposta" to pass through his text the way Ulysses passed the Sirens. Boccaccio uses this very analogy—

---

42. *Decameron* (McWilliam), 830; *Decameron* (Branca), 718. "Le quali, chenti che elle si sieno, e nuocere e giovar possono, sì come possono tutte l'altre cose, avendo riguardo all'ascoltare."

43. Ibid. "Niuna corrotta mente intese mai sanamente parola: e così come le oneste a quella non giovano, così quelle che tanto oneste non sono la ben disposta non posson contaminare, se non come il loto il solari raggi o le terrene brutture le bellezze del cielo."

44. *Decameron* (McWilliam), 829; *Decameron* (Branca), 717. "Alcuna paroletta più liberale."

not here, to be sure, but in *The Genealogy of the Pagan Gods*—to cast shame on those who claim to have been "seduced" by literature. The issue in this section of the *Genealogy* (book 14, chap. 16) is very similar to the one under discussion in the conclusion of the *Decameron*. In both cases Boccaccio is arguing that immorality comes not so much from texts as from readers, even in cases where the texts in question are not in all ways exemplary. Those who find themselves "seduced" by literature "are lured and deluded into an evil course more by their own wickedness than by that of even the less honorable poets."[45] Ulysses is held up as an example of one who could not be "lured," even by the supernaturally alluring song of the Sirens. Ulysses, of course, did not ignore that song; on the contrary, he went out of his way to make sure he would hear it; and he paid such close attention that he could later quote it verbatim to the Phaeacians. But he took care to avoid the bad effects this particular poetry is reported to have had on other mariners. Boccaccio says that Ulysses "spurned . . . the dulcet music of the Sirens, whom he passed by for fear of harm at their hands."[46] Thanks to the timely advice of Circe, the wily Greek was able to have it both ways, to enjoy the "dulcet music" and at the same time escape the harm it threatened.

The "Author's Epilogue" argues that readers of the *Decameron* can have it both ways too. Two conditions are necessary for this to happen: first, the tales must be told in a language of "onesti vocaboli," which Boccaccio says he "may very reasonably claim to have done"; second, the reader must be possessed of a mind "ben disposta" so that she can pass though the text with a mind as open to the onestà of the language as to the unseemliness of the actions described. In essence, then, Boccaccio is arguing for the importance of the literal level of his stories' discourse. He is advising us—in a manner consistent with the view of the commentators on Holy Scripture he admired—that the vehicles of the metaphors are at least as important as their tenors. The implication is that the discovery of the figurative meaning—not a difficult discovery in most of these tales—is not by any means the retrieval of the "real" or "true" meaning; it is only the recognition of

45. I cite the *Genealogy* from the English translation of books 14 and 15 in Charles G. Osgood, *Boccaccio on Poetry* (Indianapolis: Liberal Arts Press, 1956). This passage is from page 78.
46. Osgood, *Boccaccio,* 77.

another meaning. The novellas are thus alleged to operate in the space between tenor and vehicle or, to use the terminology of the *Genealogy*, between *cortex* and *sapidum* (or *velamentum* and *intentio*). Even in the *Genealogy*, where the thrust of the argument is to show that there is, in fact, a meaning "underneath" the veiling cortex, Boccaccio is careful not to disparage the intrinsic value of the veil itself: the goal of poetic invention, he says, is "to cover the truth with a marvelous and seemly veil."[47] The "Epilogue" seems to be telling its readers that the language of the novellas is just such a "marvelous [or poetic] and seemly veil" covering a truth that in this case happens not to be very seemly at all.

This defense of the literal level of figurative discourse as a crucial element demanding attention is made more convincing by the practical demonstration Boccaccio makes as part of the rhetoric of that defense. Pointing out that the frame, the fictional setting of the novellas, is appropriate to the narration of worldly material, the author reminds us not only that these stories were told in a garden, a place of secular pleasure, by and for a group of young people old enough not to be misled by fictions, but also that the entire action took place at a time when "even the most respectable people saw nothing unseemly in wearing their breeches over their heads if they thought their lives might therefore be preserved."[48] At first blush the passage, particularly in the English translation, seems a bit peculiar. Does Boccaccio really mean to say that Florentines of the mid-fourteenth century thought it proper to wear their pants on their heads? And how would doing so bring about the preservation of their lives ("iscampo di sé")?

Evidently this phrase "andar con le brache in capo" ("wear one's pants on one's head") must be a figure. According to a reliable authority on such matters,[49] the locution means "to have relinquished all modesty" ("aver perduta del tutto la verecondia"). If that is so, Boccaccio's phrase simply means that unseemly behavior was not considered unseemly when it was a matter of saving yourself from the plague, a reference to the "customs contrary to established tradition"[50] that arose

47. "Velamento fabuloso atque decenti veritatem contegere." *Gen. Deorum Gent.* 14.7. The translation is mine.
48. *Decameron* (McWilliam), 830; *Decameron* (Branca), 718. "In tempo nel quale andar con le brache in capo per iscampo di sé era alli più onesti non disdicevole."
49. The *Vocabolario degli Accademici della Crusca*.
50. *Decameron* (McWilliam), 54; *Decameron* (Branca), 14. "Cose contrarie a' primi costumi."

during the time of the pestilence, described with impressive vividness in the introduction to Day 1. An example of such immodest or unseemly behavior is the "laughter and witticism and general jollification" ("risa e motti e festeggiar compagnevole") that supplanted lamentations for the dead, even and especially among the ladies, who had learned the art especially well "for their salvation" ("per salute di loro")—compare "per iscampo di sé."[51] In other words, the significance of Boccaccio's phrase "andar con le brache in capo" has absolutely nothing to do with putting pants on heads, an act that would do nothing to bring about one's safety; it refers rather to quite different kinds of immodest behavior.

At the same time, however, Boccaccio really *is* talking about putting pants on heads, and the translator, G. H. McWilliam, was quite correct to translate the literal rather than the figurative meaning. The kind of immodesty or unseemliness one can observe in the stories of the *Decameron* is much closer to the shocking but essentiallly humorous and harmless act of putting one's pants over the wrong appendage than it is to the more deeply disturbing behavior of the Florentines in the face of the plague. It is instructive to remember here that the only character in all the hundred novellas actually to wear a pair of pants in this novel manner is the abbess described by Emilia in the second story of Day 9. Boccaccio's own précis of the tale supplies all the relevant information:

> An abbess rises hurriedly from her bed in the dark when it is reported to her that one of her nuns is abed with a lover. But being with a priest at the time, the Abbess clasps his breeches on her head, mistaking them for her veil. On pointing this out to the Abbess, the accused nun is set at liberty, and henceforth she is able to forgather with her lover at her leisure.[52]

The abbess, interestingly enough, does not wear the pants on her head deliberately, and she does not save herself thereby; on the contrary, she reveals the unseemliness of behavior she thought well hidden. Here is

---

51. *Decameron* (McWilliam), 55; *Decameron* (Branca), 14.

52. *Decameron* (McWilliam), 688; *Decameron* (Branca), 595. "Levasi una badessa in fretta e al buio per trovare una sua monaca, a lei accusata, col suo amante nel letto; e essendo con lei un prete, credendosi il saltero de' veli aver posto in capo, le brache del prete vi si pose; le quali vedendo l'accusata, e fattalane accorgere, fu diliberata e ebbe agio di starsi col suo amante."

an example of "velamento fabuloso indecentem veritatem contegere." The pants on her head are not in themselves immoral, though they expose immorality; they are ludicrously out of place. And most important of all, they do no harm to anyone but herself. Boccaccio demonstrates that a person such as the abbess who wears pants on her head is unseemly at her own expense, whereas those who joke over the death of a neighbor or relative are unseemly at the expense of others. The literal meaning of Boccaccio's trope is thus far less morally repugnant than its figurative significance. It therefore serves precisely the ameliorative function proposed in the "Epilogue" for the literal level of the discourse of the *Decameron*.

If we take this epilogue seriously—and, in spite of its jokes and ironic disclaimers, I see no reason not to do so—we are encouraged to understand the *Decameron* as a set of texts written between two conflicting readings of the same discourse, one of those readings being "honest, virtuous, seemly" and the other just the opposite. If we are the sort of readers "for whom they were written," these tales offer us the opportunity to emulate Ulysses, to experience with safety and even profit what could in other circumstances cause us harm. Those who misconstrue Boccaccio's rhetoric, however, and see only the substance beneath the veil without attending to the qualities of the veil itself, risk becoming the Sirens' victims.

Interestingly enough, the Boccaccio of the *Decameron* sees little danger of the opposite error, that is, of supposing that the text means no more than what it says at the literal level. This error, which is attacked vigorously and at length in the *Genealogy*, is not one which Boccaccio finds likely to occur in readers of these stories. In the other principal passage of self-defense in the *Decameron*, the introduction to Day 4, the author recounts a fragmentary tale ostensibly to illustrate the principle that "in order to oppose the laws of nature, one has to possess exceptional powers, which often turn out to have been used, not only in vain, but to the serious harm of those who employ them."[53] The story relates how a certain Filippo Balducci, who had resolved to renounce all worldly things upon the death of his beloved wife, gave away all his goods and retired, with his young son, to a cave, where he raised the

53. *Decameron* (McWilliam), 331; *Decameron* (Branca), 266. "Alle cui leggi, cioè della natura, voler contrastare troppo gran forze bisognano, e spesse volte non solamente invano ma con grandissimo danno del faticante s'adoperano."

boy in complete ignorance of the life of the secular world. After many years, when the boy was eighteen years old and the father had attained a ripe old age, the son convinced Filippo to take him along on one of his periodic visits to Florence. Believing that his son was by now thoroughly committed to the service of God and proof against worldly temptations, the father consented.

Once in town, the young man questioned his father about all the marvelous things to be seen there, especially wanting to know what each thing was called. At length, as was inevitable, they chanced upon a group of young women, and the son no sooner saw them than he became fascinated and wanted to know what they were called. Filippo, hoping to steer his son away from the temptations of the flesh, told him these creatures were "papere," which means figuratively "[silly] women" but literally "goslings." But the son now had eyes for nothing else, and in spite of his father's assurance that these creatures were "evil" ("mala cosa"), insisted that he wanted one for his own:

> "You can say what you like, father, but I don't see anything evil about them. As far as I am concerned, I don't think I have ever in my whole life seen anything so pretty or attractive. They are more beautiful than the painted angels you have taken me to see so often. O alas! if you have any concern for my welfare, do make it possible for us to take one of these goslings back with us, and I will pop things into its bill."
>
> "Certainly not," said the father, "Their bills are not where you think, and require quite a special sort of diet." But no sooner had he spoken than he realized that his wits were no match for Nature, and regretted having brought the boy to Florence in the first place.[54]

At this point Boccaccio breaks off his narration, allegedly to prevent the suspicion that he was "attempting to equate my own tales with those of that select company,"[55] the brigata of the frame tale, but more

---

54. *Decameron* (McWilliam), 328; *Decameron* (Branca), 263–64. "E egli allora disse: 'Io non so che voi vi dite, né perché queste sieno mala cosa: quanto è, a me non è ancora paruta vedere alcuna così bella né così piacevole come queste sono. Elle son più belle che gli agnoli dipinti che voi m'avete più volte mostrati. Deh! se vi cal di me, fate che noi ce ne meniamo una colà sù di queste papere, e io le darò beccare.'

Disse il padre: 'Io non voglio; tu non sai donde elle s'imbeccano!' e sentì incontanente più aver di forza la natura che il suo ingegno; e pentessi d'averlo menato a Firenze."

55. *Decameron* (McWilliam), 326; *Decameron* (Branca), 262. "Non paia che io voglia le mie novelle con quelle di così laudevole compagnia . . . mescolare."

probably because this part of the story, and perhaps this part only, is relevant to his argument that art is no match for the power of nature.

But the story also makes a powerful point about the slipperiness of language, even indeed of "onesti vocaboli" like "papere." Filippo's attempt to fend off the sensual attractiveness of young women to a young man by the use of a hedging trope backfires: what is for the father a signifier of brainlessness is for the son a signifier of appetite—an appetite he longs to satisfy. The seemliness of "papere" (both in its literal meaning and in the father's intended figurative meaning) is transformed into the sexual double-entendre of "(im)beccare," which literally means "to feed young birds" but has an obvious metaphorical copulative connotation as well. The seemly veil that Filippo cast over these particular Sirens has hidden nothing; it has on the contrary served to reveal what the father hoped to cover. That this happened is, of course, quite in keeping with the theory of the *velamentum* as expounded by the practitioners of biblical exegesis and by Boccaccio himself in the *Genealogy*. The poetic veil is supposed to be penetrated by the attentive reader. But this story does seem to pose something of a problem for the theory of the purifying power of "onesti vocaboli" claimed in the author's epilogue. One could argue that Boccaccio, aware that he might be undermining the basis for his defense of the *Decameron* as a moral book, broke off his narration lest he wound himself too badly with his own weapons. The ineffectiveness of Filippo's metaphorical discourse to keep his son away from unseemly matters appears to be proved.

A closer look at the story, however, particularly the point at which it is terminated, shows that the issue is not so clear. Actually, there is no evidence that the son has not taken Filippo's metaphor in the desired literal sense. His intention to "give them something to peck at" ("le darò beccare") can be read as perfectly innocent, indeed as the very thing a child would want to do with a pet bird. It is Filippo himself who construes this language sexually and who thus returns the rhetoric from seemly literality to an indecent metaphoricity. Unlike the son's "le darò beccare," the father's statment that their "bills are not where you think and require a special sort of diet" ("tu non sai donde elle s'imbeccano") will not sit still for a literal reading. All of us, including the son, know where the bills of goslings are; it is only the bills of figurative "papere" that might prove a mystery to him. And if they do—that is, if we accept the figurative import of the father's statement—then the seemliness of the son's literal understanding of "pa-pere" has been asserted. It is as if the father is saying, "You don't know where their bills are because you don't know what kind of 'papere' I'm talking about."

The son surely does want one of these goslings to take home, and he might even be dimly aware that he wants to do more than simply give it something to fill its bill; but what he does not know, as the text insists, is that this desire is evil. There is the suggestion here that, even if the son were to discover "donde elle s'imbeccano" in the father's sense and then act on that discovery, he would be doing nothing more indecent than giving a bird something to eat. What would be for Filippo an immoral act would be none for the innocent son. The ethical character of actions corresponds, as is argued in the epilogue, to the dispositions of minds and the onestà of language. What would be the worst moral breach in Filippo's eyes would be for the son no less consistent with the service of God than feeding a hungry animal.

We have good reason for supposing that Boccaccio was thinking in these terms, given the place in the *Decameron* where this piece of self-defensive rhetoric is deployed. It comes at the beginning of Day 4, just after we have heard what is doubtless the most (in)famous tale in the entire collection, the story of Alibech and Rustico. If there is any story in the collection likely to be accused of indecency, this is it. Both Boccaccio's fragmentary story and Dioneo's tale treat the power of eros in the context of asceticism and the service of God. Indeed, Boc-caccio's story and Dioneo's are similar enough to add an extra measure of irony to the author's expressed wish not to "mix" ("mescolare") his own narration with those of the brigata. While his words say one thing, his performance seems instead to be insisting the contrary, that he and Dioneo are of one mind on these matters and that we would make no great error to "mix" Boccaccio in with the brigata. In any case, it is well worth noting that the only story in the entire collection of novellas told by the author *in propria persona* appears directly after the most scandalous tale of all and is directly comparable to it in theme, structure, and technique. These circumstances suggest that the story of Alibech and Rustico has a special importance in the *Decameron* that goes beyond its *succès de scandale*.

Although Alibech and Filippo's son move in opposite directions to find love, both begin their journeys with certain key traits in com-mon. Of course both are young (she fourteen, he eighteen) and in the full bloom of adolescent sexuality; but both are also naive: she is by nature "a very simple-minded creature" ("semplicissima"), and he was brought up by his father to be unworldly. More than this, though, both have a sincere, though of course naive, commitment to the service of God. Filippo's son is described as "inured to the service of God" ("abituato al servigio di Dio") to such an extent that his father does not think the things of this world can hold any attraction for him. And of course the "service of God" ("il servire a Dio," also "il servigio di Dio") is the central issue of Alibech's adventure, since it is her quest for the "best and easiest way for a person to serve God"[56] that leads her to Rustico and to the holy rite of putting the devil back in hell.

There is an additional religious frame wrapped around Dioneo's tale in that he proposes to use it as a means to instruct the ladies of the brigata in a practice by which they might "save our souls from perdition."[57] Since the practice in question, "putting the devil back into hell," turns out to be a trope for sexual intercourse, one might wonder whether this "winning" ("guadagnare") of souls is not also somehow subverted by the worldliness of Dioneo's tenor. But actually the opposite seems to be the case, for two reasons. First, there is no clear way to read this language of saving souls as a metaphor for some secular activity; second, the reader (as well as Dioneo's audience) is not yet aware of the ribald intention behind Dioneo's "onesti vocaboli" "devil" and "hell." At this preliminary stage in the narration, then, there is no particular reason to doubt the contention that learning to put the devil back into hell will indeed enable "graziose donne" to save our souls.

If the little prologue stresses the spiritual side of the discourse that is to come, the beginning of the narrative proper quickly alerts us that we must be ready when necessary to read the same thing in two very different senses, one spiritual, the other carnal. The description of Alibech's decision to go out into the desert and of the journey itself introduces, in a brief space, an effective and relevant rhetorical turn. Dioneo ascribes her sudden resolution to seek out in the wilderness "those who put the greatest distance between themselves and earthly goods"[58] to nothing more than a childish whim: she did it, he says, not

---

56. *Decameron* (McWilliam), 314; *Decameron* (Branca), 251. "In che maniera e con meno impedimento a Dio si potesse servire."

57. Ibid. "Guadagnar l'anima."

58. *Decameron* (McWilliam), 315; *Decameron* (Branca), 251. "Che più dalle cose del mondo fuggivano."

out of a "considered wish" but rather out of an "adolescent impulse."[59] The word for "impulse" here is "appetito," employed in the Latinate sense of "strong inclination." Only a bit later in the same sentence, however, the word "appetito" appears again, but this time in its physical sense: it takes her several days to find anyone in the wilderness, and when she does she is "exhausted from fatigue and hunger" ("con gran fatica di lei, durando l'appetito"). These two forms of appetite set up the poles between which Alibech's character is inscribed, her most prominent trait in the rest of the story being an appetite of a third kind, one that is both physical and spiritual at the same time. Although it is very easy for the reader to let the power of her physical, sexual appetite efface the other, the spiritual side remains present and important throughout the narration.

It is easy to forget that Alibech's goal always remains the same: to learn the best and easiest way for a person to serve God. The religious nature of her quest is never forgotten by her, by the narrating voice of Dioneo, or by the hermit Rustico, who uses it to inspire her with a holy zeal for sexual intercourse. He tells her that the service God finds most pleasing is to return the devil to hell, where God wishes him to stay. The notion is perfectly plausible in terms of Christian teachings, especially to an innocent like Alibech, who happens to be Moslem to boot. What is somewhat less plausible—to us, if not to Alibech—is Rustico's identification of "devil" and "hell" with certain organs of the body he points out to her. This identification is made both easier and more necessary because, Rustico and Alibech having stripped themselves naked, the hermit experiences what is described as "the resurrection of the flesh."[60] Here Dioneo's sly mode of narration not only cleverly cloaks the indecent topic in the most seemly sort of language, displaying an apparent moral delicacy nicely suited to his station, it also tacitly participates in the hermit's rhetoric of seduction by using religious language to describe the most dramatic possible evidence of carnal desire. But Boccaccio's audience would realize, too, that neither Rustico nor Dioneo stands as the sole authority of what might be considered an irreverent sort of troping. By identifying the place between Alibech's legs as "il ninferno," Rustico was doing nothing

59. Ibid. "Non da ordinato disidero ma da un cotal fanciullesco appetito."
60. *Decameron* (McWilliam), 316; *Decameron* (Branca), 253. "Venne la resurrezion della carne."

different from what many a Tuscan of that time did. The misogynistic substitution of "hell" for "vagina" suggested itself for a number of reasons, some of them cultural, some anatomical, and some purely linguistic. The cultural and anatomical grounds need no discussion here; the linguistic grounds are simply that the vulgar form "ninferno" for "inferno" would surely suggest to some—and Boccaccio first among them—an association between hell and a well-known group of sexually attractive females, the nymphs ("ninfe"). Even a far less active linguistic imagination than Boccaccio's would be inclined to see "ninferno" as the proper possession of "ninfe."

The rhetoric of Rustico's seduction of Alibech is thus not his alone. It belongs also to Dioneo and to the speech community at large. This is not to say that Dioneo and all speakers of Tuscan share the responsibility for Alibech's seduction, but it does mean that both the narrator and the audience of this tale have a certain stake in its rhetoric. After all, strictly within the circle of the fiction, there is no need for Rustico to resort to these pious circumlocutions. Since Alibech is reported to be as innocent of sexual knowledge as she is of Christian doctrine, Rustico could have gratified his desires without recourse to these clever tropes. To put it bluntly, he could have told her that the thing most pleasing to God was putting a prick in a cunt, and she would have been no wiser and no more resistant to his scheme than she is otherwise. All this language of devil and hell, as well as "the resurrection of the flesh," is not for her benefit; it is for ours. It is the audience, Dioneo's and Boccaccio's, who would find it offensive if Rustico and Dioneo were not so careful to "avoid calling [these things] by their real names."[61]

Boccaccio, through Dioneo, has clothed this highly unseemly story in very seemly language indeed and has thereby made it suitable for the ears of "oneste donne," according to the principle he set forth in the "Author's Epilogue." The effect it has on these ladies, of course, is very different from the effect it has on Alibech, and pointedly so. Boccaccio takes care to show us that the ladies of the brigata differ from Alibech in two important ways: first, they are quite knowledgeable about both the tenor and the vehicle of these tropes; second, they have minds of their own and do not look to others to lead them. Both

---

61. Filippo attempted this with his son, as the narrator relates in the introduction to Day 4. *Decameron* (McWilliam), 328; *Decameron* (Branca), 263. "Non le volle nominare per lo proprio nome."

of these points are made in the little scene that serves as epilogue to Dioneo's narrative:

> So aptly and cleverly worded did Dioneo's tale appear to the virtuous ladies, that they shook with mirth a thousand times or more. And when he had brought it to a close, the queen, acknowledging the end of her sovereignty, removed the laurel from her head and placed it very gracefully on Filostrato's, saying:
>
> "Now we shall discover whether the wolf can fare any better at leading the sheep than the sheep have fared in leading the wolves."
>
> On hearing this, Filostrato laughed and said: "Had you listened to me, the wolves would have taught the sheep by now to put the devil back into Hell, no less skillfully than Rustico taught Alibech. But you have not exactly been behaving like sheep, and therefore you must not describe us as wolves. However, you have placed the kingdom in my hands, and I shall govern it as well as I am able."
>
> "Allow me to tell you, Filostrato," replied Neifile, "that if you men had tried to teach us anything of the sort, you might have learned some sense from us, as Masetto did from the nuns, and retrieved the use of your tongues when your bones were rattling from exhaustion."[62]

Filostrato is quite right in pointing out to Neifile that her trope of wolves and sheep does not fit the men and women of the brigata. These ladies are not easily led creatures; on the contrary, they do much of the leading themselves. But Filostrato makes a tactical error in suggesting that, if these ladies *were* like sheep, the men would have used them sexually. Neifile quickly points out that Filostrato's own story about Masetto di Lamporecchio (not to mention the story just concluded) put into question the roles of user and used, seducer and seduced, in the relation between the sexes. Women—even "seduced"

---

62. *Decameron* (McWilliam), 319–20; *Decameron* (Branca), 256. "Mille fiate o più aveva la novella di Dioneo a rider mosse l'oneste donne, tali e sì fatte lor parevan le sue parole; per che, venuto egli al conchiuder di quella, conoscendo la reina che il termine della sua signoria era venuto, levatasi la laurea di capo, quella assai piacevolemente pose sopra la testa a Filostrato e disse: — Tosto ci avedremo se i' lupo saprà meglio guidar le pecore che le pecore abbiano i lupi guidati. —

Filostrato, udendo questo, disse ridendo: — Se mi fosse stato creduto, i lupi avrebbono alle pecore insegnato rimettere il diavolo in inferno non peggio che Rustico facesse a Alibech; e per ciò non ne chiamate lupi, dove voi state pecore non siete: tuttavia, secondo che conceduto mi fia, io reggerò il regno commesso. —

A cui Neifile rispose: — Odi, Filostrato: voi avreste, volendo a noi insegnare, potuto apparar senno come apparò Masetto da Lamporecchio dalle monache a riaver la favella a tale ora che l'ossa senza maestro avrebbono apparato a sufolare."

women—are powerful and able to use and indeed "use up" any man thinking to follow Rustico's example. The ladies of the brigata would be as strong in their appetites as Alibech, if it came to that. But it will not, because their power includes knowledge as well as appetite. They know the difference between putting the devil in hell and having intercourse, and the knowledge allows them to both enjoy the story and keep themselves apart from it.

The story's rhetoric thus has opposite effects on Alibech and the virtuous ladies of Dioneo's audience. What draws Alibech into a situation that is as indecent ("disonesto") as any in the *Decameron* is the very thing that sets up a barrier between the audience and the indecency of the story. The religious language acts like a pair of gloves, allowing one to touch without touching, or at least without getting one's hands dirty. The ladies of the brigata can claim with a certain honesty to have heard a discourse about serving God, about the resurrection of the flesh, and about putting the devil in hell. That this was also a story about the gratification of carnal desire told in very graphic terms is perfectly true but not necessarily relevant to the question of moral contamination. The literal level of the story succeeds in doing what Filippo's language apparently failed to do: keep the listener distant from an indecent topic of discourse.

Alibech, on the other hand, appears to have been drawn by Rustico's rhetoric into an act of an unquestionably unseemly nature. Not only does she have intercourse with Rustico, but she actually develops "a taste for the sport" to such a degree that her zeal surpasses Rustico's ability to participate. She explains her feelings forthrightly:

> I can certainly see what those worthy men of Gafsa meant when they said that serving God was so agreeable. I don't honestly recall ever having done anything that gave me so much pleasure and satisfaction as I get from putting the devil back in Hell. To my way of thinking, anyone who devotes his energies to anything but the service of God is a complete blockhead. . . . Even though your devil has been punished and pesters you no longer, my Hell simply refuses to leave me alone. Now that I have helped you with my Hell to subdue the pride of your devil, the least you can do is get your devil to help me tame the fury of my Hell.[63]

---

63. *Decameron* (McWilliam), 317–18; *Decameron* (Branca), 253–54. "Ben veggio che il vero dicevano que' valenti uomini in Capsa, che il servire a Dio era così dolce cosa; e per certo io non mi ricordo che mai alcuna altra io ne facessi che di tanto diletto e piacer mi fosse, quanto è il rimettere il diavolo in inferno; e per ciò io giudico ogni altra persona,

The ill-nourished hermit Rustico does what he can, but it is not enough. Alibech has a far greater capacity to serve God than he, since (according to Rustico) "the taming of her Hell would require an awful lot of devils."[64] The innocent young girl has been turned into a creature of pure lust.

But Alibech's lust is at least in one sense special: she earnestly believes that she is engaged in the service of God. At no point does Rustico confess his deception and drop the tropes of devil and hell. We can hardly find it reprehensible that she finds this sort of service to be "sweet" ("dolce cosa"), since God's work is supposed to be agreeable to those who serve him faithfully. It is no surprise that she finds nothing sinful in what she does, nor is it shocking that she finds it a "great sin" ("gran peccato") on Neerbale's part to have stopped her from the performance of this divine duty. For Alibech, there is no distinction between the literal and figurative meanings of "devil" and "hell." Sexual intercourse *is* the service of God as far as she is concerned, and this naive belief is never challenged during the course of the narrative. There is thus an enormous moral gap between what Alibech does and what Rustico does, even though from one point of view they are both doing the same thing.

The final judge of such moral questions as these would be God himself, and we have good evidence how the God who rules over the *Decameron* could be expected to decide. The very first story in the collection, the tale of how the wicked Ser Cepperello lies his way into sainthood, is framed by a commentary in which Panfilo stresses God's interest in "the purity of [our] motives."[65] Although it is remarkable enough that such a rogue as Ceperello should be honored as a saint, Panfilo suggests, it is perhaps more remarkable that God seems to answer prayers directed to the inauthentic "Saint Ciappelletto." The mystery the story presents could be resolved in two ways:

---

che a altro che a servire a Dio attende, essere una bestia . . . ; se il diavol tuo è gastigato e più non ti dà noia, me il mio ninferno non lascia stare: per che tu farai bene che tu col tuo diavolo aiuti a attutare la rabbia al mio ninferno com'io col mio ninferno ho aiutato a trarre la superbia al tuo diavolo."

64. *Decameron* (McWilliam), 318; *Decameron* (Branca), 254. "Troppi diavoli vorrebbono essere a potere il ninferno attutare."

65. *Decameron* (McWilliam), 69; *Decameron* (Branca), 27. "Più alla purità del pregator riguardando."

For albeit he led a wicked, sinful life, it is possible that at the eleventh hour he was so sincerely repentant that God had mercy upon him and received him into His kingdom. But since this is hidden from us, I speak only with regard to the outward appearance, and I say that this fellow would rather be in Hell, in the hands of the devil, than in Paradise. And if this is the case, we may recognize how very great is God's loving kindness towards us, in that it takes account, not of our error, but of the purity of our faith.[66]

If indeed God is inclined to overlook error in favor of the purity of faith, then Alibech's actions must be understood as belonging in the same moral sphere as the literal context of the story's discourse. "He from whom nothing is hidden"[67] would have no difficulty distinguishing between the modus rectus of Alibech's speech and the modus obliquus of Rustico's, since even limited mortals like ourselves can do so. If the unseemliness of Dioneo's story has been figuratively "redeemed" by its seemly language, the unseemliness of Alibech's behavior can be understood as literally redeemed by the purity of her motives. The question of her salvation may be moot, since she is not a Christian, but it is quite clear that it is her faith, not the duplicitous piety of Rustico, that merits divine mercy.

All of the hundred novellas reside in the space made possible by the reversibility of rhetorical language. What Boccaccio tries to make clear in a variety of ways is that this is a moral as well as a semantic reversibility. While these are indeed very secular tales recounted "neither in church . . . nor in any place where either churchmen or philosophers were present,"[68] they are part of a project begun in a church and opened by a story told as proof of God's skill in reading our discourse. That the stories deal often enough with wicked doings no one would deny, certainly not the author, who recognized "Prince Gallehault"

66. *Decameron* (McWilliam), 81; *Decameron* (Branca), 37. "Per ciò che, come che la sua vita fosse scellerata e malvagia, egli poté in su lo stremo aver sì fatta contrizione, che per avventura Idio ebbe misericordia di lui e nel suo regno il recevette: ma per ciò che questo n'è occulto, secondo quello che ne può apparire ragiono, e dico costui più tosto dovere essere nelle mani del diavolo in perdizione che in Paradiso. E se così è, grandissima si può la benignità di Dio cognoscere verso noi, la quale non al nostro errore ma alla purità della fé riguardando . . ."

67. *Decameron* (McWilliam), 69; *Decameron* (Branca), 27. "Esso, al quale niuna cosa è occulta."

68. *Decameron* (McWilliam), 830; *Decameron* (Branca), 718. "Non nella chiesa . . . né tra cherici né tra filosofi in alcun luogo."

("Prencipe Galeotto") as a fitting subtitle. But there is also the suggestion that this worldly business of telling stories has a certain divine
sanction: the ladies hit upon the idea of retiring to the country while
they are attending divine service in the church of Santa Maria Novella,
whose name just happens to contain the word used to describe the
stories they will tell. Boccaccio surely had this wordplay in mind,
though he does not force it upon our attention. There is perhaps a
certain justice in the fact that circumstances have made that wordplay
more relevant today: though the venerable church is anything but
"new," it is probably best known to visitors of Florence as the place
where the project of the novellas was begun. But it is still a church, and
Boccaccio obviously thought that church was the proper, sanctifying
origin for his literary brigata.

The salvific qualities of the literal level in Dioneo's tale of Alibech
and Rustico are one aspect—perhaps the most interesting—of the saving power of language in general that is evidenced throughout the
Decameron. The story of the frame, after all, displays a successful effort
to escape from the effects of the plague by means of discourse, and
many of the novellas take as their theme the power of words to remedy
a bad situation. That is the explicit theme of the sixth day ("Those
who, on being provoked by some verbal pleasantry, have returned like
for like or who, by a prompt retort or shrewd manoeuvre, have avoided danger, discomfiture or ridicule")[69] and the unannounced but evident topic of Day 1. We learn over and over again how trouble is
averted or ameliorated by a story, "a few well chosen words," "a
clever remark," "a barbed saying," or "an ingenious answer." That the
dangers thus escaped are of an overwhelmingly practical and secular
nature should not be allowed to obscure Boccaccio's genuine interest in
the moral and even theological aspects of rhetoric. The whole collection seems to be energized by the discovery that language can be both
straightforward and duplicitous, both honest and immoral, at the same
time.

I have devoted by far the greater part of my argument to
demonstrating Boccaccio's interest in the positive moral quality of his
rhetoric on the assumption that the other side of the coin hardly needs

---

69. *Decameron* (McWilliam), 881; *Decameron* (Branca), 403. "Chi con alcun leggiadro
motto, tentato, si riscotesse, o con pronta risposta o avvedimento fuggì perdita o
pericolo o scorno."

demonstration. That other side is of great importance, however, and should not be forgotten. Many of the stories in the *Decameron* are wicked, and quite intentionally so, as is the tale of putting the devil back into hell. This is, no mistake about it, a story about an outrageously candid lust indulged in with undisguised enthusiasm. Boccaccio's trick has not been to make that wickedness go away, any more than the country sojourn of the brigata has made the plague go away, but to let it take its course without being contaminated by it. As Gilberto says in Emilia's story of Dianora (Day 10, story 5), "The power of words received by the heart through the ears is greater than many people think,"[70] and that power is to be seen clearly in those cases where the subject under discussion holds some kind of danger. We would not continue to be interested in Alibech and Rustico were their discussion understood to be entirely theological, nor would we if we (Boccaccio and his audience included) thought sex was as morally unproblematic as sneezing. Being "saved," in short, is of consequence only when there is something to be saved from.

The reversibility of rhetorical construction allows Boccaccio to develop narratives that both expose the danger and save us from it in the same gesture. The tales are so devised as to make phrases like "grinding sauces in her mortar" or "causing the nightingale to sing at frequent intervals" have a certain plausibility at the literal level. Boccaccio's figurative language of sex never seems coy or euphemistic because the vehicles of his metaphors are so regularly and rigorously connected to the plots of his stories. When Filostrato tells us about the scraping of Peronella's tub, the situation is such that the figure, arising quite naturally out of the action, demands to be read rhetorically. Peronella's husband is literally scraping one tub while her friend Gianello is busily "scraping" another, and our pleasure in the tale arises as much out of the rhetorical sophistication of the description as from the outrageousness of the situation described.

What holds our interest so often in these stories is a complication in the meaning of an action that is inseparable from the language of the narration. The case of young Caterina and her nightingale (Day 5, story 4), though not as rich in moral complexity as that of Alibech, shows this very well. The plot of the little story could not be more

---

70. *Decameron* (McWilliam), 759; *Decameron* (Branca), 659. "Le parole per gli orecchi dal cuore ricevute hanno maggior forza che molti non stimano."

simple: Caterina and Ricciardo are young lovers who contrive to con-
summate their love on the balcony of her father's house. As her excuse
for spending the night out on the balcony, Caterina tells her parents
that she cannot sleep in her room because of the heat; that she prefers to
sleep on the balcony where she would be cooler; and that she hopes the
nightingale will sing her to sleep. The father at first refuses, but
Caterina makes such a fuss that her mother cannot sleep, and the
mother intervenes in favor of the balcony. "Besides," she says to her
husband, "what do you find so surprising about a young girl taking
pleasure in the song of the nightingale? Young people are naturally
drawn towards those things that reflect their own natures."[71] Her bed
established on the balcony, Caterina awaits the arrival of Ricciardo,
who gallantly climbs the wall to reach her. "After exchanging many
kisses, they lay down together and for virtually the entire night they
had delight and joy of one another, causing the nightingale to sing at
frequent intervals."[72] The narrator (Filostrato) quietly takes up the
language of Caterina's excuse and turns it into a bawdy trope. But the
rhetorical complication only starts here. The lovers fall asleep after
their exertions, both still naked, she with one hand "holding that part
of his person which in mixed company you ladies are too embarrassed
to mention."[73] With the arrival of dawn, the father awakens and goes
out to the balcony "to see whether Caterina has slept any better with
the help of the nightingale."[74] He discovers the couple, still in the same
posture, and immediately tells his wife that her daughter "was so
fascinated by the nightingale that she has succeeded in waylaying it
[*ella l'ha preso*], and is holding it in her hand."[75] The father thus takes
up the trope first announced by the narrator in the same manner used
by Filostrato: he turns his daughter's language back upon her. But he

71. *Decameron* (McWilliam), 434; *Decameron* (Branca), 358. "E oltre a ciò mar-
avigliatevi voi perché egli le sia in piacere l'udir cantar l'usignuolo, che è una fanciullina?
I giovani son vaghi delle cose simiglianti a loro."

72. *Decameron* (McWilliam), 434; *Decameron* (Branca), 359. "E dopo molti basci si
coricarono insieme e quasi per tutta la notte diletto e piacer presono l'un dell'altro,
molte volte faccendo cantar l'usignuolo."

73. Ibid. "Presolo per quella cosa che voi tra gli uomini più vi vergognate di nominare."

74. *Decameron* (McWilliam), 435; *Decameron* (Branca), 359. "Lasciami vedere come
l'usignuolo ha fatto questa notte dormire la Caterina."

75. Ibid. "Tua figliuola è stata sì vaga dell'usignuolo, che ella l'ha preso e tienlosi in
mano."

then goes on to introduce a further complication. Because Ricciardo is rich and noble—a "good catch" for his daughter—Messer Lizio sees him as a fine piece of game she has snared: "Now that she has taken him [*ella l'ha preso*], she shall keep him."[76] Now the nightingale is no longer simply Ricciardo's penis; it is the whole man.

Caterina's duplicitous discourse employed as a way to get out on the balcony established the term "nightingale" ("usignuolo") as a figure of a desirable object. She, of course, sees Ricciardo as an object of her sexual desire, and the narrator is able to turn the trope easily into a synecdoche in which Ricciardo's "nightingale" represents what is most desired about him. But a more clever turn yet comes when the father uses this same language to signify Ricciardo's desirability as a member of the family. Messer Lizio wants this nightingale too, but in a quite different way than his daughter does. He captures the nightingale by catching the lovers in bed together and by compelling the chagrined Ricciardo to marry Caterina. This is no hardship at all for Ricciardo, since Caterina is the object of his desire, and naturally enough he too is described at the story's end as catching nightingales ("uccelò agli usignuoli") to his heart's content. The mother is shown to have been more correct than she realized when she suggested that the nightingale was one of "those things that reflect [young people's] natures."

The story of Caterina and Ricciardo develops out of the discourse built upon various interpretations of the word "nightingale" read as rhetoric and is not to be separated from that discourse. The obligation that Filostrato feels to the modesty of his audience, his reluctance to name the thing they are too embarrassed to name, begins to look more and more like an ironic flourish. The tale would be impossible if Filostrato felt compelled by some standard of candor to call things by their ordinary names. Messer Lizio's restraint in the face of his discovery would be far more difficult for the narrator to motivate and for the audience to understand had he reported to his wife that there was a penis rather than a nightingale in his daughter's hand. The turn taken by the plot is aided by the rhetoricity of the nightingale trope, which allows itself to be easily diverted from the distressing fact of Ricciardo's offending organ to the pleasant prospect of his wealth and social standing. It is perhaps not too much to say that, as the devil in hell

76. Ibid. "Poscia che ella l'ha preso, egli sì sarà suo."

figure saves Alibech from sin, so does the metaphor of the nightingale save Ricciardo from Messer Lizio's just wrath.

Constructive reading provides a remedy in both cases to situations that would otherwise be very bad indeed. In general in these novellas rhetorical construction functions as a mode of literary invention for Boccaccio and also as a powerful ameliorative force for both the members of the brigata and the characters in their stories. The beneficent power of language is shown to depend absolutely on its rhetorical capability, since that power is released only by the narrative realization of more than one potential meaning in a given piece of discourse. Both Boccaccio's success as a writer and the happiness of his stories' outcomes are due in large measure to his skill as a practitioner of rhetorical construction.

7 | *Conclusion*

"Where do you get your ideas?"

Theorists since at least the time of Plato have had an answer to this question, and it is still for many purposes a good one. Plato conceived of poetry as arising from one of two possible sources, either the imitation of the experienced world or a kind of divine inspiration. He admired poetry that sprang from the latter but leveled a sharp critique at literature that imitated the phenomenal world. Aristotle presumed that all poetry resulted from imitation and undertook to defend its philosophical value by reconceiving the notion of poetic mimesis. Since that time it has been one of the fundamental and abiding tenets of critical orthodoxy that literary structures in one way or another mirror structures in the world, either by holding the glass up to nature or by forming the text to match the contours of some aspect of the author's emotional or intellectual self.

There are excellent reasons for holding to this account of poetic invention that I hardly need rehearse here. I am not inclined to disagree with those who posit imitation as one of the basic mechanisms of the literary process. My claim is merely that it is not the *only* such mechanism. The rhetorical potential of language itself is an equally fertile source of fictional (and occasionally nonfictional) concepts capable of being developed into complex narratives. Throughout the argument, I have deliberately tried to avoid equating the language arising from inventive reading with purely poetic or literary language, because I do not believe that all poetic language arises out of rhetorical construction. But *some* literary (and occasionally nonliterary) language clearly does:

many of the stories and situations found in imaginative fiction spring from a rhetoric that both affirms and denies some difference.

How can rhetoric both affirm and deny a difference? It does so by insisting on the viability of several alternative, contradictory readings of the same discourse. These alternative interpretations arise in the rhetorical moment, the instant of uncertainty as to how to understand a text or utterance. Imaginative fictions like those discussed in the foregoing chapters come into being by harvesting all the sprouts in the hermeneutic garden without deciding which are flowers and which are weeds. The traditional practice of interpretation in literary studies aims at finding and making explicit the one right reading, evaluating and discarding other possible but unsatisfactory interpretations. Critics of this tradition, whether deconstructionists or "antifoundationalists" of another stripe (Stanley Fish, for example), have argued that the difference between a satisfactory and an unsatisfactory reading derives less from qualities inhering in a text (if such a thing as a "text" exists) than from the circumstances of the reading process, the nature of the prevalent "interpretive community," and so on. Practitioners of rhetorical construction do not adjudicate between good and bad readings; they present alternatives that seem to carry equal value, and in so doing they appear to obliterate differences. Rabelais's transformation of the rhetorical curse "le fondement vous escappe" into the narrative foundation for the account of Gargantua's birth makes comic hash of the distinction between literal and figurative. It becomes clear, however, that Rabelais's whole enterprise depends absolutely on that very distinction, just as it requires us to see a difference between faith and credulity that the narrator has just exploded with his impertinent reading of Saint Paul.

Rhetorical moments dramatize the interplay of sameness and difference in an especially forceful way, because the sameness and difference in question are both part of the conventional structure of linguistic norms. Phrases like "le fondement vous escappe" or "Ich sterbe" are apparent unities that turn out, when interpreted, to conceal a striking doubleness of meaning. They are always the same in locutionary form, but they can vary markedly, sometimes disastrously, in their significance and effects. There is always a story to be made out of such phrases, because they contain by nature issues that are potentially productive of conflict, change, uncertainty—in short, *action*. Rhetorical moments make such effective literary beginnings because they start things happening. One could even argue that they are already little actions in themselves, little nodes of energetic conflict ready to expand infinitely outward.

It is easy to see why the rhetorical moment would be such a useful starting point for a storyteller with a particularly strong sensitivity to language. Such moments unite the two elements of greatest importance to narrative—language and action—into a single impulse that is at once both action and discourse. Rhetorical writers are obviously very interested in language itself, but they are also, as storytellers, concerned with human events. Although the title *The Use of Speech* could be applied to a textbook dealing with certain aspects of linguistics, Sarraute's book is unmistakably about people in moments of great personal stress. We are interested in Chekhov's "Ich sterbe" not as an example of the problems associated with speech-acts but because Chekhov's situation as Sarraute describes it is charged with emotion and complex human meaning. Rabelais's concerns and effects are certainly very different from Sarraute's, but they too center on matters that are not essentially linguistic. His humor depends most often on reminding us of the overwhelming materiality of existence precisely at those moments when the subject matter turns most spiritual or else on the opposite, on introducing a spiritual interpretation of what we thought was an entirely secular set of events. The rhetoricity of phrases like "centuplum accipies" or of an entire text such as Psalm 124 is the hinge upon which such comic effects turn; they are not exhibited as examples of linguistic free play. Rhetorical moments happen *in* and *through* language, but the situations developed out of them by the verbal imagination happen *to* people.

The dramatized rhetorical moment accomplishes poetically what J. L. Austin sought to do philosophically: both urge us to reject the commonplace opposition between "saying" and "doing." Talk is not always a "cheap" substitute for action; it is sometimes the locus for acts of grave, even "historical" significance. Schiller sees history unfolding in a rhetorical moment manufactured by Elisabeth, who tries to manipulate the reading of her own discourse so that she can get Mary executed without executing her. The play's audience always knows what the queen refuses to acknowledge, however: that speech-acts like signing a document are genuine actions in the world, that they cannot be dismissed or denied. Rhetorical moments depend on a truth we all know but often prefer to forget or ignore: the use of speech can be as effective in the world, or as damaging, as the use of any powerful implement. Figures of speech can become "facts" in the human universe.

The relation between figure and fact, central to several of the works treated here, participates in an economy of joining and sundering, an unceasing activity of putting together and taking apart meanings that at times seems to posit the unity of language and reality, at others to deny it. Such an economy is implicit in the nature of rhetorical discourse, in which from one point of view the signifier unites otherwise incompatible significations, but from another mutually incompatible acts of reading dismember an otherwise unitary linguistic body. Is the sentence "Si ne le croyez, le fondement vous escappe" a single thing that acts of interpretation chop up into divergent meanings? Or is it really those two divergent intentions joined together by the artifice of language? The figure itself draws attention to this problem, since what is threatened (under a literal reading) is that the reader's body will come apart; but what is implicitly promised (under a figurative reading) is that, if the reader believes what is told here, he or she will remain in firm contact with the foundation of this discourse.

Rhetorical constructions often explore in an analogous—and sometimes horrifying—way this rhetorical economy of joining and sundering. When the moment of Danton's death finally arrives in Büchner's play, it can no longer be understood simply as a brute event, brutal though it may be. It occurs in a context so thoroughly saturated with figures of dismemberment that we have to find in it a rhetorical moment, an instant of uncertainty whether we should understand it as a fact or a figure. Indeed, we have no alternative but to understand it as both and to recognize that its meaning as an event is not to be separated from its function as part of an elaborate system of tropes. Something terrible happens to the physical reality of Danton's body, but even that gruesome fact has a verbal component capable of participating in a potentially limitless chain of semiotic relationships that cleave together even as the guillotine cleaves asunder. Büchner's version of the story of Danton's death proposes that the event or fact that forms its subject does not exist apart from a discourse that informs it.

That discourse is a dialogue between acts of joining and sundering, as befits a drama set during the bloodiest period of the French Revolution and chronicling the last days of one of the most distinguished leaders of a movement understood by many to seek the obliteration of distinction. Danton's great strength becomes political weakness, since the more he excels above others the more suspect he must become to a community with an ideological commitment to social leveling. In a society proclaiming as its ideal that all citizens should stand together as equals, there may not be a place for one who stands apart. The individual whom the revolution unquestionably needs to organize and direct it is sooner or later discovered to be ideologically intolerable. The revolutionary community, as Büchner presents it, both affirms and denies the necessity of uncommon men like Danton, and so its discourse to and about such people can only be uncertain, full of contradiction—rhetorical.

The rhetorical relation between facts and figures as explored in the plays of Kleist and Büchner is closely bound to the relation between society and self. The set of social norms Saussure called "langue" both determines and is determined by the individual practice he called "parole." Every act of discourse is potentially a moment of dialogue between a speaking subject and the widely shared power that resides in the community and enables discourse. Because both the individual and conventional norms may propose interpretations of commonplace expressions, the self and the group can meet with more or less equal authority in rhetorical moments of interpretive uncertainty. While there is a certain very real sense in which society can never lose in a conflict over the correctness of a reading—society is, after all, the highest court in such matters—the individual at least has the opportunity of compelling attention and perhaps even acceptance for an unconventional reading so long as some set of normal interpretive rules is employed. Penthesilea's literal reading of the cliché "I love him so much I could eat him up" does not make any converts among the Amazons, but the failure does not lie in her interpretive procedure. Her reading cannot be accepted because it implies the regular conversion of erotic desire into cannibalism.

Different as Büchner's play is from Kleist's, the two share a certain fundamental concern with the problem of how extraordinary individuals relate to the social body that surrounds them. They present rhetorical language as the medium through which individuals and social structures interact. I do not mean this in the obvious sense that people interact with each other by speaking; I mean rather that discourse represents the meeting ground between the practice of an individual consciousness and a set of norms belonging to society at large. Penthesilea makes that meeting ground the locus for her attempt to show herself an obedient daughter and a responsible citizen in spite of her abnormal behavior. Her constant striving to turn figures into facts is her method of reconciling her uncommon self with Amazon norms. With Danton a similar but opposite process takes place: a figurative structure presented in the play as so pervasive that it is virtually a social norm provides Danton with a strategy for understanding his execution—society's absolute rejection of him—as enabling a kind of social integration.

In both plays the rhetorical confrontation of facts and figures produces much of the drama. Penthesilea's slaughter and disfigurement of Achilles is unquestionably the kind of event that grabs an audience's attention, but without Penthesilea's remarkable explanation that she was merely making good everyday hyperbole, its impact would be different and, I would argue, less. Thousands of heroines have stabbed themselves at the final curtain, but how many have done so armed with nothing but a common household trope? Equally numerous are scenes set on the steps leading to the scaffold ("It is a far, far better thing"), some of them memorable. But Danton's death stands out because Büchner's play makes us understand it as another version of a figure of dismemberment that survives and thrives in the society that kills him. Figures can be more durable than facts. Events are ephemeral, but tropes live on and on.

The relation of the individual to society and indeed to the world at large can be understood as mediated by rhetoric. Like *Penthesilea* and *Danton's Death*, "Rappaccini's Daughter" proposes a kind of deep— though disturbing—kinship between the individual self and the rest of creation, a kinship suggested initially by the author's name. If a person may be linguistically indistinguishable from a thing (a plant), then the boundary between the self and the rest of the universe may not be especially firm. The commonest and most essential distinctions may not be valid, not even the most basic distinction we make among persons, that between male and female. Such a view could open up the self to the world in an exhilarating, thoroughly positive way, perhaps along the lines of what happens to Joseph and some of the other characters in Thomas Mann's novel *Joseph and His Brothers*. But the experiences depicted in "Rappaccini's Daughter" are not put in a very positive light. The potential unity of the self with the alien world is frightening, though certainly also exciting, and it tends to be fatal.

Crossing the normal boundaries of humanity leads one into exile from the land of the living. Beatrice—powerful and indeed dangerous on the one hand, beautiful and alluring on the other, human in every way, yet sister to a poisonous plant—Beatrice, and only she, dies at the story's end.

Here the darker side of rhetoric becomes visible, and it is perhaps even more prominent in the stories by Calvino, Hoffmann, and Kafka I have chosen for analysis. They remind us that the notion of rhetoricity I develop in these pages derives from a definition of rhetoric that foregrounds its more troubling features. Paul de Man's formulation of the "semiological enigma" of rhetoric stresses that it "radically suspends logic and opens up vertiginous possibilities of referential aberration."[1] Though de Man acknowledged that the uncertainty which accompanies rhetorical reading might be a form of "bliss," something in which we are "privileged" to participate, he characteristically placed the words I just quoted in parentheses, as apparent secondary alternatives to "anxiety" and "condemned."[2] De Man presents rhetoricity in such a way that we understand it first and foremost as something to which we are condemned, a kind of uncontrollable linguistic negativity that makes us afraid. I have chosen to orient my rhetoric differently, to offer first the bliss, the privilege of being able to participate in the prolific fertility of unlimited semiosis, before acknowledging the negativity that most concerned de Man.

Although my project differs substantially from de Man's, I do not mean to imply that he was wrong in this matter. Rhetoric, like any powerful force, is capable of having negative effects at least as often as positive ones. Nor was he wrong to stress that the semiological uncertainties engendered by rhetorical discourse are not entirely controllable by either authors or readers. The process of rhetorical construction is able to harness the power of rhetoric only by presenting it as already let loose. By reading so as to understand what is read as already deconstructed, a rhetorical writer diverts a certain portion of semiological negativity in the interpreted text away from the new text written out of that reading. Only by admitting in advance that incompatible, perhaps mutually destructive readings of a single text are possible does a rhetorical construction open up space in which to operate.

1. *Allegories of Reading* (New Haven: Yale University Press, 1979), 10.
2. Ibid., 19.

But that admission does not make the powerful negativity of rhetoric vanish. "The Dinosaurs," for example, has a happy ending only because the extinction of literal dinosaurs opens up a limitless space in which figurative "dinosaurs" of every kind can thrive. It is the disappearance of Qfwfq that makes the world utterly safe for expressions like "Give it to him, Dinosaur!" that were rhetorical and thus problematic while an actual dinosaur was still extant. Qfwfq's disappearance therefore functions very much like Nathanael's death at the end of "The Sandman": the problem of rhetoricity vanishes only with the elimination of the character demanding literal reading. After Qfwfq and Nathanael have left the scene, the world returns to its normal condition, in which the figurative regularly suppresses the literal. Although Hoffmann's story, unlike Calvino's, does not announce itself as a comic work, it carefully shifts the reader's attention at the conclusion from Nathanael's shattered body to the pleasant domestic scene of Klara at her country house surrounded by "two merry boys" ("zwei muntre Knaben"). The juxtaposition with the violence of Nathanael's death is a bit abrupt, but it is not entirely ironic. The two merry boys will have a much better chance to stay merry in a world where there is no one to contradict the reassuring proposition that *there is no Sandman.* The "little Dinosaur," Qfwfq's offspring, will have that same chance, knowing for certain in his heart that, if anyone should call him a "dinosaur," it would only be a figure, since *there are no dinosaurs.*

Kafka's story offers a very different conclusion. Like Nathanael, the bridge/person ends its existence shattered by a fall, but here the destruction of the protagonist does not restore order or eliminate the problems of rhetoricity. The end of Kafka's narrative leaves us in a world where there is no longer any way to "go over." The bridge's attempt to privilege the human side of its figurative equation results in the destruction not just of one form of reading but of the whole enterprise of troping. "The Bridge" makes the point that figures in which the literal is not as fully present as the figurative are no longer figures. Our speech abounds with "dead" metaphors in which the figurative meaning has so overwhelmed the literal that we no longer even recognize the expressions as figures. It takes a Nietzsche, a Derrida, or a de Man to remind us of the metaphoricity of discourse we assume to be quite devoid of rhetoric. Although it is true, as Nietzsche pointed out, that the German word for face, *Gesicht,* is a trope on the act of seeing and being seen, the word simply does not function rhetorically anymore without some kind of special contextual intervention. It may not be absolutely dead as a figure, but it can only be revived for short periods with the help of extensive life-support systems.

Kafka's bridge figure suffers this kind of destruction. It may not be quite dead—it still narrates the story of its own fall—but it will no longer serve readily as a means by which travelers and readers can "go over." With the fall of the bridge, one sort of rhetorical problem is solved in that rhetorical uncertainties vanish. We no longer have to ask: "Is it a bridge or a person? Is there a Sandman or not? Is *that* a 'real' dinosaur?" Another rhetorical problem arises in its place, however: How will we make connections? How will "intercourse" be possible? How will we go from one side of an issue to the other? Kafka's story reminds us that, if rhetoricity is an unsettling problem we would at times like to go away, its elimination—were it possible—would not be a satisfactory alternative.

But as often as rhetoric is perceived as a problem that can be dramatized in a work of fiction, it is just as often available as a powerful method for solving problems. Obviously the sorts of problem most amenable to treatment by means of rhetorical construction will be discursive in nature. The kind of difficulty I am referring to might arise, for example, when a need exists to alter the interpretation of some particularly authoritative utterance bearing an apparently fixed and widely accepted meaning. Rhetorical reading provides a way to shift the semantic ground beneath the feet of an established discursive practice without the need to negate, rebut, or somehow dismantle the existing alternative reading. This problem can come up under a variety of conditions in the course of ordinary affairs. Suppose you have said something publicly and apparently definitively that at a later time you would prefer to unsay. At the very least you wish that what you said did not mean what everybody understands it to mean. This is not at all an unusual situation: many of us face it, and many of us resort to a form of rhetorical self-reading to help ourselves out of it. Susan Noakes has pointed out that both Dante Alighieri and John Henry Cardinal Newman—neither of whom is often accused of low morals—engaged in such revisionary acts of self-reading. Dante did so in the *Vita Nuova*, where he reread his own earlier love poems in the light of his "conversion" after the death of Beatrice; and Newman practiced it in *An Essay in Aid of a Grammar of Assent*, which depends at a crucial point on his ability to treat a text he had himself composed more than three decades earlier as a piece of rhetoric subject to constructive rereading.[3]

The techniques Dante and Newman used to reread themselves are no different from those others of us—politicians or not—use to help us out of difficult situations. Self-reading of this kind is a special case of rhetorical construction in which the problem to be avoided—some form of damage to the self, such as self-contradiction—is particularly easy to identify. Many and perhaps most uses of ameliorative rhetoric involve interpreting another's discourse out of a need to put into question the ordinary, accepted meanings that accompany it.

That is certainly what Nietzsche did in *The Gay Science*, thereby providing himself with a new means for generating philosophical problems. It may be paradoxical that Nietzsche would find the solution to his problem as a philosopher in a means for discovering problems, but it is only to be expected given his own nature and the nature of his rhetorical method. We have discussed some examples of his delight in paradoxical situations, and many more could be produced. Given the amalgam of respect and skepticism that informed his conception of philosophical knowledge, he could be comfortable only with solutions to philosophical problems that were themselves also problems. And rhetoric, as he knew very well, gives and takes in the same gesture. Rhetorical solutions are always at least potential rhetorical problems, as Calvino strongly hints at the conclusion of "All at One Point." There is no internal constraint holding the process of interpretation in check; without the application of external force it will expand as quickly and as infinitely as the universal big bang. The rhetorical reading that transformed "spazio" meaning "room (to move)" into "spazio" meaning the three physical dimensions can also transform it into "distance." Qfwfq had a problem with space at the beginning of the story. Unfortunately he still has one at the end, in spite of the fact that an explosive rhetorical moment solved the earlier problem definitively.

A definitive solution does appear to emerge at the conclusion of Goethe's *Iphigenia*, however. The fall of the curtain at the play's end decisively terminates the acts of reading performed by the author and his characters and leaves one with the impression that here rhetoric has

3. Susan Noakes, *Timely Reading: Between Exegesis and Interpretation* (Ithaca: Cornell University Press, 1988).

succeeded in solving a group of serious problems without introducing others just as daunting. Thanks to favorable circumstances, a persuasive Iphigenia and a benevolent Thoas, no challenges are raised to Orestes' reinterpretation of the divine oracle. Nor does any god descend, as Athena does at the close of Euripides' play, to insist that the immortals really do want the statue back in Greece and that "Bild der Schwester" really means "statue of Diana." Those with an interest in challenging Orestes' reading—the Greek priestesses of Diana, for example, might have such an interest—are not present to make their objections known. Considering these possibilities, we might feel inclined to say here, with Nathalie Sarraute, "Really, though, it might be thought that this beautiful, this too beautiful story has in the end turned out to be no more than a fairy tale." It is not hard to imagine a sequel to the events presented by Goethe in which Iphigenia and Orestes must face a group of angry Greeks, mightily disappointed that Orestes has "misread" the oracle in such a transparently self-serving fashion. Within the compass of the drama's action, however, these matters are irrelevant. The magic circle placed around works of fiction by the fact of their having beginnings and ends allows us the luxury of accepting without reservation the rhetorical solutions offered by the play.

One does not always need the special circumstances provided by fiction, however, to find in rhetorical solutions something wholly positive. For Nietzsche, the problematic associated with rhetoricity is welcome just because of its capacity to generate problems. The difficulty Nietzsche needed to solve could be described as a kind of impoverishment in the range of questions regularly treated by philosophy. Indeed, Nietzsche believed that philosophers had erroneously set as their goal the elimination, or at least the radical reduction, of problems, while what was actually needed was a way to find new problems everywhere, even in the most familiar matters. Rhetorical reading is the perfect tool for this job, which is in effect a philosophical version of poetic invention. Whereas the question that opened this book sought to know where writers (of fiction) get their ideas, the question Nietzsche poses in *The Gay Science* addresses how philosophers might get more ideas than they seem to have. Nietzsche thus understands the principal problem of philosophy as one of invention and finds a solution in rhetorical construction. Philosophers—the best ones, at any rate—are represented as constantly engaged in construction and therefore as neither opposed to nor ethically superior to those who practice rhetoric.

It has not always been so. As Plato and his posterity represented them, rhetoricians are committed fully only to the effectiveness of their discourse and are therefore all too ready to resort to immoral means—innuendo, misdirection, outright lying, and so on—to achieve their ends. Philosophers, on the other hand, supposedly committed fully to the truth in all its forms, necessarily seek what is truly just, truly beautiful—indeed everything truly valuable. Plato thus put into question the ethical standing of rhetoric, and the question is still open.

The issue is important to my inquiry as well, even though my definition of "rhetoric" is quite different from that assumed by Plato and those who followed him. They were concerned mainly with oratory, particularly the art of persuasive discourse practiced and taught by the Sophists. Such rhetoricians worked to discover, develop, and refine methods of composing speeches that could be relied upon to win audiences' approval and belief. This field of endeavor is still very much with us today and can be seen in action daily in advertising, public relations, the law, and of course politics. Important as such activities are, and traditionally "rhetorical" as they may be, they are not my subject. The rhetorician I am studying is also one who has a need to produce discourse, but that need arises not so much from a desire to persuade as from an urge to develop the complex semantic potential of language. Rhetoricians like Goethe, Rabelais, Calvino, and the rest are people who simply cannot stop reading and will read the same text over and over again, finding possibilities for new meaning with each reading. These rhetoricians, if they are inclined toward writing fiction, produce rhetorical constructions of the kind analyzed in these pages. If they are critics, they interpret insatiably, as for instance Stanley Fish seems to do: "I hate sabbaticals," he confesses. "I don't know what to do. I run around and go out in the street and grab people: 'You want to hear about interpretation?'"[4] If they are philosophers, they reread ordinary language in such a way as to find philosophical problems in it, as Nietzsche does. They are people who cannot leave a text alone.

The ethical implications of this sort of rhetorical practice will surely be somewhat different from those of classical oratory, though the two

---

4. "Interview with Stanley Fish," in *The Current in Criticism*, ed. Clayton Koelb and Virgil Lokke (West Lafayette, Ind.: Purdue University Press, 1987), 98.

are by no means unrelated. The question shifts from the problem of the moral status of the rhetorician himself to that of the moral effects of rhetoricity. Instead of asking, "Is he or is he not a moral individual?" we ask, "Is language good or bad for people when it is understood as infinitely readable?"

The stories analyzed here do not give a reassuring answer. Instead, they point the way toward understanding the complex interrelation between rhetorical and ethical problems. In one important respect, such problems appear to be virtually identical, for both are frequently the result of the interplay between two different interpretations of the same thing. The moral character of an action often depends on what set of ethical norms we choose to apply in our understanding of it, just as the meaning of a rhetorical expression depends on the interpretive norms we bring to it. If we think of acts capable of having an ethical value, positive or negative, as composed of an intended effect as well as an overt action, we can easily see a fundamental kinship between these acts and a rhetorical mode like troping. The trope, too, can be understood as made out of an overt linguistic action—the locutionary form construed "literally"—and an intended meaning—the "figurative" purport. It is for just this reason that a phrase like "I didn't mean it that way" can function both as an explanation of rhetoric and as a moral excuse. Consider the following: A child sticks his little sister with a sewing needle. His mother, understandably angry, reproaches him for hurting her. "But I didn't mean it that way," he says. "She didn't feel good and I wanted to make her feel better." "Feel better!" the mother cries out, in tears over her child's incomprehensible cruelty. "How could you make your sister feel better by sticking her with a needle?" "But Mama, when I was sick you said the doctor could make me feel better by sticking me with a needle." "Oh," says the mother, "but I didn't mean it *that* way."

As this example illustrates, the structural similarity between an act of questionable moral status and a discourse functioning rhetorically can be extremely close. No one has exploited this coincidence of rhetorical and moral structures better than Boccaccio, whose approach to literature was founded on a perception of the importance of the difference between the outside appearance of things (*cortex* in his terminology) and their inner nature (*intentio*). No character in literature can testify better than Alibech to the complicity of moral innocence with trust in the literal meaning of discourse—no one, that is, except perhaps Harry

Ashfield. We are now in a position to acknowledge the truth of a claim that would otherwise seem totally absurd: that O'Connor's tragic tale of child neglect and Boccaccio's bawdy homage to the sovereignty of lust are both concerned with exactly the same moral problem, presented in the same rhetorical mode. How are we to evaluate behavior based on an act of understanding that is indistinguishable from an act of misunderstanding? Harry's way of reading the Reverend Summers's invocation of Christ's kingdom in the river is right or wrong depending on your point of view, as is Alibech's identification of fornication with the service of God. Very similar is Andersen's funny/scary story of the rebellious shadow, except that in this case the literal enactment of the commonplace tropes of poetic activity discloses the guilty side of an activity we might otherwise have supposed to be innocent. In all three cases we learn that innocence and guilt are matters of reading.

The close link between how we go about reading the language we hear and how we behave is frequently dramatized by rhetorically sensitive writers. Ethical construction (or misconstruction) is the topic of one of Dante's most celebrated creations, the story of Paolo and Francesca. If, as seems entirely likely, Boccaccio based the subtitle of the *Decameron*, "Prencipe Galeotto" ("Prince Gallehault"), on a line from this episode in the *Inferno* ("Galeotto fu il libro e chi lo scrisse" ["The book was a Gallehault, and so was the one who wrote it"]), the allusion is surely to the issue of morality and reading that is so often treated in the hundred tales. Although an act of reading (that might very well be a misreading)[5] condemns Paolo and Francesca, it apparently saves Alibech, in spite of the fact that the physical act in which she participates is no different from that engaged in by Dante's characters. Whether it saves or condemns, however, is not the crucial point. What these fictions urge us to recognize is that the act of reading, of understanding a certain discourse, is capable of having an effect on behavior, whether good or bad. The way we act toward those around us, whether we are poets, seekers after God, or little boys with needles, often depends on acts of rhetorical construction.

For this reason it is imperative to recognize that rhetoric, particularly the variety I am dealing with here, is not simply a matter of individual

5. See Susan Noakes, "The Double Misreading of Paolo and Francesca," *Philological Quarterly* (1983): 221–39.

style or a mark of personal difference of no consequence to others. Nor is rhetoric necessarily always a critique of the possibility of language to mediate between self and other. Rhetorical construction is at bottom a social process that attempts to put a unique speaking subject into a collaborative relationship with the collectivity of linguistic authority. I say that the relation is collaborative because the practitioner of rhetorical construction does not establish a claim to originality by denying or criticizing the commonly accepted meaning of everyday speech; on the contrary, such a writer establishes a personal voice and stakes out "new" linguistic territory by taking seriously each of several available interpretations.

This collaboration, be it noted, is by no means always wholesome or beneficial. The practitioner of rhetoric may be collaborating with the worst tendencies in society, exploiting phrases or interpretations of phrases that are themselves morally questionable or that lead to morally questionable ends. Such rhetorical activity may be reprehensible, but it is still a form of social behavior that relies on the authority of a set of pregiven norms. Here is an example. After the victory of a black candidate in the Chicago mayoral primary a few years ago, a leading defender of the white-dominated status quo remarked that the white candidate he had supported would have won if there hadn't been "someone in the woodpile" waiting to waylay the political machine. This is unquestionably a rhetorical construction, though so distasteful that one would prefer to pick it up with tongs. It exploits the presence in American speech of a commonplace trope employing a racial slur in order to make with impunity its own racial slur. When reporters asked if his remark was not offensive, the politician scoffed. What, he wondered, could be found offensive in the words "someone in the woodpile"? He could argue that he was doing the opposite of employing offensive language, that his phrase was readable as a special effort at delicacy and tact. He had, after all, left out the word "nigger."

The case of "someone in the woodpile" is a telling example of a kind of rhetorical collaboration that is reminiscent of the behavior of wartime "collaborators." The Chicago politician could not have achieved his political goal of saying something that was also readable as not saying something had the community not supplied him with a commonplace insult that could be rendered rhetorical by a minor alteration. His language did nothing to create racism, not even linguistically;

it was only collaborating with a racism that had already established itself in the commonplace tropes of American English. His slickly contrived insult was as much a social as an individual act.

The rhetorical writer may not always be admirable, then, but neither is he the self-centered, self-satisfied, and self-sufficient rebel so often depicted in romantic and pseudoromantic literature. He or she is above all someone who wants to play a role in the life of the community, to engage in individual acts that move within the limits laid down by the linguistic norms of society. The very act of engaging in rhetorical construction constitutes accepting as prior to the author's own discourse the set of norms that constitutes language, not to mention the countless individual utterances incorporating and defining those norms that took place before the author even learned to speak. This priority of linguistic norms involves both a temporal quality, the simple fact of "coming before," and an implied value. Because of the basis of accepted meanings language rests on, there is necessarily a certain authority that attaches to locutions and interpretations that have come before. This authority varies in strength according to, among other variables, the frequency of an expression's use in daily discourse. A writer would have a very difficult time, for example, altering the meaning of the word "table" but might very well be able to influence the meaning of "rhetoric." In any case, earlier usage conditions the possibilities for later usage and therefore exerts considerable control over individual speech-acts. This authority of past language over present has been for some writers, such as Flaubert,[6] a source of anxiety; for the author engaged in rhetorical construction, however, it is a circumstance to be embraced, since it makes possible the dialogue of rhetorical reading.

The rhetorical writer acknowledges himself or herself as a *reader*, thereby placing the act of writing in the temporal dialectic of all reading. This temporal dialectic is also a dialectic of power and authority along the lines just discussed. Such an implication is clear in the work on the temporality of reading done by Susan Noakes,[7] who characterizes it as an inevitable suspension between two contrary impulses: the desire to recover the utterance being read in its full, original context,

6. Sartre makes a strong case that Flaubert understood words as alien objects, and Charles Bernheimer advances more evidence in support. See Bernheimer, *Flaubert and Kafka* (New Haven: Yale University Press, 1982), 73.

7. *Timely Reading*, introduction.

and the urge to find a way to let that utterance make a new kind of sense here, in this new context. These two poles, which Noakes calls "exegesis" and "interpretation," represent appeals to two different authorities, that of the maker of the utterance and that of its interpreter. Noakes points out that the act of reading always falls between the extremes of perfect exegesis and perfect interpretation, always thus makes some acknowledgment, however slight, *both* of the authority of the author and the text's original context *and* of the power of the reader and the present reading moment. Every act of reading balances these two, however precariously. In the case of rhetorical construction, where the "author" of the text being read is so often the community at large, it is easy to see that the balance such an act of reading must look for involves the reading/writing subject and the collective author, society. If Noakes is correct that every act of reading must by its very nature be at least partially exegetical, then every rhetorical construction must also contain at least some essential element, however small, that appeals to and acknowledges the authority of the writer's social context.

There are ethical as well as social implications to the practice of rhetorical construction. By working out fully the ramifications of two opposed interpretations of a single text in a fiction, a writer can explore a morally complex issue in a way that does not support or condemn anyone. Rhetorical discourse is often used in situations where diplomacy, tact, or plain old evasiveness is called for. James Howe has pointed out that chiefs of the San Blas Cuna of Panama make use of a formal rhetorical mode of discourse "to make their opinions known on an issue and exert the force of traditional norms on its resolution without naming names, referring to it directly, or even perhaps committing themselves to a clear-cut stand."[8] The undecidability of rhetorical discourse can be a great resource, and most of us make use of it at one time or another to negotiate morally slippery terrain.[9] The Chicago politician mentioned above did so in a way that compromised his own moral position, but there are other, more responsible ways to

8. "Carrying the Village: Cuna Political Metaphors," in *The Social Use of Metaphor*, ed. J. David Sapir and J. Christopher Crocker (Philadelphia: University of Pennsylvania Press, 1977), 138.

9. See Clayton Koelb, "Parler sans Parler: The Rhetoricity of Fictional Discourse," in *The Current in Criticism*, ed. Clayton Koelb and Virgil Lokke (West Lafayette, Ind.: Purdue University Press, 1987), 159–73.

go about it. Boccaccio's *Decameron* is a great storehouse of examples showing how to do so.

The study of rhetorical construction is thus inherently a social study that often involves moral concerns as well. It does so even here, even in the context of an often theoretical discussion of literary texts. The most pressing issues it presents—the conflict between differing interpretations of the same discourse, the way new speech derives from old, the relation between individual self-expression and communal norms—are all important not just to the study of literature but to an understanding of how we relate to each other through the medium of language. Although rhetorical study may not be able to resolve any of these issues definitively, it is an excellent way of beginning.

The answer I would give to the question that opened this inquiry therefore has a social dimension from which it cannot and should not be disentangled. That answer says in its simplest form that sometimes writers get their ideas from looking at the world around them and imitating what they see; but that at other times they make their beginnings by looking at the language around them and reading it in a special way. Certain kinds of language—those possessing a high level of rhetoricity, such as tropes—are more likely than others to provoke this special mode of reading; and certain kinds of writers—those possessed of what Coleridge called a verbal imagination—are more likely than others to engage in it. But when a verbal imagination comes together with highly rhetorical discourse, the impact often ignites a rhetorical moment in which an act of reading becomes an act of writing. Out of that rhetorical moment can grow a complex discourse, an invention of reading. In the proper circumstances, then, *that* is where authors get their ideas.

Index

Library of Congress Cataloging-in-Publication Data

Koelb, Clayton, 1942–
  Inventions of reading.

  Includes index.
  1. Literature—History and criticism. 2. Reading. 3. Rhetoric. 4. Imagination (Rhetoric) 5. Creation (Literary, artistic, etc.) I. Title.
PN45.K586 1988   809   88-47732
ISBN 0-8014-2182-9 (alk. paper)

DATE DUE

The Library Store   #47-0103